*Return to Dresden*

# Return to Dresden

## MARIA RITTER

*Thank you for sharing the Asher!*

*Maria Ritter*

UNIVERSITY PRESS OF MISSISSIPPI *Jackson*

www.upress.state.ms.us

The University Press of Mississippi is a member
of the Association of American University Presses.

11 10 09 08 07 06 05 04 03    4 3 2 1

Library of Congress Cataloging-in-Publication Data

Ritter, Maria.
    Return to Dresden / Maria Ritter.
    p. cm.
    ISBN 1-57806-596-8 (alk. paper)
    1. Ritter, Maria.  2. Dresden (Germany)—Biography.
3. German Americans—Biography.  4. World War, 1939–1945—
Psychological aspects.  5. Forced migration—Germany—Dresden.
6. Refugees—Germany (East).  I. Title.
D811 .R573 2004
940.53′432142′092—dc22                    2003012683

British Library Cataloguing in Publication Data available

To my children, Peter and Lisa, and their families

All sorrows can be borne if you put them into a story or tell a story about them.—ISAK DINESEN

# CONTENTS

# ACKNOWLEDGMENTS

It takes a host of angels to raise a story from the ruins of memory. After the lifting of remnants and the sorting of treasures from the rubble comes the mending of brokenness through tears. The shared tears become the connecting thread of a new tapestry.

By now the new weave has its own story. After several years of uncovering and searching, I look back with gratitude to those persons who stood by me, offering tender encouragement, sharing sound advice, and asking questions that would resonate with elements of their own stories. Foremost was my daughter, Lisa, who simply wanted to learn more about the grandfather she never knew. Her innocent question would require a complex and arduous answer that would address the vicissitudes of her ancestors as well as those of the German people during one of the most horrid periods of human history. I am deeply grateful to her for her probing curiosity and all the practical help she provided during the process of searching and writing. My son, Peter, came to the rescue when the computer crashed and the manuscript seemed all but lost. My son-in-law, Stewart Pickard, envisioned potential readers in this country who would want to hear more about World War II and its detrimental effects on the lives of all survivors. From early on, my daughter-in-law, Julia Ritter, helped me to understand the literary concepts and leitmotivs emerging from the text (such as the silencing of the child), and suggested techniques for storytelling; it was in a coffee shop in New York that she listened, with acceptance and empathy, to my first timid reading of the border-crossing story.

Over the years, my writing became a family project in the truest sense. Each of my three brothers offered help by pasting our history together from joint memories. In 1998, Klaus Schnädelbach was our companion as we traveled to locations in the former East Germany and in Poland; together with his wife, Elisabeth, he collected maps and valuable family pictures, and transcribed Grandfather Schnädelbach's diary. Klaus also gave me a tiny brooch with a picture of our mother as a little girl, one of the few family treasures that survived the Dresden bombing. With his excellent memory, Herbert Schnädelbach recalled many names and dates as well as exact geographic locations, and thus provided a reliable sequence of events. Gerhard Schnädelbach shared with me our mother's collection of letters and her dream diary. I am so grateful for their contributions and their hospitality during my visits to Germany. My cousins Inge Alrutz and Gudrun Hilse shared letters and pictures, and Maria Mannarino put Grandmother's house key into my hand as a gift and a mandate.

A long list of readers and listeners responded with encouragement, insisting that I share my story with other people besides my family. They include Angela Moskovis, Marcus Dowd, Irmgard Frey, Hanna Sack, Ursula Sack, Janet Young, Marky Reynolds, Bob and Linda Shephard, Brigitte Thewalt, Heidi Frey, and Anna Schnädelbach. Marty and David Peck's interest in my writing led to a connection for publishing. Dr. Warren Poland offered a moving and personal response, assuring me that my story would speak for itself. At a writer's conference in January of 1999 in San Diego, California, Tom Miller saw in my writing the importance of the subject matter and handed me a green light to go on. Hana Lane helped me to develop a multilayered design for a book. A warm thank-you to each one of them!

A special word of gratitude goes to the men and women of the United Methodist Church in La Jolla, California, who gathered for several presentations and became the first witnesses to my story. Among them were Sandy and Peter McCreight, Susan Russell, Ann Harnden, D. Ann and Darrell Fannestil, Jill Tregoning, Marvin Burdg,

Rita Bell, Brenda and Tom Lester, Patsy and George Leopold, Denise and Gene Blickenstaff, Martha and Paul Jagger, Jean and Mark Trotter, and Florence and Roger Wiggans, just to name a few. Reading and storytelling led the way to a reconciling dialogue.

With the help of my psychoanalyst, Dr. Phyllis Tyson, I reconstructed the perception of my childhood in a safe and reflective way, and began to understand how surviving with unresolved trauma had organized my living. Her gift of compassionate listening and probing for previously unspoken emotions associated with painful memories formed the core of a healing dialogue. The voice of the child in the text is a tribute to Dr. Tyson's witnessing. The adult voice in the text is a tribute to the analytic process. I shared the cold ashes with her first, and I wish to express my deep gratitude.

The story can be read thanks to the diligent efforts of the staff of the University Press of Mississippi, especially Craig Gill, editor-in-chief, who understood the human voice in the face of war and tragedy. Anne Stascavage, editor, and Carol Cox, copy editor, respectfully provided excellent editorial help. The book turned out to be a truly collaborative work, and I am most grateful to all who contributed.

Finally, unending words of thanks to my husband and best friend, Winfried, who held my hand when we walked the streets of Dresden, Breslau, Damsdorf, and Bad Bergzabern. He listened and read, offered ideas and corrections, and, most of all, he put a plate of food in front of me when I was tired from the journey. A shared meal is really good!

# INTRODUCTION

## *A Small Voice*

"We certainly received what we deserved," my grandfather said after the war, and I believed him. The look on his face as he stared out the window spoke of bitterness and solemn resignation in the face of God's punishment and pity for us all.

When the fighting in Germany finally stopped in May of 1945, I did not know that the war would never be over for many of us survivors. We were fortunate to be alive, but we were burdened with the immense trauma of loss. Little did I understand that living with physical and emotional scars is costly. It would require a lifetime to recover, to salvage the remnants of a demolished past, and to weave them into a redeeming future.

As part of a nation of perpetrators we also entered a conspiracy of silence even about our own pain. Everyone around us had experienced a lifetime of tragedies; our own were nothing special. The total cost of human lives on all sides of the firing line added up to these incomprehensible numbers: forty-five million deaths, including twenty million Russians, six million Jews, and millions of unaccounted-for civilians. It was easier not to remind ourselves of this satanic history and to move on—pondering it was too ghastly. Like many other Germans, we hid under the ruins of a noxious national glory forever wrapped in shame, hoping that time would wipe away all tears, hounding memories, and nagging guilt. New life would surely cover the graves and the wounds, and surely the rise and fall of such a misguided nation would never be repeated.

Survival precedes the reflection of one's history. After the war no one took time to talk to me about what horrors I had seen or how frightened I was. It was just not done. I figured that the adults thought I was too young to comprehend anything that I had seen but not understood. Instead, my mother worried about where the next loaf of bread would come from each day, or hurried out the door to see that the correct amount of *Brikett* (coal) rations was being dumped through the cellar window to heat the kitchen. At night we sat around the table praying, heads bowed, eyes shut, and hands folded, asking for God to speak to us. I looked at my bitten fingernails instead and tried to listen for God's voice. All I heard was my own small voice. God was silent. On Sundays we went to church and prayed for the forgiveness of our sins and the strength to trust in God. We also gave thanks for being alive; we were the lucky ones who seemed to have received special protection. I did not know why us and why not my grandmother Wunderlich, my aunt Liddy, my uncle Karl, Frau Wolf, and all the others. Most urgently we prayed for our father to come home from the Russian front.

When I was five, I overheard the hushed voices of the grown-ups in Grandfather's kitchen in Leipzig. They talked about the Russian soldiers in town and their brutality toward women. I worried about my mother leaving the house, especially at night, and did not feel relieved until she finally slipped into our bed. The silence protected us like a heavy blanket, warming at the moment yet concealing the dark of memories and truths. No one wanted to remember the horrifying moments, especially not my mother. It was over for the moment and we were alive.

I joined this massive chorus of silence, hoping for a lasting peace to wipe out all reminders of the German dilemma. One family story among thousands was not worth mentioning. Our neighbors had shared the same experiences, some much worse; so I felt I no longer had a voice.

These were some of the childhood conclusions I carried into my adult years and took along with my luggage when I immigrated to the

United States in 1966. Although years passed like a refreshing breeze and I had a comfortable life in peace, nagging images and reminders of homelessness revisited in dreams and fretful sleep.

When my mother died a few months before her eightieth birthday in 1983, I said good-bye to her forever and lost the living connection to my past. There would be no more times to ask her about her family or to validate my early memories. No quiet talks to help me understand the difficulties of her life during the Hitler years. No answers to burning questions about the collapse of human decency and the rise of evil and destructive forces in a nation with a culture so rich in literature and music, science and industry. With my mother's death the final silence had fallen over me.

Over the years new facts regarding death counts were published. More horrifying stories of Holocaust survivors emerged, constant reminders of suffering and cruelty. Of the just under nineteen million Germans in central, southeastern, and eastern Europe who experienced mass deportation between 1945 and 1950, only eleven million lived to see their destination. According to a census in September of 1950, they included Baltic Germans, Lithuanian Germans, East Prussians, Danzigers, West Prussians, Pomeranians, Lower and Upper Silesians, Sudeten Germans, Capathian Germans, and Germans from Hungary, Yugoslavia, Rumania, and the Soviet Union. "Approximately four million were forced to stay in their countries of origin, and roughly three million met their death at the end of the war and immediately afterwards" (*Deutschland: Magazine on Politics, Culture, Business and Science*, D20017 F, No. 2, April 1993, E5, pp. 26–27).

They perished on the way to somewhere. The truth crushed my need to speak and ask even more. In response to all this, I held my breath. There were no words—just more silence in shame. "We certainly received what we deserved."

I belonged to this exodus. When I was born in 1941 in Breslau, Silesia, World War II had been raging for two years. In 1943 our family history as refugees began. In 1945, after an odyssey of terror, my mother, my three older brothers, and I finally found a temporary shelter in the Soviet-occupied section of Germany. After four years of cramped living and *Hungersnot* (famine) in my grandfather's flat, we fled the Communists by crossing the border to West Germany in search of freedom.

Why talk about it now over fifty years later? Why explore memories and feelings associated with trauma in my own family? Why revisit the remnants of a painful and shameful past?

Stories of liberating heroes are always sung with pride on the winners' side. Yes, there are hearts on both sides grateful for their courage and sacrifice. However, the stories of people left behind in the ashes and in covered graves on the defeated side are rarely mentioned. The Allied forces destroyed our cities, our churches, our homes, our farms and crops, our families and our fateful illusions in order to save us. After the defeat of the Hitler regime in 1945, they stayed to resurrect us. As restoration and rebuilding began, including the Marshall Plan and the program of denazification of the German people, documentaries of concentration camps surfaced and captured the facts of a systematic elimination of six million Jews and other unwanted persons. These pictures would be forever imprinted in my mind, a reminder of the evil orders of the Führer, Adolf Hitler, and his henchmen—my people.

At this time of inflated pride, hate, and prejudice, a time of war, defeat, and rejection, no one answered my cautious questions for explanations of the disasters around us. Teachers and parents alike remained silent and I stopped asking. I concluded that guilt and shame were fitting punishment for having been part of a nation that subscribed to evil and destruction. With the passing years, I felt I had no right to talk about my story, considering the plight of victims with more traumatic experiences.

The experiences of the Holocaust survivors are rightfully heard and continue to emerge from the dark corners of their memories. As time went on, other wars were being fought. From all over the world pictures emerged of refugees walking away from their homes and their

countries in times of war: Korea, Vietnam, the Persian Gulf, Kosovo—
the list goes on and on. The horror of war reveals itself over and over on
people's faces and bodies: the empty look, the frozen eyes, the wounds
untended; hungry children hang onto their parents, people are running. It is the replay of a gruesome reality, brought on by human conflict, hate, and the attempt of a few individuals to seize power through
domination—an unending human tragedy, a never-ending story, as if
no learning from past mistakes has ever occurred.

But each survivor needs to speak and be heard. The voice of each
person tells of horror, torture, and rage, while the listeners respond
with time and empathy. Adults and children alike need a heartful listener in order to heal through remembering and speaking. The utter-
ance and the cries of the survivors build a bridge for the listener
because receiving and hearing lead to the discovery and acceptance of
our humanity. This process may even hold the promise of a frank dialogue between survivor victim and survivor perpetrator so that the
suffering may finally be shared and unburdened.

This book is the story of my childhood, a small voice telling of
trauma, loss, silencing, and homecoming in the face of a diabolic history and its aftermath. In order to come to grips with my past as a
German born during World War II, I had to find out what marks this
horrible history had left on my family and on me. First, I needed to
reconstruct the events by gathering the facts pertaining to war and
violence and to explore my own memories without a blink. Second, I
revisited the past by collecting memories, listening to the stories of others, and tracing painful reminders at the actual geographic locations.
Third, and most important, I wanted to reclaim any associated emotions disconnected from these memories. On this path, I could seek
healing in the survival through confrontation, acceptance, and integration. The ashes must be shared. An experience shared with other war
compatriots is a healed experience.

During the last few years, I found my voice through the process
of spontaneous writing. Family letters, pictures, and diaries helped fill

the holes in my story. Image memories found fragmented language, while feelings took on another voice in poetry and music. Dreams and flashbacks, panic and fearful moments drove the journey. The old still pictures are interwoven with current impressions and reflections, and what emerges is a reconstructed, subjective autobiography. A reclaimed, personal history is a reconciled history, and no longer leaves one adrift through the night.

Each section in the book struggles with the burden of the political events during the Nazi regime and asks nagging questions as to what my parents might have known or how they might have subscribed to Hitler's ideology. In the end, I found no vindication for their vision or blindness, for their political conformity within their family and church denomination, or for a country that blindly and aggressively lived out an evil course of events.

I recently received my grandmother's rusty house key, which one of my mother's sisters had found in the ashes of Dresden in the aftermath of the firestorm bombing in February 1945. My cousin Maria gave it to me. With this key in my hand, I received a mandate and a permission to open up the door to the past.

The central person in my story is my mother, who led the way in the flight from Silesia, through the fires of Dresden and the postwar famine, and eventually across the border to the western part of Germany. Her story is the painful one, one of a broken heart held together by emotional scars. Her belief had a stubborn quality to it. She insisted on a merciful God, on being blessed in spite of hardship. Her prayer was like the one Jacob shouted during a night of wrestling, as told in Genesis 33: "I will not let you go, God, unless you bless me!" It was this insistence on her faith, as well as her motherly courage, that brought us four children to safety, and ultimately set us on a free path. She envisioned a freedom that could provide us with a chance to create life anew and leave the pain behind.

However, living in America, six thousand miles away from Germany, was like walking with a long, dark shadow. How was I to live with it? Other people could notice it easily, given my German accent, my name, my age. I, nevertheless, strode eagerly ahead while dragging the shadow, sometimes pretending it was not there anymore. I just wanted to move on with life, leaving memories and losses behind. But I was to discover, like every other survivor, that each one of us has to cope with the aftermath of trauma at some time during our lives, sooner or later, maybe alone, maybe with others, but definitely recognizing disturbing facts and seeking the presence of associated emotions. The permanent marks our history has left on us must be examined if we are to understand who we are now; otherwise, the shadows of the past will not vanish.

There is a way to clear the rubble of destruction and to find colorful remnants of life in the gray layers of the ashes. A new tapestry can be woven from threads of mercy and hope. The gray charcoal blends in with the yellows and the greens, the reds and the blues, the colors of the seasons of life. The journey of recovery, foremost, remains a universal one. This book is an effort to create a witness for healing and living.

# PROLOGUE

## *The Mitzvah*

"Here is your mitzvah," she said, bending down to her purse while digging out a wrinkled dollar bill. Her therapy session over, the young Jewish woman was slowly getting up from her comfortable chair in my office.

"It's a *bubba meintze*, you know, an old wives' tale." A smile brushed over her face; she had not noticed that I had no idea what she was talking about. "I'll send you on a mission with this dollar!" By now she had straightened the wrinkles in the bill and put it in my hand. When she became aware of my puzzled look and my silence, she went on, "It's a teaching—so it says in the Talmud—to do a mission, a kind act to further God's will when you go on a trip. You are on a holy mission from now on—you are a *shlichah mitzvah*, a mitzvah messenger. If you give this dollar to a needy person this summer in Germany, then your trip will be blessed!"

With that explanation and a smile, she left my office.

I paused a while, staring at the dollar bill—a mitzvah ... a mission, and with it a blessing and protection to come my way? I quickly wrote down the word "mitzvah" on my note pad so I could look it up in the dictionary when I got home. (I would later learn from Leo Rosten's *The Joys of Yiddish* that mitzvoth are regarded as profound obligations, inescapable burdens, yet they must be performed not from a sense of duty but with a "joyous heart.")

It would just take giving away this dollar, handed to me by a Jewish woman, to someone in need in Germany? "In Germany," she had said. That simple? Did she know what she was saying?

Didn't she know how many million bodies lie between her, a Jewish woman, and me, her German-born therapist? Surely she could not have forgotten; neither had I. I would never forget. The history of the Holocaust can never be forgotten. The stories of human suffering would be told from one generation to the next. I could feel my throat getting dry the more I thought about it.

*. . . cannot think about it any more, too painful, too shameful. My mind goes back to my first visit ever to the concentration camp in Dachau, near Munich, in 1996. My oldest brother, Klaus, lives nearby. The people there don't like to be reminded of their town's evil reputation; the place is tainted for good.*

"Actually, Dachau is an idyllic town, famous for its artists in times past—charming and quaint. The Americans like to travel here but only to visit the concentration camp. They never see the rest of the town—too bad!" my brother commented, his lips tightly pressed together to keep other words from slipping out.

Why had we not visited this ghastly place before? Our parents did not urge us to visit this part of the German past and our teachers did not take us on a history class outing. Couldn't we have searched for the truth after we completed our school years? We could have traveled to Dachau, and to other concentration camp sites, but we stayed away. Did we also fall under the spell of avoidance by not seeing, not hearing, not feeling? Did we, too, continue to live without confronting the ugly past, trying to avoid shame, rage, and guilt? To visit here would have been to shudder.

I had no other answers to these haunting questions, but after so many years, my time to be a witness had come.

On a clear day in August, my husband, Winfried, and I walked with trepidation through the open gate into the camp. The watchtower was still standing, the walls and the fence intact. The concrete foundations still mark the outline of the barracks on the open grounds. As a German-American, I had arrived at this place of endless human suffering to see the painful reminders for myself, to feel their horrifying impact. I had to face my own shame burdened by the knowledge that my parents had been a part of this dark moment in German history. They had witnessed Hitler's striving for power, his military conquest and domination of most of Europe, and his voracity in pursuing his grandiose goals as the Führer of a superior race; the vicious aim of his claim and pursuit included the elimination of the Jewish people.

I stared at the enormous wrought-iron memorial, symbolizing a twisted, barbed-wire fence. It was beginning to sting. The spikes would be haunting me forever and now seemed to scream questions at me: Did your parents know? If they knew, why didn't they do something to stop it?

Not too long before, one Sunday morning, the South African bishop Desmond Tutu had been interviewed on television by Bill Moyers about his efforts on the Truth and Reconciliation Commission, which brings healing to the ethnic factions of his people regarding their crimes committed toward each other. Bishop Tutu said that one has to look the beast straight in the eye in order to begin the healing process. I remembered his words well and realized for the first time the deep truth in them. My beast was right here in front of my eyes and I blinked. It was too hard to look straight at it, too horrible to see, too frightening to feel. He had also said in that conversation that people are a glorious creation with the capacity to do good as well as evil. Right now, I could only see the evil part and it made me shiver.

Our silent walk through the KZ (concentration camp) led us to the museum that housed a pictorial guide from the beginnings of the Nazi regime to the bitter end in 1945. I passed through the halls in a daze. The pictures of the German people screaming and jubilating in response to Hitler's mandates contrasted with the silent faces of human suffering. But why was there no accompanying text in English? So many foreign visitors enter this place. The German text stung my eyes.

While walking from picture to picture, I could hear the steps of a young woman visitor who was coughing every few minutes. Her scratchy rasp reverberated in the empty halls, a reminder of the illness and the distress that once filled this place. Every time she coughed, I winced. I wished that she would go away, but she took her time to look and read; her coughing seemed like an echo to my painful search into the past.

"I didn't know that besides the Jews so many priests and other clergy lost their lives here," Winfried said slowly, pointing at a chart accounting for the pastors and priests who perished during the Nazi years at Dachau. He is a member of the clergy himself, and this category of murdered prisoners touched his heart. A total of 2,720 clergy had been imprisoned, with 1,034 killed, 868 Polish Catholic priests among them. I clinched my teeth as numbness took over.

We walked in silence, the crunching of loose gravel under our shoes. I needed to take it in and sort out my feelings later. This visit was about learning and fact finding. So I stood in front of the crematorium, saw the open oven doors, entered the rooms once used for killing . . .

The statue of an old man, a prisoner, stood on a pedestal. The inscription beneath read:

*Den Toten zur Ehre*
*Den Lebenden zur Mahnung*
(In honor of the dead, an admonition for the living)

We were here to pay tribute to those who perished in this place and to take their fate as an admonition, a mandate. I was grateful for these words in the middle of my anxious reflection, so full of images of suffering. I became even more aware that during these horrible times my family had lived in Germany: my grandparents, my uncles, aunts, and cousins. How could I honor them or have respect for them?

I walked silently toward the memorial chapels sharing the same ground but separated by walls and by different faith traditions. The

Jewish memorial had been built of stone in the form of a cistern with an opening to the sky. Soft light came floating down on the cold stone—to a place of death with an open sky as the only source of hope. Walking into the cistern brought chills to my back: the rough stones, the prison walls, the filtered light in the darkness . . .

Outside the compound, a prayer chapel had been erected, maintained by the Carmelite nuns. I entered quietly and sat down on a brown, wooden bench with nothing to say to God, nothing, absolutely nothing—just silence in and around me. I could not think of a prayer to utter. Even "Our Father" seemed an unfitting address. So I just looked straight ahead. I had nothing to bring either; my hands were empty, my jaw locked. No words could express the heaviness of the moment. I wanted to hide; I was ashamed. I had come to a place where I could be held accountable for the sins of my parents' generation in a world of perpetrators and victims alike. What would I be able to utter anyway after so many years had passed? Too late for many of them to speak or defend themselves . . .

Some white candles were flickering on a pillar. The black smoke of a burning wick was rising toward the ceiling, only to disappear in the air.

I realized at that moment that my parents had taken their answers to my questions to their graves many years ago. Therefore, I would have to go on my own journey to revisit the past and find my place in it. Their journey was going to be mine from now on. In order to accomplish this, I would need help in finding their traces, in uncovering my own faded memories and, most of all, in lifting the silence of the child within me so she could speak out. Who would listen to the remnants, recognize the images, respond to the tears? What if all she could do was scream?

The woman in my office had looked at me with her warm smile and had wished me a good trip. She had stepped over a human abyss heaped with immeasurable pain, rivers of tears, never-ending grief, and the dark silence of prejudice and hate, covered by the uttered memories of the living bearing open wounds and filled with the silent screams of the dead in the deep.

But the woman had stepped over it. Her hand had reached for mine so that she could pass on the dollar. She had given me a blessing with it. All I could do was thank her, accept it, and go on my journey to Germany. I was on my way.

*Return to Dresden*

# CHAPTER ONE

# On the Road Home

The traffic was flowing smoothly on the autobahn that Sunday morning in August of 1998, as we left Munich, Germany, heading north. The late summer heat had scorched the harvested fields, which were covered with cropped stalks on a sandy, yellow soil. I was caught by the soft countryside, the villages crowded along the roads and nestled into the hills and woods. The ornamented church steeples pointed toward the hazy sky. Deep ringing bells still announced the faithful living nearby and honored the dead buried in their churchyards.

"It's good to travel on a Sunday morning," my brother Klaus commented as he read the map in front of him. "The trucks are not allowed to be on the road, and the returning vacationers are not there either."

Winfried's foot rested steadily on the gas pedal, his eyes fixed on the road. No speed limit on this stretch of the autobahn, a paradise for a California driver.

My backseat window framed the town of Bayreuth on the left. The *Festspielhaus* loomed on the hill; its huge arch towered over the city below. It had been built in 1872, without air conditioning, of course. Richard Wagner, the builder and composer, had designed it in a way to create the purest acoustics and to produce the best blend of sound ever. Never mind the heat of summer and the sweat of performers and guests alike. Every year from then on, the music had been bold and beguiling, no matter how much the critics squabbled in the newspapers about the avant-garde productions on stage, about the language, the voices, the divas, and the conductors.

The Richard Wagner Festival was in full swing at this time of the summer, with the opera *Die Meistersinger* on today's program. I have long admired this majestic piece of soaring love and celebration of German history and the country's honorable guilds. The popular overture of the opera, with its famous brass themes, started playing in my head. This masterpiece is not without controversy. Richard Wagner's anti-Semitism has been clearly documented. His image of a Jew is conveyed in the role of the klutzy Beckmesser, who unsuccessfully woos a maiden only to become the laughingstock of all the citizens in Nuremberg. This year the production had a revised text in order to take the anti-Semitic sting out. The music, remaining intact with all its colorful depth and layered emotions, is impossible for me to dismiss as background music; it speaks directly to my feelings. My second brother, Herbert, and his wife, Ursa, would be at today's performance—how lucky for them!

The town still has a bitter taste for many people. Wagner's music had been glorified by the Hitler regime and used as a leitmotif for German superiority, power, and victory. The majestic brass tunes, especially the overture from *Die Meistersinger*, were used as background music in the concentration camps. Therefore, Wagner's music is still hated today by many Jewish survivors.

During the postwar years, my music instruction at school and at home had taken a mysterious course. Wagner's music was rarely mentioned then. It was ignored at home for years because of its connection with the glory and torture of the Hitler years and the known friendship between Hitler and the Wagner family in Bayreuth. The other reason Wagner's music was shunned had to do with the "perverted" content of his stories, which stood in harsh contrast to my religious upbringing and family values. As a child, I did not understand it all but felt that something about the music was disreputable. So I ignored the music too, as instructed, and with it the stories of human tragedy—of lust for power, of greed, love, betrayal, and redemption—that were depicted in the operas. Only later did I learn why the music was tarnished, and about the denazification process after the war, even in the small town we lived in, the effort to cleanse our thinking. It was my brother Herbert who made me aware during my teen years of the tragic figure of Beckmesser in *Die Meistersinger*, his role of scapegoat in his society. Herbert showed me the musical score of the opera one day, pointing out the compositional details in Beckmesser's serenade and speaking of the human tragedy in the portrayal. The laughingstock turned into a person in need of compassion. Slowly, over many years, did I learn to separate the music from the political abuse?

Winfried and I had tried to order tickets to this month-long festival for years, only to be turned down again this year. I guess it was not our turn yet to be inducted into the society of true Wagnerian disciples. Well, maybe next year, I thought. We could come back here if we would finally be so lucky as to have tickets; we would follow the fanfares on the balcony announcing the start of the opera, and then step inside the *Festspielhaus*.

"We will soon be crossing the old border between West and East Germany," Klaus said as we headed toward a stretch of open fields. "Not much left to see anymore. They tore down all the fences and walls as soon as possible after the Berlin wall came down in 1989. To the right, you can still see some deserted barrack buildings and some cement slabs. That's where the border control took place."

"It is still hard to believe that all this is gone now," I responded. "But how do people get along with each other now?"

"There is quite some tension between the different parts of Germany. The price is enormous to restore the land. And the attitude of the people . . . well, that's another matter. Forty years of imprisonment in your own country leaves a lot of emotions and strange reactions on both sides of the border. Even now, there is long-standing jealous anger on both sides, flinches of entitlement, and pockets of hopelessness due to the high rate of unemployment in this area. Many elderly people are totally confused, their hearts full of complaints and bitterness."

*I could see their faces, just like the ones in Leipzig where I had lived as a child. Their backs were bent under the heavy load of silence, their ashen faces staring to the ground as they walked by our house. Everyone carried a handbag or a sack in which to bring home some meager food rationing . . .*

"What about the young people?" I wanted to know.

"For most of them, the transition was easier. Unfortunately, some of the teens have banded in gangs and march to the tune of the Führer with shaved heads, flags and all. It is a small group, the neo-Nazis, their actions are horrifying to us."

The soft green meadows, the rolling hills, and the patches of forest eased the pictures in my mind of border guards with their rifles, of dark windows in buildings, gates, the senseless waiting, and the flutters in my stomach when I was asked for my passport at a previous visit to the area and a border crossing many years ago; all that was gone by now, just reminders outside and memories on the inside.

My thoughts wandered back to the incredible events that started with the ending of an era, the opening of a wall.

On November 9, 1989, the Berlin wall came crumbling down. We lived in Redondo Beach, California, at the time, and the event was covered live on television. We saw thousands of people celebrating in the streets of Berlin, standing on top of the wall, hacking holes with picks and hammers, screaming and crying, bewildered and euphoric. They were breaking down the barriers between East and West Germany, destroying a wall that had separated families, friends, and neighbors, that was part of the long, painful history of the country. Huge crowds stood at the Brandenburg Gate, watching and reaching out to each other. Within hours the roadway broke open. Men, women, and children walked to the other side of the same city. No more shooting and hunting down the ones that tried to flee, who had risked their lives for the price of freedom. I realized then that I truly never expected this to happen during my lifetime. After 1961, when the wall was erected in

Berlin and the rest of the borders were even more tightly secured, we were told by our schoolteachers to accept the separation of the two sections of Germany and to stop praying and hoping for any reunification. Over the next months we accepted the political reality of the time and I stopped praying. I thought that this final division was another price Germany had to pay for the sins of our fathers during the Nazi regime—a painful punishment of separation, loss, and oppression.

But then, the wall did come down. The country that was left behind by the Russians had been trashed, polluted, and economically exploited—ready to be thrown away. But now with the exodus of the occupying force, the broken wall also opened a chance for me to revisit without fear the places of my childhood and those of my parents. A wall within me was coming down, too, bringing light to dormant memories and allowing me access to the history of my country, which had been shrouded in darkness for so many years. I, too, had to step over the rubble of a toppled wall to go to the other side and see.

The day the Berlin wall came down, I called Klaus to hear from him firsthand what was going on back home. "The wall is coming down. Is that true?"

"We can't believe it either," he replied.

"We are sitting by the television to get the latest. Aren't you worried about bloodshed?" I asked.

"Of course, but nothing has happened so far. The local police have apparently joined in the movement of liberation from the Communist regime. It is incredible! We are stunned."

I was curious about the reactions of the people to these unexpected developments in Berlin. He tried to describe the wonder of relief all around the country, the surprise on people's faces as they shook their heads in disbelief. What would a united Germany look like? Who would pay for the repair of an exploited country?

"The people on the street were already complaining about the money that would be needed," he said. "But you should see the euphoria around us. People from all over the country drove to the borders.

They wanted to see for themselves what was happening." There was a long pause. Then with a trembling voice he added, "You know, the war is over, it is finally over."

We both cried quietly on the phone. I was shocked because I couldn't remember ever having known him to cry. I tried hard to hold my tears in, to no avail. I knew what he meant. We cried for our parents and their incomplete lives, their losses and hardships, and out of relief after so many years of longing for peace. Our parents had witnessed two world wars; my grandfather fought in World War I and then lived through World War II. None of them had lived long enough to experience this special day in our history. I knew then that I was going to go back to Germany one day and trace their paths. If they could not be there to claim an end to war then I was going to do it for them. I was on my way.

Winfried hit the brakes of the Renault for another, by now familiar, *Stau,* a traffic jam on the right side of the road. Another construction site was in full swing with open pipes heaped along the shoulders; the hot smell of asphalt seeped through the windows.

The villages we passed on the autobahn took on a brighter look. Houses had been freshly painted, covered with new, red roof tiles; even small gardens were groomed with care. I could see the white lace curtains behind scrubbed and shiny windows. Fluffy down comforters, or *Federbetten,* as we called them, decorated open windows like big, white clouds. By now, we had entered the eastern section of Germany. Here, the recently repaired autobahn showed fewer stretches of the old, bumpy, noisy road. Years of neglect slowly disappeared in the black, shiny asphalt, and Winfried gladly stepped on the gas pedal.

"It was amazing," Klaus went on. "As soon as the country opened to the West, people started to plant flowers in their front yards and placed flower boxes outside their windows. You should have seen the neglect in the towns before the wall came down, nobody cared about anything. Everything looked gray and shabby. Of course, the supermarkets moved into towns, the merchants rushed in to make a quick buck!" He laughed. I liked the way he emphasized the harsh "k" sound of "buck".

"What about all these new cars?" Winfried wanted to know more, and was ever scanning all vehicles in sight, old and new. I smiled at his favorite leisure activity while he was driving; he was eager to identify the current German cars, or, better, all cars in sight. He was like a kid in a candy store, surprised and open-eyed.

"Most of the *Trabis* are gone by now. They were atrocious and stank to no end. Everyone, of course, wanted a western car after the *Wende* [reunification]." The two men began to chat about cars, models and gasoline prices.

We were on our way not only to the former East Germany and to Poland, but also to other places where my family had lived during and after the war. We had planned this trip for some time, my curiosity about our family history and my personal story being the leading force. For this adventure, I had asked Klaus, the oldest of my siblings, to join us; he would have the most vivid memories. As a geodesist, he possessed the necessary skills to decipher German as well as Polish maps and to lead the way into unfamiliar territory. I felt quite sure of his ability to guide and was hoping to connect our memories and family stories with current on-site impressions. It was an opportunity to finally revisit the location of our border crossing into the West in 1949. Our itinerary would include a visit to Dresden, the beautiful city finally growing out of the ashes. We hoped to enter Poland and the city of my birth, Breslau. Before the end of World War II, this region of Poland had belonged to Germany and was called Schlesien. Breslau had been renamed Wroclaw after the war. We also had plans to drive into the countryside of Schlesien, to a village named Damsdorf, about fifty kilometers southeast of Breslau, where we had been evacuated in 1944. I was uneasy about what we would find in the various locations. What if there was nothing left to see, no connecting memories to be found? No traces of our family life? What if my memories had concocted it all, scars and wounds? This is the summer of 1998, and my history of trauma goes back over fifty years to a time of war. Time had marched on; maybe by now it should have healed old wounds. Maybe the silence covered it for good.

I had sent a copy of my writing to Klaus a couple of months earlier. I knew his English language skills were good enough for him to understand my written text, its meaning and the outpouring of my feelings. My story is his story, too. I waited for his comments, but he said little except how amazed he was at how much material I had collected. "It is impressive," he had said briefly when we had arrived in München a few days ago.

The men's conversation about cars, gasoline, and maps had ceased, and Klaus turned around to look at me. "Maybe tonight, after we get to the hotel, we'll sit down and go through the text together. I made some comments. It might be helpful to do it before we get to the various locations."

I nodded. I was eager to hear what he had to say. I wondered about his response to our history, about his feelings and the effects of the war years on his life.

"How about stopping in Naumburg and visiting the cathedral?" Klaus looked up from his map as we were moving along with the traffic. He pointed toward the right when the steeples of the cathedral came into full view. "I remember visiting here as a boy from Leipzig. I hear that the cathedral is quite a sight again."

Winfried, glad for a break, jumped at the opportunity to visit one more cathedral on the way. I smiled at his eagerness to enter any house of worship on our trips, his seeking of the majestic as well as the humbleness in faith, and, most of all, his wanting to find a spiritual home on the way to somewhere.

Once off the autobahn, we enjoyed a closer view of the small towns and villages along the country road made of cobblestones. The hollow rattle of tires made it hard to keep up any lengthy conversation in the car.

The famous cathedral of Naumburg soon came into full view. Its two main towers announced the Romanesque and early Gothic history with narrow arched windows and massive stone walls. Spooky gargoyles bent down sharply, suspended from rain gutters, openmouthed, fanged, and winged, to keep the evil spirits away. We entered the dimly lit cathedral. Few people were visiting inside this Sunday afternoon.

"It is now a museum," the woman at the entrance hall said as she took our money. "Services are only held occasionally."

The enormous, cruciform basilica with its vaulted roof, originally built in 1213, had gone through major alterations, some completed as late as the nineteenth century. Hollow and empty, it received us—the remnants of a house of worship, its symbols of altar and cross in unattended spaces. Our steps echoed as we entered the west choir lined with the old, dark, wooden choir stalls. There they stood, carved in limestone, the life-size statues of the founders of the cathedral, twelve figures in all—the most famous pairs being Uta and Ekkehard, Reglindis and Hermann. I recognized their faces from pictures in our home during the years when we lived in Leipzig around 1947. My aunt Hanni had been so fond of them and kept postcards of their portraits around. Their frozen smiles seemed forever edged in stone. Uta's gentle face was draped by her cold cloth, her crown so delicately restive on her head. These statues came from a different world: a world of pride and celebration of the human spirit, of generosity and beauty, of minstrels' poetry, noble conquest, religious reverence, and the power of the church institution. How silently they stood in this enormous hall, still guarding what they had stood for centuries ago.

Today, the cathedral belonged to those founders again, the statues standing alone in the absence of God. The house of God was now a museum. Although years of neglect and dust blanketed this cathedral, the founders as well as the cold walls had withstood the last forty years of Communist occupation behind the iron curtain, with little money available for "the ever-needed repairs," as the attendant said when we entered. I, too, felt strangely cold and empty as I walked through the archway toward the nave that housed the sarcophaguses of knights and kings. A large wooden door led to the cloister garth. It seemed the soul of a people had departed from this place a long time ago, leaving the cold statues waiting for a new breath of life, maybe for a happier time, when the halls would again be filled with music echoing from the balconies. Maybe they were longing for brightly lit candles, for the mystery of sacrament to be celebrated around the altar, and especially for people's smiling faces. Did this poverty of spirit reflect the years of spiritual oppression, silencing the church forever?

Outside in the cloister yard, the thick wall of the cathedral framed a large patch of green grass. The late afternoon sunshine marked the stone walkways with sharp, gray shadows.

"*Ja*, I remember our trip to the cathedral in 1947 or so," Klaus said. "We walked from the train station. I never forgot about it. An outing with the train during those days was quite an event."

Klaus smiled as he followed his thoughts, and we finally headed toward the café outside the cathedral compound and sat down at one of the tables. At this time in the afternoon he enjoyed a good cup of strong coffee with several spoons of sugar. I had ordered a piece of *Apfelkuchen* with my tea. My thoughts went back to a time when, after the war, the conditories had nothing to exhibit but empty shelves. I looked at Klaus as he stirred his black coffee with a spoon, and I was glad for him that he could connect his memories of hardship with good friends and laughter way back in 1947. My memories remained so dark, and my feelings seemed to be stuck in my throat. I wanted the courage to experience both.

That night, we stopped in Quedlinburg. To our surprise, we found the inner city greatly restored to its original, medieval look. Many half-timbered houses were freshly painted. A narrow cobblestone street led up to the *Schlossberg* with the Renaissance castle where a panoramic view opened up before us. Red, tiled roofs covered the town, laid out like a poorly fitting jigsaw puzzle. Carefully tended roses in front gardens and flower boxes bursting with geraniums decorated the white houses. What an abundance of flowers! Dust hung in the heavy summer air.

"Quedlinburg is becoming a museum town," the locals told us. The people were not sure if their efforts to restore every part of the city to its original shape and color would be in the best interest of all its citizens. Old maps had been consulted, discovered paint was being matched and wrought iron skillfully restored; masonry had become an art form again. The city council had argued about the idea of returning a city to the look it had in prewar years, but finally welcomed current job opportunities in their hometown. Could a city forget the long years of dilapidation and neglect just by making repairs? The city was mending fast now. People wanted to move on with their lives, their dreams, and their hopes.

We settled in at the hotel *Zur Goldenen Sonne* in the historic section of town. The cobblestone street, cleanly swept, seemed as noisy and bumpy as ever. Our windows opened up toward a plaza with a bubbling water fountain, now a gathering place in the evening for the young people in town. They stood about in small groups, sitting or leaning on their bikes, laughing, calling out to each other by name.

The restaurant on the first floor of the hotel was decorated with cozy booths and checkered tablecloths. It served traditional regional food, which quickly sank in my stomach with a heaviness that would rule out any further sightseeing that night: roasted potatoes mixed with onions, sausage, and mushrooms, all of it well soaked in pan fat, to be washed down with the local beer. The smell of onions simmering in fat drifted like a heavy cloud throughout the dining room.

Klaus pulled my manuscript from his black briefcase as he sipped on the dark brew with its rich white foam floating on top. I could hardly wait for his response.

"You know what is so amazing about your writing," he started slowly, "is that your outpouring was triggered by a crisis in Winfried's congregation a few years back, right? I was amazed how this experience stirred up so many memories of our past."

I did not want to think about this painful time in Winfried's church when it looked as though some congregants wanted a change of clergy, which would have meant another relocation. I did not want to remember that difficult time right now. Maybe I could think about it later. Klaus looked up briefly and waited. So I said, "You are right. I reached a point in my life where I could not see myself moving one more time—maybe to be run out of town again—not being wanted in that community anymore. Just like being a refugee again, you know, in Raschau or Damsdorf." He nodded but did not respond, his hand reaching for the stein of dark, foamy beer.

"After Winfried and I left Germany in 1966," I went on, " I did not want to think much about our dreadful past during and after the war anymore. With our exodus all the war memories were left six thousand miles behind, so I thought. We had made a new beginning. We now lived in a free country. In addition, we moved five more times. Then came these trigger experiences a few years ago that did open the floodgates to my early memory so intensely, and my search began for my place in the history of my family and my country."

He listened attentively, his eyes fixed on the papers in front of him. Winfried had gone up to his room to enjoy a quiet evening of reading. He knew it would be best to leave us alone for this conversation. My brother and I were spending time together. It was like coming home.

"But that's what it takes, a crisis of similar proportions and repeated emotional themes to fully bring back the original trauma with a flood of familiar fears and reactions." I wanted to sound professional; it was easier to keep a distance from my emotions that way. So I went on, trying to invite him into the subject of emotional triggers and flashbacks. "I wonder how you dealt with all this family trauma. You were the oldest of us four, you carried so many more responsibilities, and you have so many more memories, right?"

He shrugged his shoulders. His slim lips tightened even more. "I've never spent too much time thinking about it." He stopped briefly. "You know, we all went through those years. It wasn't so different from what other people went through. We didn't have to talk about it because we all were together." He smiled.

"But after the war did our mother talk much about the war years?"

"Not really. I am not sure why, maybe we did not ask her, either."

*I knew why—because of the many years of the silent anniversaries of our flight to Dresden, the bombing on February 13, our father's death date in April, our escape to somewhere else. She did not talk because of her choked tears and her unending grief—too many losses of family members, of homes, and friends, too much to feel by herself. Maybe she was too scared to open up old wounds without a listener—her memories were too raw and powerful. Over the years, it had been hard for our mother to hold in such an overwhelming sense of fear and grief. She had several breaking points when her despair began to flow. I wanted to forget about those. I felt guilty that I could not be of much help to her during her later years. I did not know how to comfort her either. Maybe nobody could. All she said was that we were spared and protected, "bewahrt"; she did not say what for, or why. I figured it meant we were spared from dying. In her sadness she wanted to be grateful; in her bitterness she was glad to see us children alive.*

"You know," Klaus went on, "I really had a pretty good childhood." He smiled. "We played a lot, and I enjoyed school. Even in Leipzig in 1947, I liked my teacher, took piano lessons, and played outside with my friends. Oh, by the way, you are right, we boys sat in one of the ruins unattended, on a balcony, and smoked vine leaves. We even tried to clear a whole floor of rubble out of that house with shovels, but the adults wouldn't allow us to play there. I guess it was too dangerous." His eyes sparkled as he looked at me. "I took the streetcar by myself to church activities or to my piano lessons. Of course, we did not have much to eat, especially in 1947, but *das war halt so*—that's how it was."

He kept repeating this last phrase throughout our conversation whenever he needed to shield his feelings and sort of summarize his thoughts. "I don't have much to say to your memories about the border crossing because I was not there, but we will drive into the area tomorrow morning. The maps will help us to find the river. I have my own story of crossing the border."

I nodded. I knew his story, too, and had already included it in my text. I was waiting for his story, but instead he continued, "Did you know that I am not the oldest among us children, and you were not the youngest either? Our parents actually had six children."

I looked straight at him. "She never spoke to me about those experiences."

"She had one miscarriage in 1933, one year before my birth," Klaus went on, "and another one in 1943, during the war years, two years after you were born."

I had only recently read about these losses in one of my father's letters written in 1945. He had tried to comfort my mother at the time after our dreadful flight to Dresden, writing to her that a baby might not have survived the ordeal. I, however, had survived.

"You know, our parents believed in angels," he said quietly. "They called them *Himmelsfreunde*, heavenly friends, who would protect us during those years of family separation. Mother wrote to our father in 1943 or so, when I was eight or nine years old, that I had seen an angel sitting on our brother Gerhard's bed one night. This heavenly visitor was white, sort of without color. Another time, I saw a little boy in our flat in Breslau. Mother told me afterwards that this was really my little brother that was never born. I believed her. I was so sure that angels really existed; it was a proof for me that there are angels among us. Our father must have been very comforted by their presence in our home while he was absent, fighting in the war. It was such a difficult time."

He touched his chin and looked down on my manuscript in front of him. As the oldest of us, having been born in 1934, he was the one whose help I needed with my burning question. So I burst out, "How much did our parents know about the war and the atrocities committed by the Nazis? Do you know how much they were aware of what was going on in the government, the party, the . . . ?"

"That's hard to say. I really don't know what they actually knew. The reason being that every spoken word in or outside the home had potentially dangerous consequences. Under Hitler everyone was afraid to speak openly to their neighbors, even to members of their own family. You could be reported for being an enemy of the state, and deported to a labor camp—killed! Remember, even in Leipzig after the war, we still were reminded not to tell anybody what we thought, had, and ate."

I nodded, thinking of Frau Lehmann, an old woman in Leipzig who lived by herself next to our grandfather's flat.

"Don't blabber things out to anyone," Mother would say to us.

"And you little ones always did." Klaus chuckled.

"*Ja*, I know."

Even now, I felt a bit guilty for wanting to share stories with Frau Lehmann or my friend Karin across the courtyard where we had lived. Back then I did not understand why we had to keep secrets. Frau Lehmann was an old, kind woman. She was always nice to me and I enjoyed my visits in her small flat.

*The fear of spies in your own neighborhood and the presence of the Gestapo silenced all of them, including our parents. It was intended also to silence me. Fear silenced my heart and would do so for many years.*

"When you have a chance," he went on, "read Father's last letters written in early 1945. Gerhard has them. He took them along after Mother's death."

He paused for a while. Then he said quietly, "It is very clear that all our father wanted was to come home to us, to our mother, and to us children. He was never a member of the Nazi Party, but he shared the conviction of needing to protect his family and the German nation from the Russians. He called them *die Bolchevisten*, the Bolshevists. Father may not have been fully aware of the German atrocities, but, for sure, he knew of the Russian soldiers' violence: the murders, rapes, and total destruction wherever they went. And by 1944, the Russians moved west like a rapid tidal wave. At the end, he was stuck somewhere in Croatia between the Russian front and Tito's partisans. Just stuck."

We both fell silent; no words were necessary. I had to take a deep breath to go on.

*So why talk about it? That's how it was—we lived through it. Das war halt so.*

He quietly took another sip from his beer. The white foam had fizzled. The waitress came by to check on us, since we had been sitting at our table for such a long time. Klaus ordered another beer.

"You know, with very few exceptions, by 1934 most people in Germany had bought the official party line, the drive for a domination of Europe, the image of power and *Vaterland*, which included hating the Jews. They were identified as the poison in society and needed to be purged efficiently. Hitler radiated such strength and confidence in speech and presentation, it seemed as if he spoke to each individual, to each family, when he addressed the nation. The economy had recovered from the depth of depression and nobody argued with that. A global isolation of a people had been created by an infrastructure of ever-present fear. There was no telecommunication, as we know it today. I know our father feared the Gestapo, too." I wanted to know more, but he went on, "You want to know how I feel about all this?" He shrugged his shoulders. "Oh well, *das war halt so*," he said again. "It was a horrible time for all of us . . . but *das hab ich schon gegessen*."

I guess he was trying to tell me that he had swallowed it all up: memories, trauma, and losses. It was over, thank God! His memories were gone? No, he knew how to leave the past behind. We had survived and he lived in the present. Why hang on to my dark and bitter feelings? Why hang on to my nagging questions of who knew what, and how much, and when?

He could not say much more about himself and how our history might have shaped his life and our family. So I pressed on, "Didn't your children ever ask you about your experiences as a boy during those years?"

"No, not really. They don't seem to be interested in the past. They feel the whole mess has nothing to do with them. They don't feel responsible for 'the sins of our fathers'. My son is angry at the inconvenience brought on by the reunification of Germany. So many political challenges are associated with our current economic downtime, the job crunch, and the entitlement attitude of the people. No, he likes to live life and does not look back. What about your children?" He looked at me.

"One day not too long ago my daughter started asking me questions about our past. She must have felt that for years I held my memories inside. Our son lives and works in New York. His Jewish law colleagues have openly asked him, have identified his German heritage by looking at his name and asking him questions about his parents. So he had to start dealing with it. One of his colleagues is a World War II buff. Their awareness of being German by family background connects them with their families' history with Hitler. This fact cannot be avoided in the United States given the Jewish community and their unending grief following the Holocaust. Lately though, there seems to be an urgency and a willingness to break the silence on so many more fronts. Some fifty-plus years later, it is time to hear from all survivors, including us war orphans."

We pored over the text in front of us, page after page. He had made additions and corrections; even some spelling errors did not escape him.

Tomorrow we would retrace our family's journey during the war years. We would actually revisit the various sites—only this time without the imminent danger of the past looming around us. My brother, both strange and familiar, seemed to be taking me by the hand again. He was still the big brother, the one leading with little opportunity to feel much.

Sleep that night came in restless waves. I slipped into pictures of border fences, fields, and shadows, as trees and train tracks blended in with my fitful sleep. Why did I worry? The soldiers were long gone. What about the land mines in the sand strips left behind? What about being alone again out there in the middle of nowhere? Would we ever find the river, the old border crossing area past Oschersleben? The end of the train tracks?

Grandfather, fortunately, had written down the name of this town on the postcard he sent to us in 1949. I had forgotten exactly where Mother and I crossed the border to the West. Thanks to Grandfather and his postcard, we could trace the route one more time. How important it had become; it was now a reassuring guide. I still kept waking and slipping in and out of sleep. I saw the images of Dresden, the city with its famous silhouette . . . the river Elbe, the riverbanks . . . Wintergartenstrasse 31 . . . Grandmother's grave . . . the ashes . . . the bones, the key. We would go to the place of my birth, to Breslau, in Poland, then to the countryside of the bitter winter of 1945 . . .

*Where are you, all you who have lived and died here?* "Our Father who art in heaven." *A piece of my soul has been left here too with you, an aching void never ever to be filled . . . To be left alone . . .* "Thy will be done, on earth as it is in heaven . . ." *Would I meet you all somewhere during the next few days? . . .* "Give us this day our daily bread," *just bread . . . like back in 1947 when Mother was desperate . . .*

The hot summer night offered no relief, no refreshing breeze to move the sheer curtains into a flutter . . . *"And deliver us from evil . . ."* How many times have you prayed these lines too, all you who have lived and died? Uneasy sleep floated on murky reflections.

The early dawn chased away shredded dreams and fragments of prayer. The sound of cars passing outside our hotel window, their tires hitting the cobblestone roads, wakened us to a new day.

We headed north, going through the city of Halberstadt, marked by its enormous church buildings in need of repairs. Even the bright morning could not hide the potholes on the road, the neglected houses, and the construction sites everywhere. In Oschersleben, we turned toward Gunsleben, our first destination.

We entered a quiet, small town. Plain-looking, whitewashed houses lined the main street. Our car rattled even more on the old stone road, the dull sound of the tires making it impossible to talk. This Monday morning, no one walked along the sidewalks, not even the ever-busy housewives rushing to prepare *Mittagessen*. An empty silence welcomed us to the past. How different it all looks now, I thought. White lace curtains had returned to the homes, framing shiny windows. Brightly painted doors were no longer hiding lives in darkness. White paint had replaced the gray plaster hardened by harsh winters and neglect over the years.

The road led us straight ahead to the train tracks. The old red-and-white rusty-hinged gate bar stood erect, not having been used in years. I got my first glimpse of the deserted building on the right side of the street, the old train station. Now abandoned, it was partially boarded up by loose wires, posts, and fences. A covered wooden staircase still accessible from the street side was locked tight. Stalky weeds crowned by shredded, yellow flowers grew all around the building. Obviously, no one had tended the place in years. The old platform where passengers would board and exit trains was still partially visible, but the rusty, dull tracks hadn't welcomed any travelers for a very long time. More shaggy weeds covered up the harshness of the neglected site. Young, stalky trees crowded in on the back door of the building. I climbed up the stairs to the back entrance to look inside. The whole place had been transformed into a residential site. Empty, wallpapered rooms replaced the old waiting area, . . . *the brown benches we sat on, waiting for the guide to take us across the border so many years ago* . . .

The useless train station had been abandoned. No need for trains anyway, the tracks ended here, the switch tower still standing farther down to the west . . . *This was the place where Mother and I had arrived late at night in September of 1949. She had said, "The train stops here. We will have to walk from now on." I sat on the hard bench with my knapsack; only a dim light on the ceiling outlined the dimensions of the room, maybe to keep our escape from being discovered . . . I cannot remember much of the outside of the building. Of course, it was dark then . . . I need to go back to Leipzig and start my story there . . .*

# CHAPTER TWO

# *Through the Night (1949)*

The summer of 1949 passed quietly. We lived with my grandfather, Paul Schnädelbach, our Opa, in Leipzig, East Germany, and shared his apartment on Lösniger Strasse 47, on the second floor. My three older brothers, my mother, and I had moved there in 1945, and she said it was now our home, too. I was tall enough to look out of the apartment window in the back toward a courtyard with clotheslines, small patches of garden, green hedges, and balconies loaded with flower pots and chairs. The chatter and screams of children echoed from a small playground. The windows in the front faced the street, the sidewalks, and the front row of stone houses across the street whose dark windows and heavy closed doors all looked alike. The window in the bathroom was too high for me to look out, but I could see the sky. Of all the rooms in Grandfather's place, this was the scariest. A lengthy hallway led up to the bathtub and the toilet to the side. Often the light would not come on in the evening. Electricity was still being rationed during those days and we never knew when and for how long we would be without it. Taking a candle along could make things worse. Shadows of sharp and scraggly lines appeared on the walls, slowly flickering in the candlelight and then suddenly all disappearing. My steps on the hard, cold floor echoed. Some cloth-draped cardboard boxes placed in corners and along the hallway added to my fears that hidden dangers would come out with the night. Pulling the chain of the water tank was the worst; the rushing of the water and the rattling of the pipes made me flee the room in a hurry. Mother occasionally would come with me into the dark. That helped some, but then I was already seven years old and expected to manage my own thoughts and fears and be grown up about them.

Singing in the bathroom helped. The loud *hallelujahs* not only brought the walls to life, but also echoed the melodies my mother sang on many occasions—bits of church hymns, Bach and Handel themes, and phrases and scales from my brothers' piano practice. My *hallelujahs* fit any tune nicely and carried the sound into the sky. The neighbors commented on it to my mother. They told her, "Do not stop her from singing, and do not close the window either!"

I was not the only one singing. Mother had a beautiful and warm contralto voice. Her smooth phrases and sustained breath carried a mournful yet calming tone with resounding depth. However, her singing resonated such sadness and longing within me. I recognized familiar words from our church, or that had been read to me from the Bible. And there were melodies of lost love, of winter and snow, of *Abschied* and good-bye. For many feelings expressed through music, I had no words. Frequently, on Sunday afternoons, she sang in the living room while one of my brothers played the piano. Mother told us she had sung these lieder by Schubert, Schumann, and Brahms in happier times with my father playing the piano—but I could not remember those.

Grandfather's singing was more private and a bit mysterious. Every night, the melodies of muffled hymns, sung with faint, dark, and clear tones, seeped through the thin walls into my bedroom. Mother said that he was praying and holding his daily devotion, and talking to *Muttel*, his wife, who had died the year I was born. Once in a while, he invited my brother Gerhard and me into his bedroom for a brief visit before we were sent to bed. A glass of water stood on his nightstand with his dentures swimming in it. We called it the aquarium, and we were fascinated by the rows of removable and swimming teeth. Grandfather did not like us laughing at his teeth and sent us out. I think he was embarrassed.

"You must not tell anyone about it," my mother said to me one day in late August of 1949.

We were often told not to say anything to anybody out of fear of being overheard and spied on by the Communists or the *Volkspolizei*, the state police. People were arrested and sent to jail for saying something bad about the government. Some were caught trading American cigarettes and coffee for real food on the black market. Sometimes folks in the neighborhood just disappeared. I feared that the Russian soldiers in town had kidnapped and killed them. When we needed to take the streetcar, Mother cautioned us to be quiet and not to blabber out where we were going or whom we were to meet. Especially at night, darkness and warnings transformed fears into real and imagined dangers. Mother said, "It is dangerous for women to be out in the dark." Then she whispered something into my aunt's ear. I reassured myself by looking repeatedly over my shoulder or walking close to my brothers. I liked it best when I could hold my mother's hand, but since we were four children, I had to take turns.

Several of my schoolmates had not returned to class during the last year but nobody talked about it; we all knew why. I wanted to ask my teachers about my friends, but the teachers were active members of the Communist Party and could not be trusted. Being asked would annoy them. My first-grade teacher, not really a teacher by training, was given the job because he was a Communist Party member in good standing.

The summer passed and I was to enter second grade. We had learned to copy and read complete sentences written on a black chalkboard in my classroom. I memorized them. Reading street names and signs suddenly became fun; letters lined up in my mind and slowly spelled out names and places. We were taught the Russian national anthem and the famous song *"Wolga Wolga,"* with that slow, deep, and dark melody. It was a special honor in school to belong to the *Junge Pioniere*—Young Pioneers, a Communist youth organization—because as a member you were allowed to wear a red scarf to class. You were also permitted to attend a special meeting every week. I liked the bright red-colored scarf; it broke the drab gray of the day and the dark of the night. But red was the color of the Russian flag. Of course, I could not belong to this group of young people. I was not allowed to identify with and wave their flag either. My special group was my Sunday school class where there were no flags or scarves.

"Your brothers are leaving for the West and we will follow them, but not right away," she said. "You cannot tell anyone, especially not in school. Don't tell your friends downstairs on the playground. Not even the people in church. Otherwise we may be found out and get arrested."

I knew all about people fleeing into the western section of Germany. Even one of my uncles had done so a couple of years ago, and I suspected that my friends in school who had disappeared had fled also. I realized how dangerous it was. The government had strictly forbidden anyone to leave the country. The borders were closed and tightly guarded by Russian soldiers on our side. No one could obtain permission to leave this section of Germany. Mother knew that the future would be bleak for all of us here in the Russian-occupied zone of Germany. My brothers could not expect any university education even if they were qualified. Such placement would have to be approved by the local political forum and we would never qualify. I overheard my family talk about not being wanted by the Communist regime in power since Father had not been a farmer or a valued factory worker. Their children would be sent to the university instead. Our father had been a minister in the Methodist Church and had not returned from the war. We were informed in 1947 that he had died in April of 1945, a few weeks before the end of the war, in Yugoslavia while retreating from the Russian front. No one knew exactly when and where. I watched my mother quietly awaiting his return. She clung to Red Cross reports of German soldiers being sent home from the Russian prisoner-of-war camps. For many years, I shared her hope for a miracle, staring silently out the window toward the street corner and waiting for his sudden reappearance. Hope grew dimmer in time, and the sadness showed on my mother's face, was reflected in her eyes.

The waiting for my father's return became associated with another expectation and hope. Sitting on the stone steps by the front door, I waited for the second coming of Jesus Christ in power and glory, according to the lessons from Sunday school. Jesus would come really soon, the sound of trumpets announcing his final victorious entrance. My Sunday school teachers taught us about the end of the world and the end of all suffering to come. We would one day meet all our departed loved ones again, dressed in white, heavenly robes. There would be no more need to be different, neither male nor female, no evil, time without end. Eternity would receive us. So I looked out into the sky waiting patiently for redemption, only to be further scared by the droning noise of flyover airplanes, or by frightening animal screams coming from the direction of the local slaughterhouse. Yet, I waited for the second coming. Sunday school had been fun while I was waiting for Jesus Christ. We celebrated summer fests with lanterns swaying in the trees. We played games and received special treats at Christmastime, *Lebkuchen* (gingerbread cookies) and baked Santas with colorful decorations. From church, Mother brought food items for us from the American CARE packages that helped us through times of hunger.

"The time has come for us to leave next week, but you cannot say good-bye to anyone," Mother announced one day looking straight at me, her tone serious and short.

We were to leave town quietly in the night without anyone knowing. I might never see my grandfather and my aunts again. I wondered about my dear aunt and uncle in Dresden who always remembered my birthday and Christmas by sending presents in big packages. My friend Karin who lived across the courtyard would be left behind with my other friends and Herr Ottrich, a grumpy old man who was teased by the boys and retaliated by yelling and hosing them down with cold water. He scared the wits out of me and I ran home whenever he started to rage.

Frau Zieschang tried to teach me the violin but my fingers moved too slowly. My playing did not sound like the music she produced on her instrument. I was discouraged by the screeches that came from my bow. I didn't mind leaving those lessons behind. However, it was going to be difficult not to tell my school friends and my principal, Herr Mirsch, of my impending flight. Who would defend Alfred, a small and frail boy in my class, who was always slower than the rest of us and could not figure out things? Once, the boys outside the school teased him bitterly, calling him a "retard" and bullying him really badly. In the heat of this confrontation, I came to his defense and actually hit one of the boys with my fist. To my surprise, the bullies left him alone after that. Alfred stuck close to me from then on.

In September my last day in school finally came. School was out. On my way home, I walked alongside Herr Mirsch, who happened to go in the same direction. A nice man with a gentle face, he was a good listener. One of my brothers said that he had been in a concentration camp during the Nazi regime because he was a Communist. He had come away from his incarceration with a wooden leg and needed a cane for walking. I could not hold it in any longer, so I said to him, "My mother and I are leaving for the West in a few days. I won't be back anymore."

He did not reply because at that moment my mother stood in front of us. She had come to pick me up from school and had overheard my announcement. She turned white, and her movements froze; a long silence followed. Nothing else was said. She took me by the hand and left in shock. I felt so guilty and expected to be severely punished. She did not speak to me all the way home or for the rest of the day. I had done something terrible and could not make it better. I soon realized we were to leave for the West immediately, in fear of being found out and reported to the police. I had broken the silence. I had disobeyed my mother.

Two days later, my mother and I left Leipzig. Grandfather and my two aunts accompanied us to the big railway station. I carried a small knapsack with a pair of socks, a favorite teddy bear, and something to eat. Mother's luggage consisted of a big handbag, which bulged with many papers and looked very heavy. I wore my favorite checkered skirt, which I had received in one of the CARE packages from America. Only recently in school had I learned to tell time and could now read the large white clock next to the train platform: it was almost five o'clock in the afternoon. Little was said. We made no special commotion, said no excessive good-byes for fear that someone would notice our leaving and quietly notify the police. Restless, I looked back several times to the main hall of the train station, remembering my announcement of our departure to the school principal.

Grandfather hugged and blessed me, his eyes moist and his words warm; he assured us of God's guidance. My mother spoke in a hushed voice, uttering thanks and good wishes. It all seemed so final. I would probably never see them again. Mother and I climbed into our train compartment. When the train finally left, they stood waving for a long time, eventually disappearing from our sight. I waved back as long as I could.

My mother and I found seats by a window. The wooden benches were hard and cold. Smoke and dirt from burned coal filled the air. Mother sat very quietly. Silence was everywhere. Gradually it got darker and a dim overhead light came on in the train compartment. People were seated next to us but nobody spoke, their faces blurred. From time to time, the engine's whistle startled me with its shrill, loud screech; the jerky rhythm of the train wheels on the hard tracks created its own pushy, faint melody.

In Magdeburg, we changed trains. By now, the darkness of the night had fully descended over the land. Only a few people traveled with us west toward Oschersleben, until we were the only travelers on the last stretch. At last, the train came to a stop in a deserted area, Gunsleben, a railway station that consisted of one large, empty waiting room lined with wooden benches along the walls. No one met us there. I sat quietly next to my knapsack, feeling frightened. Mother said,

"The train ends here. We are soon to meet the woman who will take us across the border."

Mother frequently got up from the bench to look outside. For hours no one came. In the shadows of the night, I noticed two men standing outside; one carried a briefcase and the other one a typewriter. No one spoke. I sat curled up with our bags.

Suddenly, she stood at the door, a long brown-gray scarf wrapped around her head to cover most of her face. The woman looked at my mother, then at me and said, "I do not take children, their crying and whining will get us caught by the border guards. It is too dangerous for me."

I looked down. My feet seemed big; I could run really fast if necessary. I remembered Herr Ottrich back in Leipzig, his screaming, and my speed running home. I listened anxiously at the whispers between my mother and the woman. Now it would be my fault if we could not get across the border. We could not go back. We were on the run and could never return. Herr Mirsch might have told the police by now.

"I cannot do it . . . not alone . . . at night," she whispered. "The money?"

"We cannot go back . . . I did not know. She will be quiet . . . I promise you, she will not cry."

I stood next to her and nodded, my promise. A long pause. The woman glared at me. No one said a word for a while; Mother and I just waited. I did not move. I could hear my mother breathe. I knew that she would pray for God to help us right now. My brothers would be waiting in the West, we could not be separated, *Dear God* . . . Mother slowly bent down to her bag, took out her wallet, opened it carefully, and offered the woman a bunch of folded bills in her open hand. I was surprised by so much money.

"Did you bring the cigarettes and the coffee?" the woman finally asked while she acknowledged the bills and looked for the goods. We both nodded.

"You have to pay me now, all of it!" she said sharply.

I watched while my mother took out the rest of the money from the envelope in her wallet and gave it to the woman; then she added some extra for taking a risk with me and handed over the coffee and the cigarettes. She had saved them from the CARE packages back in Leipzig. I knew how valuable they were, and how much real food they could buy on the black market. The woman took the goods from us as part of her pay. I was relieved that my mother trusted me and believed in my strength to be quiet on the way across the border. She had promised for me.

The two men outside the station were waiting their turn to talk to the woman and to pay for their border crossing. I could not hear their conversations; their backs were turned toward the entrance door.

Soon thereafter she waved at us to get up. We started walking into the dark—the woman ahead of us, my mother and me, the two men behind us. None of us knew where we were going, not even my mother. Some dim light came from the risen moon and threw long shadows into nowhere. The leaves crushed under our shoes. I tried to walk carefully, not to stumble or fall down. Not a word was spoken. We reached an area with high trees and several trails leading away. In the dark, human shadows moved, appearing and quickly vanishing. We were not alone in this spot. The woman stopped us and asked us to sit down. She went toward the shadows and conversed with someone. Then she returned and said, "We will take the left route. The Russians are guarding the right one too tightly tonight."

We continued our walk away from the trees and sought the protection of the dark forest. A narrow trail led us into an area of wheat fields, not harvested and now thickly overgrown. Telephone wires dangled above us, suspended loosely between large wooden poles. The sound of blaring sirens hampered our progress. From time to time, the shrill waves and hacking alarms pierced my ears; they must have meant danger because the woman hushed us, telling us to sit down and wait. I figured that the shrill sirens announced our presence to the border guards. I hoped for silence. I was afraid that the woman might be a spy for the

Russians and would eventually deliver us to them once we got closer to the border. I knew we would have to go to jail, at least my mother, and I would have to go back to Leipzig. I closed my eyes to chase away my worries.

Finally daylight was breaking and the sunshine felt warm and comforting on my back. I could not make out where we were. All I could see was the blue sky above us, the shimmering sun, and the orange-yellow stiff stems of thick grass next to the dry wheat. I sat close to my mother. The lingering silence made me sleepy. I leaned on her; she put her arm around me. We must have sat there for hours. I did not cry. I had promised my mother and the woman.

An intense rustling moved closer and closer to where we all huddled; the wheat stems crackled and bent sharply to the ground. Someone was approaching. Suddenly he stopped sniffing: it was a dog, a big, brown German shepherd, the soldiers' guard dog, trained to sniff out fugitives. He continued to move fast, his nose to the ground, his tail wagging. I tried to be quiet and small, looking down on the ground in order for him not to notice me, but my heart was pounding in my throat. When I looked up, I noticed his sharp, white teeth in his open mouth, his red tongue hanging out. I heard the panting. I was very afraid and froze, not sure what to expect next.

Just sit quiet . . . don't move, don't cry . . . don't make a sound . . . I do not take children, the guide woman had said last night. I had promised . . . dead silence.

I knew so little about dogs. I had met only one or two dogs in Leipzig and before that I had seen a large dog, Bruno, in Damsdorf, where we had stayed during the war. I felt cautious and curious at the same time. I thought dogs to be unpredictable yet friendly, protective yet able to attack when told to do so. Sitting in the fields, I was not sure at all. Any barking by this guard dog would signal his find to the soldiers and we would . . .

He suddenly stopped sniffing and rustling. His brown eyes fixed on us sitting there on the ground and—he did not bark. Not one sound came out of his open mouth. He looked one more time, then turned away and disappeared quietly from our sight. I believed that the dog had wanted to help us and therefore had remained silent. Finally, the sirens stopped and we were told to move on quickly.

"Walk, rush, hurry on! Over there . . ." Our guide pointed toward the woods.

The right moment was here for us to forge toward the border. The woman guide urged us one more time to cross a clearing in the woods, run across a meadow with an open view in all directions and head toward the river Aue. After she whispered something into my mother's ears—"Over there . . . straight . . . cross the river . . . then the tracks toward the left"—she disappeared.

From that point on, we were alone; no more guide to help us find the way. The two men who had been with us headed west and left us quickly. My mother and I ran across the open meadow alone, hand in hand—full sunshine, blue sky, trees over on the right side, green grass to step into. It was so quiet among the trees . . . so different from Opa's place in Leipzig.

Three Russian soldiers stood at a distance to our right, leaning against a tree. They were smoking, talking, and handling their guns. I recognized them by their olive-colored uniforms and their red-crested caps. One of them turned his back toward us; the smoke from his cigarette floated up in white clouds in the air. His rifle hung over his right shoulder. I know they noticed us running toward the river, but they looked away and did not shoot at us. I believed our guide had given them the cigarettes and the coffee as a bribe so they would ignore us.

Finally, we reached the riverbed. I wondered how deep the water would be because I could not swim. I remembered the time I almost had drowned in the Bagger See near Leipzig while going swimming with my family two summers ago. The summer of 1947 had been so hot and the water promised relief for all of us. While in the shallow end of the water, I kept losing my balance. My feet could not find a grip and I slipped and slipped. My face was hitting the water. I tried to call for help and waved my arms at my mother who was sitting at the shore, but nobody seemed to notice. I expected to die because I could not breathe anymore. Finally, my oldest brother ran toward me into the water and fished me out. I cried bitterly, but they all laughed at me and said it was not that bad. "You were not drowning!"

"I was slipping and couldn't breathe anymore, my head was down!"

"No, no," they all said.

To no avail. They talked me out of the idea of anyone drowning in that shallow water. "You were not drowning. You were not under the water; we could see you the whole time. The water was not very deep anyway!"

Mother and I were now preparing to cross the river. "Take off your socks and put them in the knapsack," she whispered. Next she tucked my dress into my underpants in order to keep me dry. Then she pulled up her skirt and took off her shoes, too. Her big handbag dangled from her shoulder. The water was shallow as we started to step into the river, which was cool and refreshing; it was not as deep as I feared. I could see the steep, green banks straight ahead of us, the river lined by small pine trees and thick brush on the other side.

In my mind, I had prepared myself for a much wider and deeper river, one that you had to swim across or be pulled through by your arms. Mother would have to drag me along, floating, while she swam. I would not be drowning if I floated on top. My brothers had said, "You are not drowning!"

Scares and worries had to be pushed aside for the moment. It was so quiet here. Except for the gurgling flow of the water in front of us, no sound disrupted the clear September air mixed with a touch of fall. The glistening reflections of the sun danced on top of the ripples. I looked into the water—all the way down to the sandy, brown bottom and the floating, long green grass moving in the slow current. How deep was the water going to be?

As the ripples touched my thighs and my feet felt the slippery rocks in the smooth sand pockets, I held on to my mother and my mother held on to me. We had stepped into the river. Step by step . . . no deep sand pockets to slip into. She did not have to drag me across after all. I walked all the way by myself, holding her hand, looking down into the clear water for the ripples of the stream. And I was not drowning!

Halfway across the river, we passed the official border between the eastern and western parts of Germany, the latter occupied by American forces. I knew all about it. I remembered Mother telling me that the border was marked that way: an invisible line in the middle of the river Aue, to be recognized by all Allied military forces. We passed this magic line with the next few steps and reached the other side. Our backs were turned toward the soldiers, turned toward Grandfather too, and my aunts, and all my friends—Karin, Alfred, Herr Ottrich, and the rest of them. Mother's back was turned toward her Motherland, the place of her birth and her childhood. She would leave behind her fondest memories in life, including those of my father and their music making, and Dresden, the place where her heart broke. We left it all behind now . . . wading through the water to a promised land. We could not look back; it was too painful and scary. Ahead of us were the trees, the unknown, safety and freedom—and my brothers waiting for us at the relatives' homes. At this moment, we were about to walk into a new land, a new life.

Together and safe at last, we stepped out of the water onto the green, grassy embankment and climbed up to the trees and bushes, to hide behind them quickly, out of sight of the soldiers.

"Are we safe now?" I looked at my mother.

"Shhh, we are safe now, but still in shooting range!"

We stepped farther into the brush. In the protection of the tight bushes and low trees, we sat down in the grass. I opened my knapsack for that pair of socks and my dry shoes. Mother smiled and we ate the food she had carried in her purse: some bread, boiled eggs, and an apple. After a while she said, "We are safe now, we can talk out loud. You don't have to whisper any longer." Mother and I had come across the border, together, hand in hand.

The forest was peaceful here. An open view revealed large fields and trees toward the west. No more alarms and scary shadows. The sun warmed my back. No more foot trails, no more roads going nowhere, no more soldiers, and no more people running. Mother turned toward the train tracks on the left, and we followed those for a long time. I balanced on the shiny, narrow edge while she held my hand. Then I stepped on each of the railroad ties, but my legs were too tired to keep it up for very long. So I walked behind my mother along the side of the tracks, on the banks of fine rocks and sand. I was told never to walk on train tracks—ever! Train engines could not stop very easily and people had been killed for not paying attention. I had been warned a number of times. Today, Mother did not seem to be much concerned about it. Maybe no trains had been running here lately. I was getting sweaty and thirsty.

"We should be at the train station pretty soon," she said.

After a long time of following the tracks, which overlooked wide fields and patches of forest, we saw the first houses of a village come into view.

"Is this the train station?" I asked her and pointed to the first house on the right along the tracks. I was getting tired, and my feet ached.

"Just a little farther this way." She smiled at me. "There is the station, just ahead of us where the sign is." It read "Jerxheim."

We walked toward the train station. Mother bought our tickets at the counter and we boarded the next train to Bad Wildungen in the Kassel area. My mother's sister, my aunt Hilde, and her daughter, Inge, expected us eagerly. Later that day, we arrived there safely, tired and hungry. It was dark by the time we reached their home.

A warm welcome awaited us. Mother told them over and over how I admired the bright lights in the clean and fast train on our way to Kassel. Everyone had laughed at me in our compartment for being so excited. I felt embarrassed and blushed. During the train trip in the West, I had observed that people did not mind speaking out loud while talking freely to the other passengers in the compartment. Were there no more spies to watch for? No dangers lurking in the dark?

Mother believed that we had experienced a miracle that night because the dog did not bark, and God had protected us as we walked to the other side of the river. The two men who had been with us during the flight never made it to the train station in Jerxheim. Only later did I learn from my mother that the Russian guards right at the border had caught them; one was the man with the typewriter. I feared they were sent to prison or killed. I was scared thinking about it, imagining what could have happened to us had we been caught. I never asked my mother how she knew about the fate of the two men at the border crossing; I did not want to know. Instead I wondered why the man had tried to take a heavy typewriter across the border. Maybe he couldn't run as fast as I could.

From then on, not much else was said about that night. Mother remained silent about the traumatic events during those years, and I did not want to ask her and remind her again of her grief and horror. Silence became a soft blanket covering gently all the fears and hiding the dark moments of terror to let us go on and see the full, blue sky, sing familiar songs, trust in God, and laugh again. We were far away from the border—but also far away from our grandfather.

I often thought about what night this had been when the dog did not bark, the soldiers did not shoot, and the water was calm. I did not cry—I had promised. Grandfather's blessing was with us.

During the week following our border crossing, Grandfather wrote this postcard to my mother:

September 23, 1949

Dear Leni!
The telegram you sent from Bad Wildungen was a real answer to my prayers . . . Now after many dark days of fear and worry, you have arrived in a place of outer as well as inner peace, and you may trust the Lord with your future plans. You must be happy,

especially to be reunited with your children. May you be led by God's hand into the future as he has done so in the past.

With warmest greetings . . .

Your father-in-law,

Paul Schnädelbach

One week later, we were reunited with two of my brothers as we moved to Bergzabern. My third brother joined us shortly thereafter. Each one had his own border-crossing story to tell. One year later, Mother purchased our first dog, a German shepherd named Ria. I loved her soft ears, her smile that showed her white teeth, and her gentle nudge.

I never saw my grandfather again. He died in 1951, without us, alone, back in Leipzig.

So now here I was, where our journey to freedom had begun, the dilapidated train station a witness to the beginning of a scary and liberating journey. I was not sure how much time had passed, but Winfried and I walked around the deserted area one more time. The outer silence continued to open my inner world of still pictures, full of shadows and rekindled reflections. Winfried put his arms around me as we walked the tracks for a while in silence. The traces are still right here; the station is still standing, the way to the West accessible again. I was comforted to find these concrete remnants of my memories. *It happened here . . . I know it . . .* I bent down to pick up a rusty metal bar, useless, yet something like a souvenir to hold on to and to take home with me.

Klaus stood across the street conversing with a gray-haired man whose outfit reminded me of a purchase from a thrift shop, the pieces wearable but unmatched. I always admired my brother's ease in striking up a conversation with anyone out there, even in a deserted border town like Gunsleben. When we walked up to him, he had obviously introduced himself and was already involved in a serious conversation.

"*Ja, ja,* I have lived here since right after the end of the war. It was a bad time, no food, no heating supply. Not much better now, the government is not doing much for us at all since the *Wende. Ach ja!*" He threw his hands up and then looked away.

"Do you still work?" Klaus asked.

"Oh no, I am retired and there is no work for any of us anymore. We don't get much help from anyone. And then, given our measly pension, the price of food has gone up—everything has gone up."

"What about the young people in town?"

"They have to leave the area in order to make a living. Too many changes . . ." He looked up at me and sighed.

After my brother had introduced us, he said, "My sister and my mother crossed the border in 1949 somewhere here in this area. Do you know anything about this time when people fled from the East to the West?"

"Oh sure, we all knew about the access to the West from here. Many people used to go *hamstern* from here, to bring back food for their families. Some people went as far as Hamburg to bring back fish. They even called this area the *Herring Express.*" He started to smile. "You know, during the first few years after the war, it was fairly easy to cross the border, starting out here at the train station. If you take the dirt road over there, you can drive straight up to the river Aue, where people just crossed the river and went on to the next train station, Jerxheim. Today, you find a bridge there for the farmers' vehicles. That was the place to go back and forth. By the time you and your mother crossed the border in the late forties, the Russians guarded the area so tightly that people were caught right and left. Finally, the borders were completely shut down and became deadly." He was quiet for a moment and pointed past the train station.

He continued, "Over there is an area called the *Grosse Graben,* a water-land project initiated under Hitler to drain water properly from the swampy fields. Right along there, the dirt road will lead you to the border-crossing area. I hope your tires can take the potholes and the rocks." He began to chuckle. "You can also find the area via Ohrsleben and drive along the border if you don't mind the old cement slab path and bumping along through the fields. The border control used these roads to control the area." By now, he wanted to be helpful.

But then he continued to complain once more about the poor living conditions in town compared to the western part of Germany, the summer heat, the many years of political isolation, and his limited pension. The bitterness had left deep lines on his face. Happiness must have been a rare guest. However, his memories had matched mine with validation of this place and time. I was grateful for his words and his directions to the border.

"We are here only once, so let's take the dirt road," Klaus said as he started the engine of his car. I felt uneasy, nervous, and excited all at the same time.

Not much was said as we drove toward the open fields past the old train switch tower where the end of the tracks was marked by a barrier. The meadows on both sides of the dirt road had turned into dry, yellow blankets offset by groups of trees. The fields had been harvested this summer, the cut stalks remained. I thought of the word *Nomannsland*, a land that belongs to no one and is located near any border, is inhospitable to everyone, a warning land, often a dangerous zone meant to keep people apart. That's what we had entered, a bare land, with an open view into nothing . . . *We sat in the overgrown fields for a long time with the sirens over us. The yellow shimmer of the sun and the shelter of the high grown bush around us . . . waiting to go, run . . .*

A young farmer on his tractor was plowing along the old death strip. We stopped to talk to him, stepping into the black clods. Klaus was the first one to climb up the footrest of his tractor.

"Yes, this was the old border strip. The soil was raked thoroughly each day to reveal fresh footprints to the soldiers and their dogs. You are driving on the road that was used to control any movement close to the border. I am trying to plant for next year. All the border fences are gone now . . ."

"What about the mines?" I asked.

"They, too."

He smiled. I began to feel more at ease after what he said, no more mines hidden in the ground.

But I could see an old watchtower hiding behind the green thickness of bushes. Built of wood and old window frames, it was a meager shelter for the soldiers against any cold weather or burning sun. It was their special place to hide; they could hunt down humans, and later on, the border guards could keep watch of the death strip straight ahead of us. We passed the freshly plowed land, running north and south, parallel to the border. The black soil had been opened up wide in order to receive the new seeds for growth next spring. The old death strip was coming back to life. Instead of mines, a new crop of feed was being planted. No more searches for footprints of strangers and fugitives, no guard dogs sniffing out intruders.

*The dog had found us, but did not bark. Then he disappeared from our sight . . . a miracle . . . We must have walked about four kilometers that night . . . through the forest, through the fields . . .*

From there we headed toward the river Aue. Just as the man had said, our car tires hobbled along the cement path until we stopped at the most idyllic spot. The sun shimmered through the trees, the river curved ever so gently out of sight, the banks were green.

*It does not really matter where the exact spot is, but here it feels so true, the water, the trees, and the green meadows. This tranquil picture in front of me could cover the fears and panic that were nestled in my memory of the crossing so many years ago. But here in this spot, it was easier to remember my feelings, long put aside, the dread and the terror. I had worried about how deep the water would be because I could not swim. I had to be silent because talking out loud could have cost us our lives; I promised not to cry and to hold in my feelings. I had to be brave because the future had no other path and there was no way back. I had to forget because my questions about loss of home and friends found no answers. Most of all, I learned to live with fear, always anticipating that the worst would happen. By rehearsing the worst, I could prepare and claim a bit of control in my mind.*

I stepped carefully up to the riverbanks. Between the trees I could see the provisional bridge to the left, just as the man had said. People had used the old train tracks to build this crossing to the other side— a small bridge, but it made it easier to cross the river.

Of course, the river was not as wide as it was in my memory— maybe ten to twelve meters at this point—but the sloping, green, grassy banks on both sides were just as I remembered them. The water in the river was moving ever so gently, drifting grass covered the riverbed. I could not guess how deep it was. The sun's reflections played with the ripples in the clear water like a slow dance to a soft tune. The silvery surface glistened with the mirror images of trees bent close over the water, the long grass blades of the banks pointing toward the river—*somewhere here in this area, maybe down this way by the trees out of sight . . .*

I walked over the bridge, crossed the river, and went along the dirt path on the western side, my eyes fixed on the reflections in the water. The sun was shining on both sides of this once-divided country; the rain or snow had fallen on the same soil, during the same winter. People on both sides of the border prayed to the same God in their churches or their homes. Soldiers had guarded the dividing line on both sides. Families could not get together any more once the walls and fences were erected. For many people hopes had died and resentment had grown on both sides of the fence.

Today there were few traces of trauma here; no more barbed wire and cement posts, no mine fields, no soldiers with guns—just the two deserted watchtowers and the plowed death strip. I bent down to pick some flowers, dry thistles, and yellow, blooming *Butterblumen* to press into my notebook, a token of the living soil to take home with me.

*Our mother had been so courageous to take us out of this part of Germany at that time. What a risk she took! She had held my hand as we walked through the river to the other side, which promised freedom and hope . . . Her faith must have carried her then . . . We had survived with scars . . . I never forgot that night, the dark, my fears, and being alone with my mother. Was our father left behind forever?*

We left the area soon after that, having paused at the bridge for the rest of the *Streusselkuchen* in our bag and the water we had brought along. I needed the silence to let the pictures sink in.

"It's probably not a place you will come back to again," Klaus said, "so take your time."

*In order to retrieve the past, I have to be willing to go to the other side, sometime in my life, eventually wade through the water, holding some-one's hand. From now on, it would be easier to go even further back into our family history, now that I had retraced our way out, the way to free-dom, the way of escape. I needed to start with the top layer of my memory, the events most concrete in detail and image. It will be harder to go further back into my childhood but I will take one step at a time.*

We arrived at the train station in Jerxheim after a short drive. The platform was empty but the shiny tracks told us that the station was still in use. Old, gnarly oak trees in front of the main entrance carried lush, green foliage. Were they the only witnesses of our passing so many years ago?

We found our way to the old autobahn, newly paved and repaired of potholes and neglected shoulders. We passed the city of Leipzig on the right, the enormous *Völkerschlachtdenkmal*, the war memorial of nations, rising above a sea of roofs and steeples.

So much of my family history belongs to the city of Leipzig: my grandfather's home, my parents' life together, times of happiness and sadness, times of tears, a time of refuge . . .

I need to go further back to the years before all our lives changed forever. I need to go back in time, long before Mother and I crossed the border in 1949. The crossing became a pathway to another time, to the murkier waters and the faded images of my memory. Yes, we had escaped to safety, yet we had not escaped our memories. It became more and more difficult to look back on those dark days in

Leipzig and Dresden and feel what I could not feel then, break the promise not to cry.

When did the dam of silence finally break? Why so late in my life?

While many memories remained dark and heavy over the years, the waters of the past, the difficulty of living with the German question, the burden of the past, and my feelings of guilt and shame had been stirred up by recent traumatic events back home in San Diego.

It all happened a few years ago during a crisis in Winfried's congregation, where he was the pastor. The resulting tension in the church affected me more than the usual squabbles that go on in any such organization. I had seen it happen over the many years he had served in various churches. But now, I watched with great fear the confrontations among church members debating Winfried's future with this congregation, heard the harsh criticism behind his back on the parking lot, and saw the tension written on people's faces. Our personal future was at stake. I felt so helpless in the face of this upheaval. Rejection and depression rekindled the much deeper fear of becoming a refugee again: a person not wanted in the community, a family to be chased out of town, if necessary. I found myself set back in the middle of a battle zone with people fighting around me. But this time, I could not run anymore. There was not another place to flee to. Where should we go anyway? Pack up again and move to another church assignment? Leave the first home we had owned after years of parsonage living? We thought we had finally moved into our own home to stay. Pictures hung permanently on the walls. No parsonage committee!

I was ready to give up.

My body was speaking, too. I could not eat—I was not hungry anymore. Nightmares entered my sleep again. I wanted to crawl into my closet and stay there for a very long time. Tears flowed uninvited. My intense feelings, overwhelming and at times irrational, forced me to recognize the ongoing affects my childhood was having on my current state of mind, which included panic and despair. I began to think about death. Sleep problems and nightmares had always been there to some degree, but I had ignored or forgotten them. Tormented sleep with recurring images of attackers and fear of the dark were quickly pushed aside with each breaking day. Intense worries came like a stranger with the night shadows.

"You just worry too much," my daughter, Lisa, had said on occasion. I had ignored all these warning signals until now. I had gotten used to them. I had practiced to be strong, look straight ahead, and swallow my feelings of dread; and I had promised not to cry.

The crisis in the congregation passed with painstaking slowness but also brought unexpected support from many parishioners. A fragile peace remains here too, as all peace hangs in a precarious balance.

Two other events occurred to trigger awakening memories and unresolved feelings. During those turbulent months in the congregation, Lisa announced her plans to marry and asked for an album of her German ancestors. On several occasions, she had cautiously asked what happened to all of us during the war years.

"How did you get to Dresden? What do you know about Opa's death?"

I had usually answered her in a general way, leaving out the painful parts so she would not be burdened. But at this time in her life, she wanted to claim her German family history, and I had to answer her honestly.

"I will write it all down for you. It is too much to talk about," I promised her. She was about to start the most exciting chapter in her life. "I also need time to translate some of the letters written by your grandparents in 1945," I told her to buy some time.

Having given her that promise, I began to look for pictures and documents. During her later years, my mother had carefully collected a bundle of papers for me that would provide a starting point, and a road map for revisiting the past. One evening, I sat on the floor surrounded by letters and pictures. I started to read about my maternal grandmother Wunderlich and her experiences as a minister's wife in a troublesome and fighting congregation in Dresden, way back in 1915. I read about her plight and felt deeply connected to her, sensing her comfort. She would have understood. My tears told me so.

One more experience triggered my words and memories. It happened during a family gathering in 1996, at the birthday party of my brother Herbert in Hamburg, Germany. The day after the festivities, my three brothers and I sat outside in the garden where the summer weather presented its best in colors and sunshine. Maybe for the first time in our adult years, we started to talk about our childhood and our joint experiences during the war years. I learned from them the extent of my injuries during the bombing of Dresden in 1945, details my mother had spared me. I, though, had a deep sense of injury beyond the scars I could see on my body.

I did not hear much of the rest of that conversation because I started to shake and cry. I was shocked, angry, and relieved. Why did my mother not tell me? Maybe she assumed that I had not noticed nor remembered much of the trauma because of my age at the time. Maybe she thought she could help me by not bringing it up, ever. That way, it would be forgotten as if it had never happened. And really, it was not so bad when compared to other people's experiences. We had survived to move on, hadn't we?

The night after my conversation with my brothers, a sense of overwhelming dread came over me and I feared life. It was triggered by what they told me about the extent of my personal injuries, the background being the most horrific time in the history of this century. I spiraled into a place of paralysis. I could not sleep, my frozen emotions began to thaw and spill, even Winfried's presence and warmth that night could not shield me from the waves. I shivered under the warm down comforter throughout the night and I realized that I could not go back into the past alone, nor could I go ahead into the future, either. It was too much to untangle alone, too scary to go there. It would take too long because so much had happened, maybe it would never end, or

I was not going to survive a second time around. I could always continue to scratch the surface and limp on, but that I had done.

Upon returning to San Diego from this significant family gathering in 1996, burdened with discovery and dread, I walked into the office of a psychoanalyst.

"Why are you here?" she said calmly, waiting for me to begin.

I started crying. I had been crying for a long time on the inside but the tears were stuck in my throat. My feelings had tightened my jaw rather than finding their way out through my eyes and spoken words.

"I was born during the war in Germany . . . ," I started. "My daughter is getting married next month . . . The church my husband is serving is disgruntled and fighting, and wants him out."

I could not see much anymore because of my tears. It was like a dam had burst. The broken words and the silent, listening presence of the psychoanalyst made it seem possible to put meaning and reflection into my scattered story. Her simple offer—"You need to take time to talk about all this"—opened the door to the past in a safe way.

That day, I received the gift of understanding and compassion and I accepted it. I began to take one step at a time to explore memories and connect emotional events. Layers of memories revealed subjective reflections and contaminated conclusions, interwoven with images of light and darkness, surface and depth. With the writing came more crying. In order to continue my inner dialogue between therapy sessions, I wrote down my reflections and thoughts. My time to speak had come. I began to write word after word, sentence after sentence, sequential and fragmented, full of images and poetic lines, carried by music when my words stopped, until a tapestry appeared in full color. It will hang next to other weavings of life.

There was one more event that made this trip to my past so special. I had been given a mitzvah, the dollar bill, a blessing given to me by the Jewish woman back in my office. She had gladly blessed this trip. "Be a *schlichah mitzvah* and have a safe trip." Now, I quickly checked in my wallet where I had stuffed the blessed money. It was still there.

Winfried, Klaus, and I entered the city of Dresden, bathed in the warmest glow of the late afternoon sun. The famous silhouette of towers and steeples lined up along the river Elbe. We had come home to the city of our parents, our grandparents Wunderlich, a place of painful memories and losses; today, we entered a city in full recovery.

"The whole town still looks like a construction zone," Klaus said slowly but with a gentle smile, pointing to whole city blocks of fenced, crater-looking, barren land.

"Parking the car here is a nightmare. No space available any-where." It was easier to be practical than comment on the historical homecoming.

He had his own plan on how to enter the city; he had been here before. Within a few moments we arrived in the center of town, turn-ing right on Holbeinstrasse, the street where our grandmother's house once stood. He stopped the car—no one spoke for a while as we got out. I closed my eyes in the bright sunlight of the afternoon, or was I afraid of what I might see? For sure, I was afraid of what I might see on the inside.

As the three of us stepped out of the car, an eerie silence met us.

"This is the area where her house stood," he finally said. "Right over there, where these ugly apartment buildings are."

We both knew our story even in the face of the resurrected cement houses lining the street. The old Wintergartenstrasse was no more, just a plain road, blocked off by more fences that surrounded a barren land, fully overgrown by weeds. A street intersection was visible in the far distance. No traces were left of rubble, ruins, and ashes, except in our inner pictures. Grass and weeds had grown from the remains of the ashes, the firestorm, and the terror—nature had covered them all up. The barren land had been watered by rain and snow, new grass and weeds had sprung up year after year, and a fragile life had returned to the old city. My hardened soil had rested, too, for more than fifty years, and time had passed with the rhythm of the seasons.

*Why did we escape this hell? Maybe so we could tell the story.*

"*Ja*, that's where it all happened," he said quietly. His face was motionless as he tightened his lips, seemingly staring at nothing.

I could not say much—my throat was too tight. My eyes scanned the area so intensely that they began to hurt. I could find no words. There was really nothing to see in this place that belonged to our past. I could only see a street in front of us with the ugly apartment buildings in the spot where our grandmother's house once stood, and an empty street corner fenced in by meshed wire. Grass had covered up more than the piles of rubble and ashes. It obviously had covered memories and words attached to buried feelings, hiding the harshness and brokenness of the experience. I did not want to interrupt his silence as I watched my brother standing there. He seemed to look at his experiences with such calmness and acceptance, or was he merely holding his feelings out of range? Winfried busied himself taking a few shots with the camera, really pictures of nothing. He respected our quiet time and wandered around the area, shaking his head at the postwar, socialistic architectural building style of the late fifties: bunker-like houses, cookie-cutter cement boxes with dirty cracks in the walls, dirty streets and broken sidewalks where weeds grew tall. Even a war could not stop nature.

"*Ja, das war halt so,*" Klaus said again quietly, looking at a prewar city map.

I was glad he was with us in this historic place. It seemed he was still holding my hand, needing to be strong for us by not showing too much emotion. It was easier for the moment. If he was not scared then I didn't have to be scared either. I would have to sort out my feelings later on at home. Now would not be the right time, too much heaviness around us and not enough words. But the silence was strong in this eerie place, too much for me to put aside and postpone. My tears welled up in my throat but I swallowed hard.

*What about the impact, the lingering images, the fears, and the fragile girl in that childhood picture I have back home? Her eyes hold the key to the inner frame, the mouth closed tight for many years to come. Just look at* it. Just stand there for a while—it will be enough. No, I had not talked about it enough at all.

I looked at the strange burial ground for my grandmother and Aunt Liddy and all the other bodies right here on Wintergartenstrasse. We walked away from it then—only to come back today and remember. I must tell my story of Dresden.

# CHAPTER THREE

# *Out of the Deep (1945)*

I have two silver spoons lying on a shelf, back in San Diego, next to all the special family mementos: the two Meissen china vases, the fluted flower plates, and the family Bible. The tablespoons, once shiny and polished, are now burned black and deeply scorched. But the thin, delicate design on the handle is beautifully preserved. A faint, filigreed monogram reveals a *W* entwined with an *L*. The black spoons were found by my mother in the rubble of the city of Dresden, on Holbeinstrasse 28, a few days after the Allied forces destroyed the city during the nights of February 13 and 14, 1945. The initials stand for Lydia Wunderlich, my grandmother, who lived and died there during that night of terror.

I can hold the spoons and a few pictures in my hand—they are a grim reminder of the end of a beautiful city. They also symbolize for me the beginning of a painful search for the impact of the faintly orange and ashen-clouded memories of that night on many others over the years. Memories of trauma have a way of sinking deep into the body, without words, and as life goes on, all that remains audible is a sigh and a cry.

Erich Kästner, a German novelist who survived the night of the bombing, wrote these personal reflections in November of 1946:

> For one day, I ran aimlessly through the city, following my memories. The school? Burned down . . . The boarding school with

its gray school years? An empty facade . . . The Dreikönigskirche [Three-Kings Church], where I was baptized and confirmed? And in its trees, where starlings, exhausted from their practice flight each fall, fell to the ground like shrill, black clouds? The tower stands there like a giant pencil in the vast emptiness . . . The Japanese Palais, in its library I crammed as a doctoral student. Destroyed . . . The Frauenkirche [Church of our Lady], the old magical building where I sometimes sang the motets? A few pitiful ruined walls. I have controlled my pain. It does not grow larger with the number of wounds. It reaches its limits earlier. Whatever pain is still added does not resolve into emotions any more. It is like the heart falls into a deep coma (in . . . *oder Dresden*, Ev.-Luth. Superintendentur Dresden-Mitte, 1987).

I, too, could recognize my own emotional coma that had fallen over me at the end of these events in 1945, gracefully covering wounds and pain over the years. Even now, knowing the outcome of survival does not make it easier for me to enter this time in history and revisit the memories. I had been on my way to Dresden with my family in 1945, and I was now on my way to Dresden, once more.

Winfried, Klaus, and I found our quarters for the night near the inner city of Dresden. An old patrician house had been transformed into a bed-and-breakfast hotel with a restaurant on the ground floor. The door to our suite opened into a flat, complete with sitting room, bedroom, and kitchen; I felt at home as soon as I walked in. The hot summer air blew the sheer curtains into the room; they fluttered toward the high ceiling and the elegant stucco molding along the edges.

"Grandmother's flat must have looked like this," I said to Winfried later that night after dinner. "Look at the high windows, the white ceilings, and the wooden floors. Isn't it strange to revisit a home in Dresden, a house that has survived the bombing? A house that may look like the one that Grandmother once lived in?"

Winfried had busied himself with the television set and hardly tuned in to my musings. Back home in the United States, President Clinton had admitted to an affair with a White House intern, Monica Lewinski. The news reporters were having a field day. The topics of sex, lies, and morals filled their endless talks like waterfalls. The president was leaving on a vacation with his wife and daughter to escape his past.

I walked around the flat some more, opened the balcony doors wide to let the breeze in. I can remember so little . . . but it all feels familiar . . . Grandmother's flat on Holbeinstrasse . . .

"Don't open the windows yet, the mosquitoes will eat us alive."

Sleep during this hot summer night visited me with faint pictures of grass and fences, rocks and faces, fanned by the rushing traffic of the early hours the next day. Fatigue and stillness carried me in and out of sleep. I hoped to be visited in my dreams by some of the loved ones who had once lived in this town, but no one came.

We had to visit them the next day at the family gravesite at the *Tollkewitzer Friedhof*. The cemetery is like a park, with old trees and flowering shrubs in the midst of ornamented gravestones. Rows and rows of graves were framed by neatly cleaned walkways. A funeral was in progress.

"Look at that," Winfried said. "People here still dress in black for a funeral."

We passed by the mourners standing together at the large gate. Death and endings never stop. We, too, were paying our respects to painful endings and loving memories.

The gravestone of our grandfather Wunderlich headed the small plot. It read:

> Here rests in the Lord my dear husband,
> our unforgettable, truly loving father,
> Preacher Engelbert Wunderlich,
> born January 11, 1859 and died July 27, 1918.

My grandmother and Aunt Liddy are commemorated here. Another sister of my mother was buried here too, many years later. The old city greeted us with a marker of our family, reassuring us of our roots right here amidst the graves. The chirping of the birds in the trees and the cool morning breeze filled our silence. I gave thanks for their lives as I bent down to pick up a small stone to take home to California. This grave contained their history and therefore mine; now it was time to tell our story.

In 1913, my grandfather Engelbert Wunderlich and my grandmother Lydia Wunderlich moved to Dresden, following Grandfather's acute vascular health problems caused by "exhaustion." He was a minister in the Methodist Church and had served as a superintendent in the Saxony area. His ministry had required much traveling and hard work. The congregation he was assigned to in Dresden was rather small, and the family hoped for a time of reprieve. Instead he found himself in a congregation full of foul gossip and closed social cliques. In addition, the housing for his family was marginal. They lived for a short time behind the *Schauspielhaus* (the theater), on Feldherrenstrasse, and later on Grandfather moved the church and the parsonage flat to Ostraallee 25.

Mother remembered and talked about the years of World War I, when her oldest brother, Friedrich, had to serve his country as a soldier. Her face would light up with a smile whenever she remembered Dresden during those prewar years. Street names and historical locations were mentioned over and over in her stories and have remained imprinted in my mind. I know them by heart and recognize them easily: the *Grüne Gewölbe*, or Green Vault, the *Taschenbergpalais* (Taschenberg palace), the *Vogelwiese*, an amusement park, and the *Striezelmarkt*, the famous Christmas market (*Striezel* is stollen). Here you could find the *Dresdner Christstollen*, a traditional Christmas bread, among crisp gingerbread cookies and small chimney-sweep figures made of baked prunes with black top hats and ladders. My mother said that clouds of gold glitter came from nowhere and the scent of fresh pine and roasted almonds hung in the cold winter air. She explained to us that the long, bread-like form of the *Dresdner Christstollen* was to symbolize the swaddled Christ child; a thick cover of brushed, sweet butter and white powdered sugar over the most delicious yeast dough sent off a whiff of lemon, *kirschwasser*, almonds, cardamom, cloves, and raisins. She was convinced that her mother's recipe was the best in town. I know why my mother kept Christmas always so close to her heart—because she remembered her home, her family, and her city in that special way.

Mother said that Grandfather had been a kind but stern man. "He was a man of solid faith and strong convictions. He did not hesitate to speak out on both." He was a blazingly patriotic man, deeply convinced of the political goals of the Germany of his time. He believed in a God who would not forsake the German nation, a God who would eventually provide justified victory over all its enemies.

Mother said that her life in Dresden had been exciting and stimulating amidst its rich history and cultural beauty. Grandfather had warned all his six children about the recent signs of decadence and decay of a once strong German cultural heritage. He did not allow his children to attend certain theater productions, including performances of Shakespeare at the *Schauspielhaus*, or to listen to operas at the *Semper Oper*, not even *Carmen* or the popular *Cavalleria rusticana* by Mascagni, the hit of the times. He was convinced that these shows portrayed seductive, loose lifestyles and promoted perverted relationships. He himself came from a family tradition of strict devotion and righteous living in the country estate of Rüssdorf. He observed Sundays with devoted and regular church attendance. No card games were allowed in his home, no alcohol was served, and no loud laughter seemed necessary on Sundays, the day of the Lord. Grandfather was a teetotaler all his life.

The story goes that Mother's older brother Paulus had a way of sneaking out of the house at night anyway, to see the latest theater productions, the modern ballets, and the trendy operas. He watched the productions from the standing gallery in the theater for just a few pennies. My mother joined in at times, more so in the later years when Grandmother was a widow. Grandmother had become by then more lenient and did not seem to mind frivolity so much.

My grandparents had met during Grandfather's pastoral internship in Heilbronn. Lydia Lämmle had been born on May 16, 1864, the daughter of a cooper who owned a grocery store there. She married Engelbert Wunderlich on June 19, 1886, in Heilbronn. While Grandfather was serving as an intern pastor at the Methodist church there, he co-officiated at the wedding of Karl Striffler and Emma Bausch on November 23, 1882, and co-signed the family Bible. Karl and Emma Striffler are Winfried's grandparents. How did their paths cross? Did they ever dream of their grandchildren's marriage eighty-three years later?

Lydia Wunderlich started her married life with the knowledge that no pastor, including her new husband, would be assigned for more than six years to one congregation while receiving limited financial compensation for his dedicated work. Grandfather and Grandmother lived for a short time in Bayreuth, where in 1886 they witnessed the funeral of the famous composer Franz Liszt, the father of Cosima, who was married to Richard Wagner. What a historic moment!

Parsonage life has never been easy for anyone, given the frequent moves, limited financial compensation, and unlimited work hours. God's work does not fit into a forty-hour workweek. As a denomination, the Methodists in Germany were not fully recognized by society in general or the government, which meant that only people who had officially exited the Protestant church were allowed to be present during Methodist worship services. Therefore, on Sunday mornings, a policeman sat in one of the church pews and registered who was present. If a violator was spotted, he was written up and Grandfather had to pay a fine for this violation. Since his family had little money with which to pay the fine, certain valuable objects in the home of my grandparents were pawned, and each sticker, called a *Kuckuck*, was stuck on the piano bench, on Grandfather's clock, or on his desk. Grandfather's parishioners later went to the public auction and bought back their pastor's household items. My mother told this story with a loud laugh, shaking her head, her voice full of wonder. I just shook my head; what a different time it was.

I waited eagerly for her to talk of her childhood, especially to tell about the emperor during her early years. She would smile and her eyes begin to sparkle. "You know, I remember Emperor Wilhelm's birthday celebrations each year. There was a huge parade in town and festivities went on all day long." She lived during a time when Germany had an emperor! Her stories seemed like those from another century!

"My brother Friedrich, who was an officer of the army, had to salute every time an official would pass by. He would hide in any hallway he could find to avoid saluting all day long."

She snickered about her first conversation with her friends in the neighborhood on the subject of the "birds and bees." After she had listened for a while to what the kids on the street were whispering about what men and women do between the sheets, she shouted to all, "The emperor and my father are no such swines!" That was the end of that subject.

Another story goes that Grandfather loved Christmas preparations very much and personally saw to the decorations on the live Christmas trees in church, a few days before the holidays. One year, he climbed up a high ladder to decorate the tree and suddenly slipped and landed on the floor between ladder and church benches. Fortunately, he walked away without any injuries except for some serious bruises. On Christmas Eve, however, he was able to get out of bed and open presents with his family. During the service on Christmas Eve and the reading of the Christmas story, the Christmas tree caught on fire, ignited by the burning candles. Grandfather jumped up to put out the flames despite his condition!

That year, there were gifts for the kids. The boys in the family received the latest technical items of the time, such as an accumulator with which to build a radio, some tools, and a joiner's bench. As the youngest in her family, Mother admired her brothers, Friedrich and Paulus, and their technological adventures. She talked about their efforts to place wires in and out of their rooms with several antennas fastened to the window frames. Everyone gathered in their room to listen to the first screeching signals of the radio waves muffled by static. That Christmas was memorable for all!

The war years, with their devastating course of hardship and famine, ravaged Grandfather's health. He suffered from dysentery, malnutrition, and a heart condition, and died in 1918. Mother was only fourteen years old. His death was deeply felt by all. Fortunately, he was spared the devastating end of his hopes and dreams for a *Vaterland* in victory and honor.

After Grandfather's death, Grandmother remained devoted to her church activities. She continued to sing in the choir; Mother remembered that she had a beautiful voice. Later in life, she loved to read stories to her grandchildren and showed much interest in music and the arts. She was active in mission work and Sunday school education, and she remained devoted to the *Frauenmission*, the Women's Mission Society. Mother said that she was never too tired for another trip to one of the regional meetings.

The work for the Lord had to come first and the household chores were often left up to my mother. Saturday was the day to wash and scrub the stairwell. She complained that she had to polish the wooden floors with a *Blocker*, a hand-pushed polishing tool that weighed a ton. I detected in her voice that she did not like to do it all by herself. The rugs had to be aired out in the yard; they were hung over the clothesline and beaten with the *Teppichklopfer*, a wicker paddle.

What about her sisters and brothers? Why weren't they helping out? "I was the youngest," she would mutter.

She sounded resentful. I figured that she wanted to be outside on Saturdays like other young girls, having fun with her friends in the city. There was so much to see . . .

The next morning Winfried, Klaus, and I entered the city of Dresden on foot after a hearty breakfast of strong *Kaffee*, fresh, crisp rolls, and *Schinken* (ham). There was still so much to see.

"So much progress has been made during the last few years," Klaus said, holding an updated city map in his hands. "I only remember it gray with grimy walls and hollow windows in bombed-out houses. Spooky and dead."

Klaus did not seem to notice my hesitation and led the way, following his map. He had figured out some shortcuts so that we could avoid crossing the streetcar tracks and the heavy morning traffic. The sunlight had settled on the lush green of the trees, seeming like an opening curtain to the city before us. Each street sign seemed so familiar; I knew them by heart. I recognized Tzschirner-Platz and Rampische Strasse—it was like coming home with butterflies in your stomach. What was I going to see?

The *Frauenkirche* showed walls and outline completed, partly visible through the bars of a huge scaffold, and from the *Brühlsche Terasse* I saw the river Elbe housing the *Weisse Flotte* once again. The *Stallhof* of the royal palace sparkled with newly completed white and blue wall paintings in sgraffito style. People walked by and pointed to the fine artwork. Vendors sold guidebooks and postcards of the city in 1945; restaurants advertised potato soup and plum tart for lunch; the city felt alive. With each street corner I walked more steadily, taking in the sounds of recovery. I stopped to buy a selection of the old postcards. Of course, I had seen them before. But buying them today was like acknowledging a harsh memory again and again and again.

We headed toward the *Augustinum*, which exhibits a collection of paintings, and the *Grüne Gewölbe*, the Green Vault, the royal treasure chest. Glass case after glass case was filled with the finest jewelry, silver, gold, and ebony—treasures collected from all over the world by the royal House of Saxony.

Klaus and I walked toward the *Zwinger* and the Gallery of the Old Masters, while Winfried took a tour of the rebuilding of the

*Frauenkirche*. Revisiting the famous collection of old masters has become a sort of homecoming for me on every visit to Dresden. This time, the walk through the gallery with my brother became a special trip back to our childhood. It is a place that our parents knew all about and had frequently visited during their lifetime—a piece of home.

"Mother loved the Madonna and child paintings in this gallery. We always had postcards or pictures of these paintings in our house," I said to him. He smiled and nodded.

"*Ja*, the baby Jesus in all these Madonna paintings is not always so pretty," he chuckled, hardly listening now to my musings. "Look at this one over here." He stood in front of Tizian's *Maria with the Child and Four Saints*, dated 1505. "And here is Mantegna's *Holy Family*. You see real people with everyday faces, old and young, from the year 1495."

"I read the other day that over 150 paintings in this gallery perished in the bombing," I said to him as we walked into the next exhibition hall. He knew and was silent.

Many of the paintings had burned on the trucks leaving the city too late.

*We walked through the burning city, too, could not flee fast enough. I could not walk any more. Klaus carried Mother's bag, our few belongings . . . my mother carried me. "You were very sick those days!" More raids in Strehlen. We walked away alive . . .*

"This painting hung in our home in Bergzabern." I stood in front of *The Holy Night* by Carlo Maratti, done in 1652. "It was in that brown, wooden frame. I don't know what happened to it. Do you?"

"My daughter has it."

"Mother must have loved it, it was a reminder of her hometown."

I began to understand the small remembrances we had in our home—a piece of Meissen china, a special book with old city photos—and the comfort she must have drawn from them, even just one postcard of the Madonna with child from this gallery.

"I must stop at Raffael's *Sixtinische Madonna*. It has become a ritual," I said.

I entered the hall alone, leading up to this masterful painting from the year 1512. I sat down in front of it. I have long been fascinated by the Madonna's lightness. She is floating on a bed of clouds. Her facial expression is so soft and innocent, framed by the flowing fabric of her cape, her blue-and-red dress. She holds the child with so much tenderness while the pudgy, winged angels are watching from below. As a child, I thought those to be our guardian angels. I had always wondered about the deep, green curtain hanging on a rod, suspended from nowhere. Why a curtain in heaven and what about the meaning of the kneeling saints in front of her? I would have to read up on it later.

The painting had survived the war and been returned to this gallery, its home for so many years. The city had survived and was coming back to full life.

*The child carried to safety by someone, too. The pudgy angels watched at the bottom of the picture, the guardian angels in my memory . . .*

We wandered from painting to painting and finally stood in front of Bernardo Bellotto's painting *The Ruins of the Kreuzkirche in Dresden*, which was obtained in 1765. The towering cathedral had once before been destroyed in a war, and in the painting was in the process of being rebuilt, just like the one outside in town. I felt calm and hopeful in the presence of these familiar pictures and the knowledge that Dresden had emerged from the ashes.

I paused awhile by the open window looking out toward the *Schloss*, where Saxony's last but enormously popular King Friedrich August III had governed in a simple and earthy style. He had walked among his people and spoken their dialect, had gone hiking with his family in the local woods, the *Sächsische Schweiz*, and lived a rather normal life in the palace. Mother said that, in 1918, with the beginning of the Weimar Republic, he had lost his job and title. He had left the monarchy quietly without bloodshed and violence, and was said to have told his ministers when he departed, "Well, then, take care of your own mess!" (*"Nuu, macht eiern Dreck aleene."*)

Mother told us about the king's departing speech and repeated this story often, all in full Saxon dialect, of course. She would laugh out loud, her voice full of wonder.

"Do you need some help with something?" someone said to me, disrupting my floating images of Madonnas, Mother, grandparents, and the king.

There she stood, the gallery attendant, a woman about my age, dressed in a brown work uniform. A warm smile greeted me. I looked at her, not knowing what to say next. I pointed to my city map, so she would not notice my tears.

"I am trying to figure out where my grandmother's home was located before the bombing in 1945. It must have been in that direction. I was there during that night," I blurted out. "My brother and I are visiting . . ."

"Oh *ja*, I was there, too," she said calmly. "We lived across the river, over there, about eight kilometers away from the inner city. I was eight years old then. My mother took me to the window of our house that night and said, 'See over there, the city is burning!' I remember the red sky and the smoke."

I could hardly hold back my tears; they began to ache in my throat. I could not say much in response. Her words had touched me. This horrible history of the death of a city connected the two of us, right here in the gallery, in the presence of Madonnas, famous portraits, lovely landscapes, and inspiring altar paintings. She stood next to me, looking out toward the *Theaterplatz*, and said quietly, "It's better now. The city is rebuilding . . . coming back to life."

She was right. I could see the crane high above the palace, the scaffolds around the *Schlosskirche*. Even the streets had been dug up; wooden barriers blocked and rerouted the never-ending traffic. The *Augustusbrücke* was intact again; we would walk across it this afternoon.

When I looked up again, the woman had disappeared. I could not even thank her.

Gerhart Hauptmann, the famous German writer, once said, "Whoever forgot to cry learned it again at the destruction of Dresden" (in *Der Wiederaufbau der Frauenkirche zu Dresden*). My mother quoted him at home but I did not understand what the words really meant. She did. He knew that the sight of a dead city would trigger tears, shock, pain, and the recognition of unending loss. Maybe I had stopped crying over the years; maybe I had forgotten the pain and needed to return to Dresden to cry again. Maybe I needed to start here with my story. I had been on my way to Dresden before, to my grandmother's house . . .

It started in 1941 when I was born in Breslau and my three brothers and my parents welcomed me into the family. Germany had already been at war for over two years and the initial military victories were turning gray and heavy. In 1939, our father had been ordered to participate as a soldier in the Polish invasion, but then was sent home to take care of his church and his family for some time. He was home at the time of my birth. I know for sure because my brothers told me so, much later.

I have always wondered how my parents perceived the political world they lived in. Were they aware of the totalitarian state they belonged to, the loss of personal freedom? Did they know of the persecution of the Jews, undertaken in order to protect German blood and German honor? I am not sure how much they knew about the Nazi propaganda and the actual atrocities. They must have known of the *Kristallnacht* in October of 1939, when most Jewish synagogues were burned and shattered and when people unwanted by the government suddenly disappeared. Many of those citizens had previously been their neighbors or local merchants. My parents must have known of the full-scale censoring of literature and art and the book burnings to sterilize the German soul. I don't know what they thought about all this. Letters and documents are gone forever.

I know my parents were familiar with the goals for the German nation brought about by the country's miraculous economic recovery after World War I under Adolf Hitler. Along with the economic resurgence came the creation of a great German empire and the resurrection of the German spirit, the goal being to raise pure bodies and pure souls. The tight infrastructure of the Third Reich lifted the national depression of defeat and lethargy, and the future began to look bright, with an identity of power and pride. As part of this goal, the internal enemies in Germany had to be liquidated; these included the Communists, the Marxists, and the strong Jewish community, perceived as the controlling force of the national money market. Many religious denominations, including the Methodist Church, were supportive of the Führer's ideas. My parents, along with their spiritual leaders, thought Hitler stood for a strong *Vaterland*, for family, and for God. Many church members perceived the Führer as having been sent by God to be the fulfillment of scripture, and an answer to their hopes for a great leader of a great nation. My paternal grandfather, Paul Schnädelbach, had described Hitler in his diary as a "corner stone . . . a miracle before our eyes" (the words are a reference to Psalm 118: 22–23).

I am convinced that my parents saw the historical events of their time from an anti-Semitic point of view, widely shared throughout Europe and fueled by the two-thousand-year-old Christian belief that the Jews had killed Jesus Christ and therefore carried the curse by the blood shed on the cross. That is what I perceived through the teachings of the church during my early years.

The necessary liquidation of internal enemies during the Third Reich also targeted politically outspoken church members, Freemasons, politically dissatisfied people (so-called "grumblers"), members of the national opposition, reactionaries, members of the Black Front, economic saboteurs, common criminals, abortionists, homosexuals, mentally disabled persons, retarded children, and those accused of high treason. How the government liquidated these elements was not widely known. Nobody was allowed to talk about any suspicions they had. Even the slightest comments were punishable by arrest and prison. Ever so slowly, people must have become aware of rumors of atrocity and terror, with more silence and horror to follow. My mother later on told me that she knew of the assassination attempt on Hitler's life on July 20, 1944. All suspected individuals involved were immediately tried and executed; the official newspaper carried the story with public outrage. By then, hope for an end to terror and war conflicted with the official vision of a final victory to come, the *Endsieg*. I am convinced that my parents did not and could not talk about what they thought and felt about the political regime. I don't know what they whispered to each other when they were alone. Intimidation and fear for their lives and ours set in as denial and despair followed. I have gone back again and again in my mind to our life as a family and tried to reconstruct the political clouds of evil hanging over us all. There are no answers to be found. My parents were there and got swept away with it, all the way to the bloody end.

From early on, we were told not to share with neighbors and friends what we thought and what was talked about in the home, not even the mundane details of family life. I was born into a world of necessary and prescribed silence.

One day, our father returned from Poland with a goose as a special treat for the family. We were all told not to let the neighbors know about it so that they would not be jealous or invite themselves to the feast. Later that day, my brothers Herbert and Gerhard said to Frau Wolf, who lived in the basement of our house in Breslau, "We are not supposed to tell you that we have a goose for dinner tonight!"

The two of them were known to chat (*quatschen*), and loved to visit with neighbors and friends. My parents' silence served both to cover the evil and to protect our fragile lives.

Our family's life was closely interwoven with that of the church my father served. Many visitors came and went; our flat bustled with the clatter of activities, laughter, and talking interwoven with music, prayers, and quiet hopes. This early time in my life is shrouded in mist. My first image memory is of looking out from behind the wooden bars of a playpen, placed in the corner of a room, and watching a tumultuous family life. I observed what was happening on the outside of my world but could not comprehend it on the inside. I responded to it all with my eyes, my body. Such a hectic time, so many people around . . .

They tell me that, from early on, I liked the warmth around the Christmas season. One time, soon after the holidays, no one could find me in the flat. They finally checked the living room, where I had drawn the curtains and sat on the couch, crying bitterly, "See the little men go around and around!" I was waiting for the propellers of the Christmas *Pyramide* to move all the shepherds, sheep, angels, wise men, and camels around the manger scene. I must have thought the magic would come alive if you pulled the curtains and invited the dark. I had not discovered that it was the heat of the candles that would set the holy scene in motion. My brothers laughed about it and remember it well to this day. They also say I already liked clothes way back then. Mother actually found time in all the turmoil of family life, congregational duties, and worries of war to sew a dress for herself and one for me using the same fabric. I called it my "Sunday dress" and was excited about the matching outfits.

Kurt Kriegler, a friend of our family and later on the teacher of my older brothers in Damsdorf, visited us one day in Breslau in 1942, and wrote down the following memories and reflections about our family life during those years (my mother received these notes from Herr Kriegler in 1961):

> On a Saturday—it must have been in early September of 1942— I traveled with my wife, Lens, to Breslau, to visit the Schnädelbach family which had kindly invited us. Our grief about our youngest son, Dieter, seemed to ease during the spiritual conversation we had. [He had recently been killed in the area of Charkow; his parents had encouraged him to join the army voluntarily, and now felt deep guilt for having done so. He was eighteen years old.]
>
> The whole atmosphere in the Schnädelbach family with the children whose age ranged from two to nine was intended to lead us

into a world of peace. When the children were tucked into bed, their Mother sang a lullaby to them, and then they prayed so innocently in their own words, seemingly undisturbed by our presence. We were so moved by it that we thought we felt their guardian angels amidst us all, a presence the parents strongly believed in. It became suddenly clear to me how this spiritual world had also touched our lives with a special celestial radiance. I was so deeply touched that the following night in my dreams I found myself in their world where I met loved ones long deceased. What a good fortune it is when couples agree on the education and the religious upbringing of their children. That was the case with Mr. and Mrs. Schnädelbach. A special blessing rested upon them. We respected Mr. Schnädelbach so very much as a pastor and as a counselor. His sermons could be understood by everyone and had such depth; they stimulated our own thinking. I can imagine what a blessing his work was for his congregation. He was also a fine counselor who showed concern for his parishioners, and always found the right word to lead them from darkness into light.

What an idyllic picture is painted here at a time of war. Such a normal family: songs and prayers, grief and comfort. Shielded from disaster and harm?

Life in the city of Breslau became increasingly difficult. The flat we lived in had no garden for us four children to play in. The air was heavy and polluted with soot from the coal-burning stoves in the houses. Winters were long and dark. We all were quite ill with colds and bronchitis, including Mother. She contracted a nasty blood poisoning in her hand and suffered periods of acute infections. At one point the doctors even considered amputation. She was in severe pain and cried with the anticipation of losing her hand. Fortunately, she slowly recovered without surgery but was left with feelings of fear and anxiety. Despite these worries, she tried to care for the congregation during our father's absence the best she could.

Grandmother Wunderlich, back in Dresden, was quite aware of my mother's plight and her ongoing health problems. She expressed her worries in many letters at that time, including the following to one of her daughters, Hilde Alrutz, written in 1944:

> Dear Hilde,
>     . . . And then came the news that Leni [my mother] was supposed to have her appendix removed last Saturday. She underwent surgery and is doing as well as can be expected . . . She was in the hospital again, she had hurt herself.

A relapse following Mother's surgery must have required a second hospitalization. Major children's illnesses such as diphtheria, measles, and smallpox were quite common during those years. Both Klaus and Herbert spent up to three months in the hospital in Breslau with smallpox. Our parents had to stand outside the hospital building while they waved from the window.

With the ongoing war, the food supply and proper nutrition while we lived in the city became an increasingly serious problem. The doctor suggested that all of us should leave the city and spend some time in the country where the air would be clean and the food better. We spent the summers of 1942 and 1943 in the countryside in Jenkau, Silesia, on the estate of a baron, Freiherr von Richthofen, who owned several mansions and the adjacent land. Our parents' friendship with the Richthofens' daughter, Barbara, went back to the prewar years, when they had met at a religious conference in Switzerland.

The summers in the country brought new experiences for all of us. I can't remember much, but there is a picture that shows us all sitting in the grass, barefoot, smiling, and in bright sunshine. Mother is wearing an apron.

One day, my oldest brother, Klaus, was walking with my mother through the fields near Jawor and saw a group of men, wearing blue-and-white striped outfits, working the railroad tracks. They bent over their shovels and pickaxes as they quietly scraped along the gravel banks.

"What kind of people are they?" he asked my mother as they came closer.

"They are *K̟ler*," she replied, which meant prisoners from the concentration camp in Grossrosen.

Nothing else was said about the incident, but he knew what he had seen and never forgot about it. Their blue-and-white striped outfits had marked them as prisoners for all to see. They were prisoners on work duty, just prisoners? Later on, the heaviness of the image sank in, the truth to be revealed in time. The Baron of Richthofen, too, employed prisoners of war from Poland, captured by the Germans, as laborers in his fields. Mother later on remembered that they had been treated well and had received free shelter and food. Some of the workers settled in the area after the war was over.

*Mother wanted to tell us that not everyone during that time was cruel and harsh. There were moments of kindness and sharing between stranger and friend, between master and servant.*

The estate in Damsdorf and the ranch are only partially imprinted in my mind but actually account for my first clear memory. One day, the old Baron von Richthofen arrived in a fancy, open horse buggy in front of the house we lived in. He was holding a whip in his hand for the horse.

"I'll give you a ride," he said several times to me with an encouraging smile.

My mother had greeted him and felt honored by his visit. When I heard his invitation, I hid behind her. I was terrified of the horse, the whip, and the high seat of the open buggy. I started to cry bitterly, and would not be separated from my mother. I held on tightly to her apron.

"There is a blanket, if you are cold."

Despite the baron's friendly invitation, I would not get up in the buggy. My mother felt embarrassed by my tears and my refusal to accept a ride from him; it would have been such an honor. She tried to urge me to climb up to the seat. It was a gray and rainy day and he had offered a blanket—to no avail!

The other memory is vivid in my mind: intense, screeching bedlam and visions of white, flying feathers. My brother Gerhard and I were playing by the pond one day and had gotten too close to a group of geese. The gander unleashed all his fury on us; we must have infringed on his territory. His charges joined in the honking and hissing as he chased after us down the driveway. I was terrified and ran as fast as I could. After that, I did not wander too close to the animals or the pond anymore.

Starting in 1943, the clouds and screams of war came closer and closer. The horrors had reached a shocking culmination in Stalingrad with the defeat of the German army. From that time on, the Red Army, the Russian front, was moving west. Breslau, located conveniently in that path, was targeted for Russian takeover and occupation. There were threats of bombing raids. The war had arrived everywhere, including the cities of Berlin and Dresden.

Grandmother wrote these notes from Dresden in January 1944:

> Dear Hilde,
> Every time they start raiding Berlin, we also get the siren alarms. We have to go to the basement. They are dropping tons of debris. The Grosse Garten [the Great Park] is full of it, even up to Lange's garden. To wake up alive each morning is a gift from God. The raids have even started in Breslau but Leni and the children were able to celebrate Christmas together. Thank God for that! . . . Did I tell you that Karl Schnädelbach was killed in action? The parents of his young wife were also bombed out in Leipzig. They lived near the railroad station. Mourning is everywhere. In Berlin, with the exception of Imkerstrasse, all our churches are destroyed, even Tilsiterstrasse . . .

One month later, Grandmother wrote an update, this time about our life in Breslau:

> Herbert [my father] left for the Balkan. Leni was still able to visit him in Bohemia and helped him get settled on the train, but

they were not sure where he was deployed. It is very hard for Leni to care for her family, for the congregation and all the visitors. She has no au-pair girl right now because Rulla is still sick with diphtheria. Yes, she has much hardship to bear . . . In addition, I learned that Leni contracted an infection in her hand and needed surgery on her thumb. Her condition got increasingly worse, and the pain became excruciating. And she has no assistance. Klaus was taking care of the whole household, bathed the little ones, washed dishes, etc., until Gudrun arrived. May God help! . . .

Since the political situation had become increasingly threatening on the eastern front with the Russians marching west, we were ordered to evacuate Breslau for good; we were now refugees. We packed a few belongings, fled the city of Breslau in May of 1944, and again found help and a place to stay on the Richthofens' estate in Damsdorf, Silesia.

Earlier that year, the young baron, Karl von Richthofen, had been severely injured in the war and had returned to the estate and his parents to recuperate. The old baron and his wife said that their son had been clinically dead after being shot, and that he had been left dying on the battlefield for a whole day before he was finally rescued. We all heard that, during those traumatic hours, he had seen the angels around God's throne. Because of his severe injuries, he needed speech and reading rehabilitation, and his parents were there to help him.

"He was like a child when he first came home," my mother told us.

But he had seen the angels and God's throne! I wondered about all that. He had actually had a vision of what we had been taught in Sunday school and what we believed in. The young baron took a special liking to me and told my mother that he wished I were twenty years older, so that he could marry me. I felt his presence by my crib bed one day when I woke up from my nap. His loud breathing close to my face scared me . . .

We were on our way to Dresden, a place of refuge. Grandmother wrote this letter in July of 1944, again to her daughter Hilde, documenting her thoughts:

> Leni is in Damsdorf since the second day of Pentecost. She is near Striegau, staying in the Schloss with the Richthofens. I hope she has more rest there especially now that her help is back . . . Leni sent me about one and a half pound of freshly picked, red currents; it was enough for 2 small glasses of jam and a small cake. It was delicious! Here, thousands of people went to pick blueberries, even camped out in the forest. The trains were jammed. The people threw themselves in front of the train engines in order to be allowed on the train, and all in the middle of a thunderstorm. That first Sunday must have been terrible when the berry season was opened. We were not able to participate in that . . .

Worries about blueberries, jam, and crammed train rides became trivial when, on July 20, 1944, news reached us of a failed attempt to assassinate Hitler.

Disbelief and silent disappointment were written on my mother's face as she huddled with Barbara and her family outside the mansion. Publicly everyone condemned the attempt, but events during the following night revealed true sentiments.

After night had fallen over Damsdorf and we all were asleep, a group of men dressed in full military gear knocked at the door of the mansion and were let in by the baron. They turned out to be German officers fleeing their Nazi pursuers because they were part of the anti-Hitler conspiracy that had detonated a bomb in the Wolf's Lair in an attempt to kill Hitler. Mother told us later that these men were fed by the Richthofens, given civilian clothes, and quickly sent off with money and supplies to flee into the night. Since my mother had been a witness to this visit, she had to promise not to tell anyone about it. We never learned the identity of the officers; nothing more was said to my mother. Her suspicions, though, were confirmed that the

Richthofens had some secret connection to the resistance movement, a daring stance that put their lives in danger. Indeed, most of the conspirators were captured and hanged, and Mother worried about the safety of the Richthofens from then on. A few days after the failed coup, a postcard from Opa Schnädelbach reached us in Damsdorf. He wrote, "God sent us this man (Hitler) and therefore protected him!" Nobody dared to contradict him.

During our time in Damsdorf, my two older brothers went to the local school, where their teacher, Herr Kriegler, taught classes until January of 1945. My third brother, Gerhard, who was five years old, loved to go along to the small school in the village, but frequently had to be sent home because he asked too many questions and disrupted the class by talking out loud. Herr Kriegler described our life in Damsdorf with these words:

> We enjoyed a quiet Advent season at the end of 1944. In December, on the second Sunday of Advent, Frau Schnädelbach and Pastor Krämet, who held religious services and devotions in our nursery school, were guests in our home. We sang Christmas songs while enjoying candlelight, and we thought about our dear ones on the front, our Helmut, and Herr Schnädelbach, who was enlisted in Yugoslavia. Frau Schnädelbach said, "It is all so hard to comprehend, and hardly right to sit here in this peaceful atmosphere of Advent while our cities are bombed, thousands are dying each day and the soldiers are giving their lives on the front." She was correct; we were better off than many others. So far we have been spared from the bombing raids; only once did we see a big air raid on Breslau from a distance when the Christbäume [flares that resembled Christmas trees] lit up over the city.
>
> At the end of January of 1945, our village received evacuation orders. A tumultuous meeting was held in the brewery. The majority of the citizens present refused to leave their village whatever may come. Others thought we should organize a trek to Bohemia, in Czechoslovakia. Only a few people followed the official command, among them, Frau Schnädelbach. She was on her lonely way . . .

Mother had planned our way to Dresden, a place of refuge . . .

We prepared to leave in a hurry at the end of January of 1945, in the middle of a bitterly cold winter. The next train station was located about sixteen kilometers away and all public transportation had stopped for good. The baron and his family—his son, Karl, and his daughters, Barbara and Irmela, or "Innchen"—had been packing too, and carefully planned their evacuation. Sleds were being loaded up and the horses were ready to pull away from the estate. Furniture and extra supplies were stored and locked up in a hurry. Would they take us along on their trek? No one answered. The baron did not invite us to join the exodus. A silence fell over us all. Mother was devastated; she did not understand why he excluded us. The baron did invite a few other people to leave with them, among them a couple of musicians, but not us. Mother was deeply hurt and never told us what was the cause for their action. We children, though, figured that *we* were the reason for his decision. Small children on the trek would mean one more problem to reckon with. So they quietly left without us. In the meantime, the Russians were approaching fast, the sound of artillery already in the air, a thunderstorm in the winter.

Mother prepared for our exodus in a hurry and with a heavy heart. She packed two sleds with our most important belongings, some blankets, an orchard basket stacked with boiled eggs, apples, and bread for the next few days. We had to wear triple layers of clothes, just about everything we had. During the early morning hours on January 28, 1945, my mother led us four children and Rulla, our young au pair girl, out of the village toward Striegau. We pulled our sleds into the snowstorm on the icy road, covered with deep snow, and headed into the freezing air. People stood alongside the road, especially at the end of the village, and watched us walking away, our backs turned. We heard them yelling at my mother and us, "Those poor children . . . how could you . . . in this freeze!"

Another mother with her three children had decided to join our little trek. Frau Schumacher was alone too, and had decided to leave the village the same day. Not only did she take a sled along, but she also pushed a stroller with her sick three-year-old child under the blankets. The walk was treacherous on the narrow road to Striegau. The road, slippery and snow-hardened, was leading us uphill toward the woods, past the Domsberg on the right, and along a ridge with the wind picking up an icy whistle. We walked past the Kohlhöhe estate that belonged to the baron's brother without stopping once. We were used to walking. As the smallest in my family, I got to ride on the sled for some time and held on tightly. The road was leading us to Dresden—all of us—together.

We were not the only ones on the road. Figures moved swiftly in the white blizzard. The bitter cold, the deep freeze brought death quickly to other small children on the road, a sudden end to the elders' suffering, and the collapse of animals.

We were on our way to Dresden, to my grandmother's home, a place of refuge.

Darkness had come when we finally walked into Striegau. The food on our sleds was frozen hard and impossible to eat. My brother Gerhard, age five, was hurt. He held on to his knee and whimpered. It was strained from the long walk, the cold, and the fatigue. The train station was crowded with refugees, people pushing and shoving, rushing along the platform, waiting anxiously for an arriving train. People were screaming, the noise was deafening. Mother noticed a Red Cross station in the waiting hall and asked for help for my brother. They massaged his leg but not much could be done, the nurses said. While we were waiting, one of our sleds was stolen—the one with the food basket on it!

A train of freight cars had finally been assembled and was ready for departure to Frankfurt/Oder. We all climbed aboard one of the freight cars; it had no windows. Someone slammed the heavy, wooden door shut. There was straw on the floor so we could all lie down to rest. A single candle up on a ledge lit the compartment that night. Finally, the train set into motion with slow, jerky puffs. The compartment was crowded with other refugees. Someone started to sing an old camp song: *"Ich wäre so gerne geblieben—aber der Wagen der rollt . . ."* ("I would have liked to stay longer—but the wagon is rolling along . . .").

Food was shared. I fell asleep, rolled up in a blanket on the straw. A place of refuge . . .

The rattle of the train, the steady motion, the noise of squealing iron wheels, and the warmth of people provided a fitting lullaby; I entered an uneasy darkness. Time began to stand still in sleep, dream, and motion.

Mother planned to change trains with us in Glogau, the next station with a connection to Dresden. However, when we were ready to exit the train, no one was able to open the doors from the inside or the outside.

"The doors are frozen shut—you have to go on to Frankfurt!" someone finally yelled outside in the middle of the night at the station in Sagan.

Slowly, the train started to move on, carrying us north, ahead of the Russian front in the east, with the sound of battle, the explosions of the artillery clearly within earshot.

We reached Frankfurt/Oder sometime the next day or so. The city was in a state of panic and paralyzing fear. The train station was crowded with thousands of refugees—women, children, and old people—and everyone's luggage. Confusion and chaos marked people's faces. Everyone was trying to flee to somewhere, we were all refugees here. Where could we go now? Mother was told that there were no more trains leaving for Dresden, or anywhere else for that matter. Maybe a train would be leaving for Berlin sometime during the next few days. She knew by now that the Allied forces had bombed the city of Berlin and that it would be a dangerous place for us to go to.

The stationmaster and his assistants still ran frantically from one train platform to the next, hollering information at anyone around them. "There are no trains! There are no trains leaving anymore!"

Where were we to go now? Where to flee?

Despair, resignation, a realization of total helplessness in the presence of chaos sharpens the senses, chokes the soul, and numbs emotions. There she stood, my mother, with us four children, alone, in the train station with nowhere to go.

"I do call unto thee, O Lord; Lord, hear my cry!"

She clung to her faith with such insistence and bitter complaint while her soul began to harden.

One of the train officials passing by looked familiar. Mother knew this person, she thought. He turned toward us, their eyes met, and he too noticed her. They knew each other from way back when they had gone to the same Methodist church in Langensteinsdorf, in Saxony. They had attended the same youth group. It all seemed so long ago now; it was a different time then, a time of peace. A warm, brief reunion followed in this place of chaos, full of screams and panic. He listened to our plight, saw our need, and led us away from the main train station to a sidetrack near the depot where a new train was being assembled. The train was to go to Dresden . . . a place of refuge . . .

Somewhere in all this confusion, my brother Herbert got lost. I don't know how it happened, maybe he had gone to the toilet; whatever it was, he was gone. He was nine years old and lost. People started pushing and shoving around us to get on the train. We climbed up into one of the open freight train compartments that even had a stove on board for heating—but my brother was not with us; he was gone. The train was already packed with people and others insisted on getting into the small compartments. The noise was deafening, screams and fear mixed with the thick air of smoke and coal. My mother yelled out his name over and over, waving her arms so that he could see her in the crowd. My brother finally located us on the train but could not get on. The doors were blocked with heavy luggage piled up too high to pass through. Finally, someone lifted him up, handed him from one set of arms to the next, and then shoved him through the open window nearby. My mother sighed, *"Gott sei Dank!"* The panic on her face was beginning to lift. My own fear of losing him had moved into my stomach and my throat. I had imagined the worst—but he was back!

The train finally started to move with the familiar sound of the engine's rattle and the puffing of the rhythmic steam exhaust, going southwest towards Dresden. We were together. We arrived in Dresden during the early morning hours on February 1, 1945, tired, hungry, and shaken. The exodus had lasted five days.

We were in Dresden, at my grandmother's home, a place of refuge . . .

Later on we learned what had happened to the small trek of people in Damsdorf who had left for Bohemia. Very few survived the ordeal; the Russians quickly caught up with them in a violent way. Damsdorf itself was destroyed and plundered soon after we fled. The people who remained in the village were herded into their church, terrorized, and the women raped by the Russian soldiers. The Baron von Richthofen and his family reached the West safely. Mother had no contact with them, their friendship irrevocably broken. Many years later in a correspondence with Barbara, the baron's daughter, we found out that the young baron, Karl, had died very suddenly, succumbing to his head injuries.

A warm welcome awaited us in Dresden. Grandmother, who had turned eighty the year before, and Mother's sister, Liddy, who lived with her, had anxiously waited for our arrival. Their prayers and worries had filled their days of waiting while they watched the city crowd each day with thousands of new refugees arriving from the East, fleeing the overwhelming threat of the Russian army and their feared occupation. The city had lost some of its lightness and charm while housing the additional six hundred thousand people who were seeking refuge here, mostly women, children, and the elderly. Dresden with its historical and architectural beauty did not pose a threat to anyone; it was not a strategic military site. Surely, it was a city to be spared the ugliness of destruction and war?

As we learned from Grandmother, Dresden had already experienced one major air raid in the fall of 1944. The attack had not been mentioned by the government despite its severity and destruction. Grandmother, however, had written about it to her daughter Hilde, in October of 1944:

> On the Freiberger Platz, a whole wedding party of 40 people was piled up in their long gowns, all dead. They had been in a restaurant celebrating. The Hitlerjugend assisted well. They helped to lower people and their belongings down from the upper floors of their houses with rope ladders. Frequently, the windows in the upper floors were intact while the ones further down were shattered. In general, only one windowpane will be replaced, all the others have to be boarded up with wood or card board.

Grandmother and Liddy had anxiously waited for our arrival and wrote down their impressions of our plight in this way:

> January 30,1945
>
> Leni is not here yet, we are waiting anxiously. We called her ten days ago. She (Leni) thought they were still safe there and if necessary would leave with the trek, since they would not be able to leave by train, and in the bitter cold of winter. I am really worried. She wrote us a daily note, though not during the last days anymore.—I hope they did not leave too late. We will try to call again.

Two days later, this note:

> February 1, 1945
>
> Dear Hilde,
> Just a brief note to let you know that Leni, her children, Ruth and another family, a total of twelve people arrived here last night. They were on the road for several days. Thank God for their safe arrival. More details later.
> Warm greetings,
> Mother

Finally, a letter summarizes the events from Liddy's view:

And now the latest on our refugees! They walked through a bitter blizzard with minus 15 degrees Celsius for 15 km, had to leave everything behind. Leni joined up with a family of five, unknown to her, and an old woman walked also with them. There were a total of 7 children: the youngest was 1½ years old; a 3-year-old was sick lying in the baby carriage; and they pulled the sleds in the snowstorm. Little Maria always walked bravely. What indescribable fears and anxieties they must have experienced; it is hard to imagine. In any case, they were able to get out of Frankfurt/Oder in a miraculous way. They were traveling from Monday morning until Thursday morning. Now they are here, thanks be to God, although all of them are sick with colds. Leni suffered from a severely infected finger which gives her severe pain, and all other fingers are spilt open from the freezing temperatures—but they will be at home here. The "empty" room is now quite full because they all want to sleep together there. My sleeper bed is for Leni, the two old beds from the attic with air mattresses are for the two big boys, and the two crib beds are for the little ones. The table from the pantry, covered with linoleum has become a vanity table. Ruth is sleeping in my small room. The big living room has become a real family room. Slowly but surely, we are getting organized. It is amazing what they were able to transport on those sleds: 2 featherbeds, 2 comforters and 3 pillows, how lucky . . .

In the mean time, the situation here has changed again. The Russian front is moving in and we are discussing all day long what to do to bring Mother and the children to safety. We don't see a solution since we have no car and there is no snow to use the sleds. Where could we go anyway? They are digging trenches outside Dresden in the area of Moritzburg and Bühlau. How can that help? . . . You are better off in the middle of a bombing raid than us here who know about the atrocities of Russian occupation. May we be protected from the worst . . .

Mother and Liddy

A place of refuge . . .

Then on the nights of February 13 and 14, 1945, all hell broke loose. It was late at night when the sirens went off to warn us all of impending bombing raids. The shrill, piercing sound broke deep sleep and calmness of mind. Everyone was prepared to hurry down several floors to the basement to sit out the announced raid. The sound of approaching airplanes in the darkness of the night was followed by sudden crashes and explosions.

The raid was carefully orchestrated by the RAF, the Royal Air Force, flying out of England under Churchill's command as part of the Allied forces' attempt both to force Hitler and his men to final capitulation and to show off war muscles to the powerful Russian army that had infringed upon valuable territory in their move west toward the Rhein. Whatever the intentions that night, and whoever was to blame, the city and all of us in the middle of it were systematically and intensely bombed for the next fourteen hours with about three thousand tons of various explosives.

The following section contains shredded memories, incomplete phrases, and powerful images woven into a painful account of this fateful night—forever fragmented and too horrible to revisit at any length:

The first of four air raids started around 10:15 P.M. that night . . . out of sleep and calm . . . all of us spent time in the basement waiting . . . We were all safe . . . Mother went up to Grandmother's flat to put out the fire on curtains and windows . . . waiting and listening for the sirens to signal the end of the attack . . . Silence . . . They say, "Let's go back to bed!"

It is over . . . More sirens at 1:30 A.M. that night . . . Back down to the basement . . . many layers of clothes, warm stockings, and shoes . . . Sleepy and scared. More bombs to ignite the houses, drapes, windows and attics, flames burn quickly down through all floors . . . falling . . . horrible noises. The firestorm starts outside, whipping up flames . . . sucking cinder, flying . . .

"We have to leave, the house is burning!"

A *Sprengbombe* has hit the ground behind the house, Grandmother's garden, rocking the house back and forth . . . We cannot escape anymore, the basement door lock is melted shut. Finally, we all get out, wet sheets thrown on our heads, hold hands, walk together. Grandmother and aunt, too . . . Orange shears, wind and heat . . . Mother's other sister, Mariechen, and her three daughters, who live nearby, are also standing on the street. Their house on Elisenstrasse in full blaze . . . Go where? . . . Walk toward the Elbe and turn left on Wintergartenstrasse into a house entrance to seek refuge. Klaus is carrying Mother's big leather handbag, tied over his shoulders by a rope. Too scared to cry . . . fear is cropped by the moment. Other people are huddled in the hallway. Door is closed . . . Sitting down to rest and wait . . . wait . . . Firestorm rages outside . . . Hell is here . . . Breathe shallow, a little bit of air at a time . . .

"We will die here!"

Herbert knows we are dying . . . Falling asleep curled up, down . . . *Into the deep* . . .

Klaus floats in and out of sleep and vision . . . "bright colored, orange palm trees . . ." Floats and wakes, both brothers call my mother again and again: "Are you awake?" . . . "Are you still awake?" . . . "Mutti, are you still alive?" . . . "Klaus, are you still alive?" . . . "Herbert, are you still alive?" . . . "Gerhard?" . . . "Mutti?" . . .

Grandmother and Aunt Liddy are very quiet. We sit there for hours, waiting . . . waiting. Flames come down the stairway. With them . . . a man with a knapsack on his back steps down the stairs, he is engulfed in flames, collapses quietly . . .

"We need to get out!" Mother yells.

She walks up to the door . . . locked tight, locked in, less air . . . Fire has burned two holes in the door. The end is here . . . Fire is all around us now . . . no air . . . The lock has melted. Mother is grabbing the door, pushing with all her strength, the door opens wide . . . air!

"Get out of the burning house!"

I run toward the open door, my mother . . . I step—phosphor ignites me. "I am burning!" . . . socks and stockings catch fire, fast around me, orange licks, cry . . . I burn like a torch . . . Mother rushes toward me, takes off her coat and wraps it tightly around me . . . flames out . . . hot . . . not that bad. Outside, on the street, standing together. An old man walks out, too . . . don't know who he is. Grandmother and Aunt Liddy are not with us. Frau Wolf screams, she is missing her sister-in-law, Frau Seibelt, inside the burning house.

"I have to get her out," she cries, runs back into the hallway . . .

At this moment, the whole house comes crashing down with seventeen people left inside . . . dead . . . Grandmother and Aunt Liddy, too . . . Frau Seibelt and Frau Wolf never return.

Daylight is breaking; we are walking toward the *Grosse Garten*, the park, along streets. Stepping over debris, bodies there . . . smoke and ashes, horse dead . . . don't see. Orange, no more firestorm. Hot asphalt, shoes get stuck, left there. We all walk into the park . . . trees are burning, charcoaled stumps.

"Better here than by the banks of the river, thousands are dead there. Easy targets," Mother says.

Hollow houses, empty windows, rubble, boulders in the way, ruins . . . We rush toward the Methodist church on Wiener Strasse. They bandage my arms, legs and back. Cannot stay—still too dangerous. We walk a long time toward Köttewitz. In Strehlen, outside the inner city of Dresden, another air raid is announced by the siren. Roaring airplanes approach above us. We have to wait it out in a basement somewhere . . . It is passing by us this time. I cannot go on any more. Mother has to carry me the rest of the way on her back, fifteen kilometers . . . Klaus is still carrying Mother's handbag with a few personal items in it, that's all we have . . . To a refugee camp . . . *Out of the deep* . . . In Köttewitz they look at me for the first time, take off clothes . . . The wounds are there on my hands . . . I can see them . . . burns on my legs, my back, and my chest. Then they notice the wounds between my legs . . . I did not know.

"Second- and third-degree burns. Not that bad," they say. "Others are worse off."

They put cold ointment and powder on my wounds; wrap and cover . . . squeeze my legs together.

"It hurts!" . . . Don't cry out loud, whimper . . . can't help it . . . Urine helps soothe it . . . sleep, feverishly . . . forget . . . alone and dark.

We are in a warehouse of a factory; there is straw on the floor to lie on and food. They say we have to move on after a few days, they have to close the camp. We move on to Heidenau. I can't remember . . .

"Wound infection," they say . . .

It is dark for days . . . They say my wounds are finally getting better when I ask for some *Wurst* . . . They share and laugh about it . . .

"You were very sick during those past days!"

Mother wrote the following letter to her sister thirteen days after the night of the bombing of Dresden. Here are her words to add to my vague memories:

> Dohna by Heidenau, February 26, 1945
>
> Dear Hilde,
> Since I will be unable to write down again everything that has happened, I ask you to forward this letter to Neheim. You probably know that Oma and Liddy are dead. It happened this way.
> Suddenly alarm, no pre-warning, we had just gone to bed. Everybody up—straight down to the basement. The radio wire urged to hurry. We barely made it down when the bombs started rattling.
> Schreiber's house burst in flames right away, as well as the small Burg Ecke and Wintergartenstrasse and Striesener Platz. Our house was rocking; we were all lying on the floor. Finally, the "all clear" signal—upstairs, our house was not burning, our flat was a chaos, without windows and doors and what a fire storm! Protect our home! Oma and children to stay in the basement! One hour of desperate fighting. Raging firestorm outside. Peterman's

house was burning and foremost Langes' which truly shocked us. Then a new alarm. Quickly downstairs. We thought the world was coming to an end. The first raid was nothing compared to this one. The house rocked back and forth and caught fire, there wasn't a house that was not in flames—up and down the street. Smoke, smoke, off to the Grosse Garten. Not possible, fire everywhere, fire, fallen trees.—In a hallway, Wintergartenstrasse 31, our first protection. But that house was also burning, we all huddled together. Oma and Liddy tried one more time to go outside but quickly returned. I saw Maya and Inny outside, all very exhausted. Oma and Liddy lay down, totally exhausted. Liddy said, "We are all going to perish here." The fire came down the staircase, everything was in flames, the house door, everything. Oma gracefully suffered a heart attack, she looked so blue. Liddy suffocated, I saw it but could not help. Everyone suffocated or burned. I, myself, was only kept awake by the children asking, "Mutti, are you still alive?" With my last strength, early the next morning, I tried to rip the burning house door open. I succeeded. The children out— Ruth out. Maria was fully ablaze, extinguished her with my coat— get out. Everybody else was dead.

Our house had burned down to the basement. I found mother's china and some spoons, everything else lost, all the suitcases and belongings burnt. A few days ago, I returned to Dresden. The house did not shake me up that much, but the hallway, full of rubble—Mother's and Liddy's grave! 120,000 official deaths, only Blasewitz is still standing, everything else a pile of rubble. Zwinger, etc. Royal Palace—everything, everything destroyed. Incomprehensible, 3000 aircraft! We still do not know where to go, we are in emergency camps. Maria with third degree burns, getting better. The Grosse Garten in total chaos, particularly targeted, because there were so many people there, satanical! I wish we could leave Saxony, but where should we go?

Love,
Leni

The bombing raid was a success, fifteen square kilometers in ruins and ashes, rubble and smoke. Thirty-five thousand people killed that night, many, many more unaccounted for by cremation. Seventy-five

Wintergartenstrasse 31, Dresden, February 1945

Maria, Jenkau, 1943 (this photograph survived
the Dresden bombing)

Maria with Opa Schnädelbach, Leipzig,
1947

Grandmother Lydia Wunderlich, 1907

Grandfather Engelbert Wunderlich, 1885

Family portrait: Klaus, Father, Herbert, Mother, Maria, and Gerhard, 1942

Herbert Schnädelbach, 1944

Grandmother Wunderlich, 1944

Family portrait: Klaus, Herbert, Maria, Mother, and Gerhard, 1946

Wintergartenstrasse, Dresden, 1945

Holbeinstrasse, Dresden, 1945

Herbert Schnädelbach with Maria, Breslau, 1942

Methodist Church entrance, Breslau, 1998

Maria and Klaus, Breslau, 1998

Klaus, Herbert, Gerhard, and Maria, Bad Bergzabern, 1951

Maria and Ria in front of the Children's Home, 1951

Baptism of cat Morle; left to right: Heidrun, Maria, Mother, Almut, Fräulein
Kitzmann, and Gerhard, 1950

Mardi Gras, Bad Bergzabern, 1950

Mother at seventy, 1973

Gerhard, Maria, Herbert, and Klaus, Hamburg, 1996

thousand homes destroyed, the inner city leveled or left with standing skeletons, strategic and military positions in the area left intact. Someone said it was meant to punish the people who lived in the city and worked in the military factories outside the city. I don't know.

About ten days after the death of the city, Mother took my oldest brother, Klaus, and traveled with him by train back into the bombed area to look for Grandmother's remains. My other brothers and I stayed at the refugee camp. The train station was a disaster beyond description; the bombs had sunk whole train engines into the underlying bunkers. They walked the streets toward Holbeinstrasse 28 and Wintergartenstrassse 31. Dead bodies were lying everywhere. Corpses were burned beyond recognition, brown and shrunken.

"Are there any streets without bodies?" he asked my mother.

She had no answers. An eerie silence all around them engulfed them. They arrived at the burned-down home of my grandmother, *a place of refuge*. The basement was still partially accessible. They walked into the ruins. Mother started to dig with her hands to look for something, some sign of survival; the ashes were still warm, even after so many days. She knew the place where her mother had stored some personal items. She found the fine Meissen china still packed in the crate. And there in the ashes—the black, charcoaled soupspoons! She recognized the familiar monogram *L* and *W*. With tender care, she put the two spoons in her handbag. The china seemed useless at the moment so she left it there. Klaus thought of taking the china along, but it was too heavy to carry. They walked into the opening of the hallway at Wintergartenstrasse 31, which now looked like the entrance to a tomb: black, hollow, and final. They turned away, deeply shaken by what they had seen. They had paid their respects, their tears frozen in time without relief. As they prepared to leave the city, another bombing raid was announced. They sat out the alarm in another doorway nearby. Waiting and hoping.

While in the refugee camp, Mother had read a public notice instructing people to inform officials of the whereabouts of any victims under the rubble. She reported the location of the hallway on

Wintergartenstrasse 31, mapped out where her mother and sister had been lying. She had left them behind, crouched along the left side of the hallway, next to each other. Despite their efforts, no human remains could be found, only ashes and rubble. A mass cremation had taken place. Someone found Grandmother's big key to her flat in the ashes and boulders, black and burned. Grandmother had taken it with her that night. It seemed so worthless and haunting. No use to open a bombed-out home. A useless key at the time.

*The key is in my hands now; I have it here with me. A gift from the ashes but a grim reminder of fire and destruction, a mandate to tell the story.*

During the following week, nine thousand bodies were cremated in the middle of the city to keep disease from spreading. Other body remains were collectively buried in a mass grave in the *Heidefriedhof* (Heide cemetery) in town.

Mother led us out of the burning city that night, leaving behind our ruins too, and carrying away wounds, grief, scars, and memories. The life of the city ended in ashes, rubble and stench of death, and punishment. Her city and her history were destroyed there that night. She turned her back on the dead city, on her mother's grave in the rubble pile, and never, ever returned. No time for tears and grief. Klaus carried her only personal belonging, her handbag. He carried it on his shoulders. With that he carried her burden too, her pain, and many unspoken memories. My two oldest brothers saved our lives that night by calling out, "Are you still alive? Are you awake?"

I was three years and five months old and did not understand or remember beyond images of pain and scars. Memory, though, retains feelings in the body and buries them there. Sometimes I wonder why we did not perish too that night, along with Grandmother and Aunt Liddy and all the others in the hallway; it would have been so easy. Mother said it was a miracle that we survived and we should be grateful to God for it. Maybe God saved us for a purpose. I look at my left hand . . . they said it was good that it was not the right hand . . . the skin is very thin and tender. The warmth and protective coziness of

the night with its magic and shine are gone forever; recurring nightmares and fear of the dark linger on. Uneasy rest alone remains. Who
were we that we needed to be punished so severely? What had we
done to be haunted by bombs and fire?

There comes a moment when words cannot describe anymore
the thoughts and feelings attached to trauma. However, the ancient
words of the psalmist, when carried by music, can do so, allowing the
layers of sound to resonate with the depth of the experience. The text
keeps haunting me, especially when sung in John Rutter's *Requiem*,
composed in 1985. Here are some of the laments in Psalm 130:

> . . . O let thine ears consider well the voice of my complaint.
> If thou, Lord, wilt be extreme to mark what is done amiss:
>   O Lord, who may abide it?
> For there is mercy with thee: therefore thou shalt be feared . . .
> Before the morning watch, I say, before the morning watch.
> Out of the deep . . . Hear my voice.

In the moment of grief the old words belong to all of us and
speak for us all.

An odyssey followed. We were homeless again. While in the
refugee camp, Mother wrote a postcard to her sister Mariechen in
Tschopau, where she and her daughters most likely would have fled
after the Dresden bombing.

> Dear Mariechen,
>     Mother and Liddy are dead—Maria is severely burned—we
> are housed in Dohna, in a school. The refugee camp will be
> closed. Can you please pick us up?
>     Leni

My aunt arrived at the refugee camp and helped us move on to
the Methodist hospital, Bethanien, in Chemnitz, on March 4, 1945,
where we would stay for a few weeks. I still needed medical care.

On the way to Chemnitz, the train passed the city of Dresden. The two sisters sat next to each other as they looked out the window of the train compartment and saw that the once familiar silhouette of the city with its famous towers was gone forever, erased to the ground. Nothing was left—just ruins. They both wept. Their city was dead, along with their mother and older sister.

One of Mother's cousins, Mariechen Körner, and her husband, a Methodist minister, lived in Raschau, Erzgebirge, in the countryside, away from the city. Word came that they could offer us temporary shelter. Maybe the air and the food would be better there.

As soon as we all arrived in Raschau, Mother had to take me back to Chemnitz one more time by train to Bethanien, for more medical treatment. The brothers stayed back. One night in Chemnitz, the sirens announced another bombing raid; this time we were in a strange city. My mother carried me down into the hospital basement, bandages, clothes, and all. Down the stairs again . . . droning airplanes coming closer and closer . . . I am not scared anymore . . . My brothers are not here . . . Don't feel anything anymore . . . Can be brave . . . be still . . . Breathe a little . . . *Into the deep* . . .

Mother and I were spared that night. The hospital was only slightly damaged by the raid. I heard my mother and the deaconesses talking about it: "Only windows were shattered, the building is standing . . ."

I had expected worse, more fires and rubble. I was a bit disappointed when nothing else shattered around me because I wanted to be brave. My wounds started to close up with new, tender skin but numbness moved deep inside. Mother and I returned to Raschau, to be with my brothers.

Initially, the American soldiers had marched into that area of the Erzgebirge, bringing victory and supplies, including food. Soon after that, however, they left the whole region, waiting for the Allied and Russian commanders to divide the land into sections for occupation. The American forces took part of the city of Berlin and gave up Saxony and Thüringen to the Russians. In the middle of this political maneuvering, we found ourselves in no-man's-land, an area that did not receive any supplies or rations of food because nobody was in charge anymore.

We were refugees, homeless and unwanted in Raschau. We lived in the home of Mother's cousin and her husband, shared their flat, infringed on their precious space. Downstairs, the Fischer family from across the street lived with their grandfather, while another refugee family occupied their home; it was all so confusing. People had a hard time scraping by for themselves; there was so little food to share. Mother knew that we were in the way at her cousin's home. Their small flat on the first floor was located right above a hall of the Methodist church in Raschau, a basement that served as the gathering place for the congregation. All five of us occupied one small bedroom, which we could get to only by walking through the Körners' bedroom. The sparse heating came from a tiled corner stove, a *Kachelofen*, which reached into our bedroom. During the night, we all had to use the bathroom because our food consisted mainly of soups and stews. We had a bucket for peeing into close by the beds. It got filled up fast. Klaus remembered missing the pail one night; he was half asleep, and aimed at his shoe instead. I wet my bed . . .

Winter was all around us. None of us had shoes that were appropriate for the bitter cold and snow in the area. My brothers had to wear some sort of wooden clogs, *Holtzlatschen*, most likely the kind used for working in the fields. They were made fun of by other children in town, laughed at, mocked. Stones were thrown. "You *Flüchtlinge* [refugees]—now you'll starve to death!" they screamed at us.

Their wish almost came true. There really was no food for us. We ate a lot of *Rübenschnitzel*, discarded beet peels that were used for animal feed. Mother cut the peels into small pieces, browned them in the pot without fat and added water and *Otterzungen*, greens that we had gathered in the fields. It was bitter and did not taste good; I did not like it.

"We have nothing else." And we were hungry. No complaining!

Gerhard checked out the garbage of the people who lived downstairs. He found their discarded potato peels and ate them. I was not allowed to go outside much because of my ongoing recovery from the burns on my body. Maria, a neighbor girl, visited me upstairs and watched as Mother and Aunt Mariechen took off the white bandages wrapped around my chest, back, and legs. They wanted to change the cod liver oil dressing. The blisters were still there. Sometimes, the bandages stuck to the skin, and it hurt when they had to peel them off; I stiffened up. They said, "We have to pull it off fast, so it won't hurt that much."

One day, Mother and Klaus went into the nearby woods to search for mushrooms. They actually found a nice bundle of *Steinpilze* and stopped by a farm where some friends of Mother's cousins lived. The mushrooms were cleaned and sautéed in the pan with real butter. What a treat! Klaus ate his share and became sick soon thereafter, throwing it all up. It was too rich, too much butter!

Otherwise, there was so little food for all of us. Mother would go begging to the farmers in the area, hoping that they would share some meat, milk, or vegetables. One day, she carried a heavy knapsack into the house. A farmer had allowed her to take a stillborn calf. The women boiled it, and we all ate that day.

In April, Klaus received an official note instructing him to join the Hitler youth organization, the *Hitler Jugend*, which all ten-year-olds had to join. He never made it to one single meeting because he did not want to go. He preferred to play with the other kids by the railroad station, putting pennies on the train tracks and waiting for the train to flatten them into thin metal pieces.

Only a few bombing raids targeted our area. When the sirens went off, we would run into the basement of the house and huddle together. Gerhard and I screamed and covered our ears with our hands.

Finally, in May of 1945, the war came to a screeching halt. It was finally over.

"It's over," they said. "We have peace now, no more war!"

They smiled and laughed. I knew what they meant: no more bombs, no airplanes flying low, no more fleeing refugees. My brother Gerhard and I were playing on the street the day the news reached us. People came out of their homes; they talked to their neighbors. They smiled. The sun was shining. I was healing. We skipped higher and lighter. Gerhard had said many times, "When the war is over, I'll jump all the way to the ceiling." He jumped and jumped.

That evening, our mother made us all kneel down on the floor to give thanks to God for the end of the war. Our prayers for peace had been answered. However, our prayers for the safe return of our father had not been answered. Each day, Mother waited anxiously for his return. She sent the boys up the street to the train station to wait for his arrival on the afternoon train. We waited and waited. He never came.

As the German soldiers returned from the East, groups of disheveled, hungry, and defeated men walked through the village. Gerhard ran alongside the ragged parade and yelled, "Did you see our Vati? Did you see our Vati? He was last in Yugoslavia!"

No one answered him. They just kept on walking.

Klaus and Herbert learned to knit during our stay in Raschau. Klaus knitted a pink-and-light-blue sweater for himself and one for me with a fancy design, a *Zopfmuster*. It had stripes of different colored wool. He was always proud of that accomplishment. The yarn had shown up in the Körners' house in small bundles that were often tangled. These wool skeins had to be carefully untangled and rolled up into a ball, a *Wolleknäuel*, before the knitting could start. I tried so hard to sit still and hold the tangled yarn, a *Wollefitz*, with my hands. They said, "You have to stop wiggling around!"

*One yard at a time, Mother untangled just one yard at a time. You can't do it alone. You need someone to untangle it, one yard at a time. I had to sit still in order to make anew . . . I can't remember much. I don't know . . . numb.*

In July of 1945, the American forces left Saxony, which then was taken over by the Russians for occupation. We were finally able to travel out of the region to Leipzig where our grandfather Schnädelbach lived. He had invited us to live with him in his flat. We left Raschau with an official permission to move to Leipzig, a place my mother called home.

Mother wrote this letter in December of 1945 to her brother and his family:

Leipzig, the 2nd of Advent, 1945

My Dear Ones in Neheim!

Your dear letter, dated in October [1945], reached us finally after a long silence. This was the first sign of life from all of you after all these horrible events. A few days ago, a letter from our brother, Friedrich, also reached us here, telling us that you are all alive and well. I was so relieved. I am so glad that you are all healthy and together as a family. It's a true miracle and a gift. I am sure you think the same way.

I can't tell you how often I tried to write you but nothing seemed to reach you. I would have liked so much to come if Maria would have been able to. When she finally recovered from her injuries, nothing was working—no trains, no telephone—so we could not travel. For sure it would have been better to be with you than in Raschau where we experienced a true famine. God helped us through it again and again when we were close to despair—it was so difficult with four children. As soon as the Russians arrived in Leipzig, we were allowed to move to Opa Schnädelbach. That was a real joy and a gift, and it is still so. Even our cramped quarters do not bother us. We are at home here; that's what counts.

During the first few days here in Leipzig, the children kept asking, "Mutti, are we now at home?" My affirming answer lifted whole mountains of worries off their backs. The worst is being homeless and having to be patient. We lived through bitter times.

We are much better now. Klaus is attending Oberschule. He is doing well and enjoys playing flute and piano. He accompanies me quite well when I sing: Bach, Handel, etc. Herbert is learning to play the violin. Hilde gave him a violin, and since his instrument had to be left behind in Damsdorf, the gift made him happy. He is taking lessons from a chamber virtuoso player, just great! Gerhard started playing the piano all by himself, his music score is a picture book; he is finding harmonies, etc. All day long, it's music. I, myself, went back to my old voice teacher, Frau Kubel, who dug up my singing voice I had lost during the carbon monoxide poisoning in Dresden. I am traveling with her, a violinist, and an organist on concert tours to sing in churches. This is bringing me some happiness. The horrible experiences are covered up by music; even the children can be happy again.

It is so painful that our Vati is not here yet. We don't even have a sign of life or death from him. We are still hopeful! . . .

Leni

Music remained the connection to the past and the hopeful sound of the future. It was a constant in all this chaos of war, in homelessness and hunger. We could recognize the beauty of life in harmonious sounds and familiar melodies. Our history was alive through hymns and words, instruments and songs. Music went beyond the home we had lost, the belongings that had burned. Out of the ashes the music emerged again; it had never left our souls. Through music, our parents and grandparents expressed love, comfort, and faith. It would be up to us children to carry on the tradition.

Mother grieved over the deaths of her mother, her sister, and her home in Dresden as long as she lived. In her diary entries, written much later, she spoke from the heart. The following one is from 1983:

Dresden, especially Holbeinstrasse 28—that's where my Mother lived. It was my home, even after I was on my own. Other people went on vacation somewhere, I went back to Dresden. Even today, I think of the time in Dresden with such longing. I was always welcome there, even after I was married. There was always room—until the destruction of this beautiful city.

The heaviness of her experience, even after many years had passed, is evident in this entry from 1974:

> Today, January 28, is the anniversary date of the day we left on our flight to Dresden . . . It was also bitter cold, minus eighteen degrees and snowstorm. This day means two things to me. First, a reminder of the whole terror and tragedy of walking into the freeze with four little children, Klaus, the oldest, had just turned ten years old, the youngest, Maria, just three years. Second, a reminder of the help and inner strength when we were stuck in Frankfurt/Oder, and I found this station employee: he was a neighbor of our father, 400 km away. He helped us and took us along . . .

Klaus had carried my mother's handbag through the night in Dresden. It contained all we had, a few portable items to assure us of our identity, our history, and our family. The papers, the red savings account card, number 8.212.025* with the swastika on it, a few family pictures—one scorched photo of me standing in a garden—and the *Mutterkreuz*, the medal given to my mother by the Nazis in honor of my birth.

"A child for the Führer!"

The blue cross with the swastika on it hangs from the blue and white ribbon. Why did she take it along? My birth celebrated by the Nazis, a reminder of the bitterness in a family of faith and love? A few simple pieces of silver jewelry were stuck between more papers. She had received these tokens of love from my father: a bracelet, a pendant of finely designed stems of lilies, and an amber brooch. Deep down in the bag, a small pin was put. It is smaller than a quarter. Its ornamented metal frame shows my mother's picture, enameled, at the age of one or two in 1905, innocence forever imprinted on her face, the sweetness of childhood in her eyes, the gentle flow of her fine hair to her shoulders. Could it be a reminder of life and beauty in the fire? It became a tender symbol of our history, like the soul of a family alive, carried through the flames and finally brought across the border to freedom.

Klaus gave me the little brooch not too long ago. He thought I should have it now. Another piece of the burden he carried with her . . . *Out of the deep.*

I have the two silver spoons lying on my shelf in San Diego, next to all the other special mementos there. They are burned black, but the design is beautifully preserved, the letters *L* and *W* faintly visible to those who look closely. My mother gave them to me during one of my last visits with her in Germany in 1983. They are a reminder of the dry bones. I understand now that mitzvahs come in many different ways: sometimes they look like a dollar bill, sometimes they come with scorched pictures and spoons, sometimes with candlelight and songs.

"Take them with you." That was all she said.

Out of the deep . . . hear my voice!

CHAPTER FOUR

# *The Open Window*

The three of us headed toward the Polish border past Bautzen and the town of Liegnitz. The autobahn became bumpier, the hot summer air mixed with the exhaust of heavy trucks passing by. We began to see villages in the far distance. The sun had washed their roofs and steeples with a gray, misty cover. Wide, open fields along the road seemed unattended except for a group of storks parading along the watery ditches.

"I have not seen storks since the time we lived in Bergzabern. Their red legs and knobby knees are so funny. They look like down comforters with legs. I am amazed how they migrate to the same place each year to make their nest. Their presence usually brings good news, right?" I seemed to be talking to myself while in the front seats Klaus and Winfried discussed the local car manufacturing, the newest models on the road, and the advantages of air conditioning at this time of the year.

"We'll stop in the countryside this afternoon before we go on to Breslau," Klaus finally said to me.

"Will this give us enough time before it gets dark?"

"Oh, *ja*, it is not that far. When I was a kid, these distances between Breslau and the countryside seemed enormous."

Thank God for his skills in map reading and his preparations for finding the area around Damsdorf, to which we had been evacuated in 1944. His memories became increasingly important to my story as we crossed the border into Poland, since the images in my mind were getting fainter. This area was called Silesia until the end of the war when it was German territory. After the war, the land was returned to Poland.

We passed Bunzlau, where the local merchants sold their famous blue-and-white ceramic ware; it was a popular place to bargain for that special bowl or teapot. The colorful display of pottery on shelves provided a welcome relief from our efforts to seek traces of our family's past at a time of hardship and war. Open stands along the road displayed the fresh produce of the season: red apples, yellow potatoes, and full baskets of freshly picked, golden mushrooms. I had not seen such a harvest of fresh mushrooms for many years. We passed by a dirt parking lot with a large selection of colorful ceramic gnomes for garden display. Hundreds of bright red hats shimmered in the hot midday sun. Their grotesque postures and frozen grins offered us a stiff welcome. I wondered how I could transport such a gnome back home to the United States, but quickly gave up on the idea.

We exited the highway in the area of Weissenleipe, heading east toward Lohnig. A narrow road ended next to a row of fields where several men maneuvered their tractor along the dusty trails. Klaus stopped our car next to a group of old oak trees, where the ground was littered with papers, general trash, and discarded condoms—a meeting place of sorts.

"There it is," he said. "The train platforms are over here, you can still see them, and the tracks running south. This used to be the train station where we exited the train many times coming from Breslau on our way to Jenkau or Damsdorf."

"You remember this?" I was so surprised.

"Of course. From here we walked over to the country estates of the Richthofens, where we stayed a number of times before and during the war. It is about seven kilometers from here."

"We all walked from here?"

"Quite often. That was nothing unusual, come rain or shine. We were all used to it, you too. Sometimes, the baron himself or a farmhand would pick us up with a horse carriage. I remember late in 1944, when our mother and I went back to Breslau to check on our flat there. It was already dangerous to go back into the city. While we were there, we got caught in a bombing raid and sat it out in the basement. When it was over, I looked out of our roof window in the house—I spotted six or seven fires from where we were." His voice was animated now. "All our stuff remained there, who knows whatever happened to it."

"Were you scared?"

"No, not really."

My thoughts started to spin into a world of air raids and the consequences of danger and separation from my mother and brother at that time. What had he done with his feelings?

Except for the rusty tracks and the cement platforms, all traces of a train station had vanished. No remaining walls—nothing, just litter and dust. Klaus's memories of more than fifty years, however, were alive in his mind. The old oak trees in the hot summer breeze had remained the only witnesses to the coming and going of travelers—including my mother and us four children.

Just a few miles down the road, we entered the sleepy village of Jenkau. The estate of the Baron von Richthofen was located at the north side, the gate unattended and open. The once proud and lively country estate looked like a neglected burial ground. Parts of walls and hollow windows outlined the former stables on each side of a large courtyard. A filthy pond reminded me of the sparkly water the geese and ducks once owned. The high piles of dirt, overgrown by grass and covered by trash, contained the ruins of the country house where we had lived. A dirt road surrounded the grounds but was lined with more paper trash and discarded, rusty metal parts. No one cared for this place anymore. The once flourishing estate was in ruins, had been left dismantled many years ago. Only one house was still standing next to the entrance gate; people lived there. Someone had spotted us as we walked up to the door. An old woman, a man, and a young woman greeted us. Their warm smile welcomed us. The young woman spoke about eight words of German; Klaus spoke a pigeon Polish that opened their hearts. I pulled out some old family pictures from my bag and pointed at us and at the houses. "We used to live here during the forties, before the end of the war, with the Richthofens."

They nodded and smiled in recognition of the name Richthofen and asked us to enter their home. We sat down in their living room. The man brought out a bottle of brandy, someone set some glasses in front of us, the woman asked if we wanted *Kaffee*. I was touched by such a warm welcome in this desolate place.

Despite the neglect outside and poverty all around us, the people received us with such kindness. They had moved into the area after the war was over, they said. Their home had been in Czechoslovakia. They were refugees, too.

"Not much has changed here," Klaus said to us. "Even the door-knobs on the doors are the same, the long dark hallways between the rooms are well imprinted in my mind." His eyes wandered around as we shared that special brandy.

We had found more than bare traces from our past as we left our hosts to move on to Damsdorf, the larger estate in the area that had housed us before our exodus to Dresden.

"Look over there." Klaus started to chuckle as he pointed toward the stone wall next to the entrance gate. "I ran into this wall with my bike and I needed stitches. Someone drove me to the doctor on the back seat of a bicycle."

He knew the spot, the date, remembered the pain. He walked over to the village church to peek through the window, and he talked about the large gardens and the times of carefree summer play by the ponds and the closeness to the animals. I felt frozen here. The sunshine, the silence was all around us; so many images floating . . .

*So few memories I can hold onto: the picture of Klaus sitting next to me in the grass of the gardens. My hand is resting on his leg. He is wearing*

*Lederhosen—we both are barefoot. A happy time to be with my oldest brother. He smiled at me. I am holding on. What a special moment now to trace the past, the play, the warm summer air . . .*

A few miles down the road was the large country estate in Damsdorf, which was easy to recognize because of its remaining park. A large entrance gate led to a hill that buried the remains of the once beautiful manor and the arched entryway. The large trees had retained their majestic crowns; the hardened trunks had survived the seasons.

"We spent much of 1944 here and lived down there in the basement," Klaus said to me as we passed the hill to walk around the property. Along the way, a few huge boulders stuck out from under the rubble and its soft grass cover. "Did you know the whole estate was ransacked after the war was over?" I nodded. Mother had told us. "People just tore everything down. They took whatever they could use: wooden frames, bricks, furniture, everything . . ."

It was so quiet here in this place, almost lifeless. The importance of this moment stood edged in time, most likely never to return. I wanted to hold on to all my impressions in order to fill the gaps in my memory, to put together my history and gather the one of my family.

*We sought refuge here. The baron and his family offered us a safe retreat from the bombing raids in Breslau and the approaching Russian front. My first memories are here too, the horse buggy and the dog Bruno. My fear of the horse and the screeching of the geese still vivid, I could see them with my inner eye. Later, our flight out of the village . . .*

Winfried had remained by the car on the street. Everyone in Germany had told us not to leave a western car unattended, anywhere. So he stood guard while Klaus and I explored the estate. We walked along the paths that had once housed the most beautiful gardens, the large pond for the geese, and the stables.

I saw Winfried waving his arms and gesturing impatiently for us to join him by the car. "Someone wants to meet you!" he yelled across the street.

I really was not that keen to be interrupted in my nostalgic musings, and made sure I had seen all I could before returning to the car on this warm and strange afternoon. Winfried could hardly wait for us to cross the street. I wanted just another special moment to myself, to chase the silence some more, take in another picture of a dark past. Klaus had wandered off the old path one more time and slowly headed toward the entrance.

As I crossed the street, I saw Winfried standing next to an old woman dressed in a simple, faded housedress, wearing old felt slippers. Her gray hair was held together with a comb, although strands were hanging freely down her neck. She greeted us with a warm smile despite her many missing teeth.

"This is Wanda Freitag. She speaks German," he said. We shook hands and introduced ourselves.

"We lived here with the Richthofens in 1945 . . . ," Klaus started right off.

"I lived here, too. I was a little girl then," the woman said. A shy smile brushed over her face.

"Did you go to school here in Damsdorf?"

"*Ja*, over there to the old schoolhouse around the corner."

"Me, too," Klaus said.

"What grade?"

"Fourth grade."

"Me, too," Klaus said.

"Our teacher was Herr Kriegler, right?"

"*Ja*, he was a friend of my parents."

Frau Freitag looked at us and started to weep. Her tears just ran down, her red eyes having held tears more like streams over the many years of hardship. She and her mother had fled the village, too, she told us, in 1945 on the trek to Bohemia, but later on returned to a world of shambles and poverty. She was not allowed to speak German for about forty years, never ever to honor the hated Germans by using their language. Her mother did not survive the ordeal. The words just poured out; a sparkle in her eyes touched my heart.

Frau Freitag led us through the park estate of the Richthofens, along the paths to the old pond that once housed white swans and was now covered by green algae to feed the mosquitoes. The village children used a large part of the park as a playground. A makeshift basketball court and a grassy soccer field offered a place where they could run and play—a new generation of children playing on top of the rubble, children who had no memory of war.

Frau Freitag invited us into her flat in a large apartment house across the street. Her small apartment on the second floor housed her daughter and her two grandchildren. The living room was just large enough for us to sit on a couch facing a television set. At night, the couch served as a bed, we were told. The only running water was in the bathroom, one faucet over a cracked bathtub. There was hardly room enough to get to the commode; the floor was stacked with laundry, brooms, and cleaning rags.

Our host sent her daughter to the local baker to get some cake while she fixed coffee for us, a delicacy for her and special friends. We sat down on the couch to share the family pictures I had pulled out of my purse; the children laughed at a picture of our cockatiel, Joe, whom they called "*babuski* Joe." The little boy, maybe five years old, showed us the new slippers he had just received. Actually, he showed them to us two or three times; he was so proud of them. What was to us a simple pair of felt slippers was to him a colorful treasure.

"Barbara von Richthofen came to visit her old home about two years ago," Frau Freitag said as we shared coffee and cake. "She looked at everything but did not want to come back here to live. After her visit, she went back to Germany where she lives."

What an impact such a visit must have had on her, to see the old family estate in ruins, erased, overgrown, and discarded. Nobody said any more about it. Words could not describe our feelings. Our presence with each other, however, said more than language ever could.

We remembered and looked at each other some more. I was so relieved to have found the area of the country estate that housed my first memories and the fragmented life of our family. We had found another piece in our history, a place that had been home for a while in 1944.

*I thought of the mission I had been given back in California—the gift of the dollar bill handed to me by the Jewish woman in my office. She had said to give a mitzvah on the way, to share with someone in need, to give quietly, to leave a blessing, to give it joyfully as a sign of peace. Right here in Poland? Right here in Poland, in Wanda Freitag's home? I remembered it well and to fulfill my mission I left a mitzvah for her . . . put it in her hand. She accepted it quietly. My mitzvah had grown in numbers; one blessing had multiplied. I was not sure who was the giver and who was the recipient anymore, who was doing the blessing and who was being blessed. Maybe it did not matter at all. The woman had said, "Your trip will be blessed!" Right now, on this warm afternoon, it was.*

After many hugs and good-byes, we headed toward the edge of the village to find the road leading toward Striegau. The warm feelings at Wanda's home turned quickly into icy weariness. I stared at the narrow road. It was empty now—snow covered and icy then; we are visitors now—refugees and unwanted then; a silent recognition now—fearful and helpless then. I must have stood by the road for a long time, moments turned into timeless waves.

"Just take a picture," I finally said to Winfried as I stared at the road. He could sense the importance of this place and began to set up the camera to shoot some pictures, busying himself with the zoom lens. A woman was walking toward us with her baby in a stroller enjoying the warm summer breeze of the day. She passed us by, heading toward the fields.

*Those poor children . . . "How could you . . . in this freeze?" Our exodus to Striegau with the sleds started right here. We walked. The baron had left without us, a treacherous walk. Cold. Mother's worst memories right here: alone with us kids, abandoned by her friends, fleeing toward Dresden to my grandmother's home, a place of refuge . . . Mother did not talk about those days. I often worried about her silence. Maybe something terrible had happened to her that she could not speak about? Maybe she was threatened by someone, I can feel her fear. How did she get through all this hardship and terror? Who listened to her, who held her hand?*

The three of us climbed back into our car and started on the road to Striegau, leading up the hill toward the Domsberg area. The tree-lined street opened up to a panoramic view toward Grossrosen, the location of a concentration camp during the war. My throat began to tighten more; the dry summer heat made it hard for me to swallow. The pictures of the concentration camp in Dachau began to haunt me again, a painful reminder of the suffering, much more devastating than what my family had to go through.

*For many years I thought my story was not of any importance in light of the suffering of the millions of victims. Then one day, it became clear to me that it is not important to compete for victimhood with those who have lived through their trauma but rather to celebrate the life that is left, one person's story of survival at a time—one person at a time, one tear at a time. The dead would have to be mourned forever and ever by the tears of the living. But living did not have to be a state of permanent victimhood. Survival does not have to become an art of suffering for the rest of my life in order to maintain a sense of identity and dignity. I would need to think about how I have tried to live a life more in atonement than in joy.*

None of us talked as our car hobbled along the narrow road. I looked back toward the village of Damsdorf as the houses slowly disappeared in the distance. We stopped in Kohlhöhe, about halfway to Striegau, where the Richthofens had owned another country estate. The buildings were still standing. The richly decorated family crest was left intact on the walls of the main villa but the grounds and building were neglected and dilapidated. Nobody had kept the grounds up, no flowers were planted in gardens. Apartments had replaced the stately country home. Broken tree trunks and dust marked the remnants of a groomed park. Poverty and neglect had become the current owners. A young woman sat on the steps of the old mansion's entrance, smoking, ignoring us. I tried to imagine the villas in their splendor—the horses, the gardens, the parks. The original owners had abandoned it all, more than fifty years ago.

We found our way along the rolling hillside toward the highway. I wanted to hold on to all the images I saw that day; most of all, to the memory of Wanda Freitag's face, our laughter and our tears. I was so relieved to know that the remnants of our history were there. We remembered and validated them, Wanda Freitag remembered them, and together it would be easier to accept the losses and heal.

We entered the city of Breslau late that afternoon with the bright evening sun on our backs. I had finally arrived at the city of my birth. What a strange and exciting feeling it was. Here began my wearisome, adventurous, lengthy and traumatic journey, which would eventually take me all the way to California and then back here to validate my family's history. I hardly noticed the late afternoon rush hour traffic as we entered the city, now called Wroclaw, where about 650,000 people lived.

"Turn right here," Klaus said as we entered a side street and stopped in front of a large, stone house. "This is our house. We lived here on the third floor. Our father's church stands right behind this building."

Not much had changed in the last fifty years or so. The building had survived the massive bombing raid at the end of the war in 1945, but had only seen marginal repairs since then. Grime and pollution had eaten into the walls, leaving cracks and holes. Some of the window frames had never been replaced. The large gate was half open, the heavy wooden door broken. This was my first home.

An elderly woman opened the window to check on us strangers standing on the sidewalk and staring at the house. A large group of children began to gather and watch us on the street. Finally, a man who spoke German approached us.

"We used to live here during the war . . . ," we started. "Our father was the Methodist minister for the church there in the back of the house. We want to visit the current minister who still lives in the flat."

"He is not home. He took his daughter to the hospital. They are out of town," he replied. "I may be able to show you the old apartment you lived in, at least a part of it."

He was glad to welcome us to the home as we entered the dark hallway and climbed up the old wooden staircase.

"Frau Wolf lived down here in the basement apartment," Klaus said. "Herbert and I loved to go there to visit her. She had the best *Streuselkuchen*. Hmm. She would cut it in long strips right off the baking sheet and we ate it from both ends."

Frau Wolf had been the janitor for our father's church. She died in the fires of Dresden. Mother and my brothers had seen it happen.

"The flood last year devastated the whole area," the man said. "This house may have to be removed because of the heavy water damage." He pointed at the wall to show us the floodwater crest marked by grimy water suds that had turned into a black mold.

He knocked at a door on the third floor. A young man opened it and invited us to step into his world of two dogs, a cat, and a motorcycle amidst old clothes and general junk on the floor.

"Step over here," Klaus said. "This was our living room. The piano was standing there and the couch over here. Rulla, our au pair girl, slept there in this large niche." The space looked more like a closet. It was hard to imagine.

The windows were open. The rays of the summer sun shimmered into this junky room. I recognized the open window, the place where my father had stood in 1942, holding me as a baby in his arms—the only picture I have of him holding me. I had found the spot. He had been here with us. We were still a family in those days. I don't remember but I have the picture to prove it.

The chatter around me had stopped. I stood by the window, my hands reaching out into the empty space, seeking the outline of a person once standing there, gently following the motion in the air. The warm sun carried the eternal light of the moment. Time was standing still . . .

Klaus and I had our picture taken by the window, a proof of our homecoming after fifty-some years.

"We used to have a cat who liked to sit on the sofa," Klaus said.

We stepped over the dogs and the motorcycle parts to explore the apartment. The long hallway leading to the rest of our old flat had been permanently blocked off by a wall.

*This was the place where Mother received the* Mutterkreuz *from the Nazis for having given birth to us four children. This was the place where our father played the piano, our mother sang. He wrote his sermons here. Our mother could still laugh here. This was a place where we could love and pray, a place where angels had visited Klaus one night—a small oasis of a home in the middle of a chaotic world.*

As we climbed down the creaky stairs to the backyard, I felt relieved of my worries, having found nothing left in this place, but I was also wondering about the puzzling experience in the apartment. I had opened my hands to touch someone . . . I would think about it later.

Our father's church was still standing. I marveled at the Gothic window frames and the wrought-iron crosses on the façade. The sign at the entrance door announced the time of the worship service on Sundays, in Polish, of course. It had been a flourishing congregation during our father's time, a busy place of worship—today, the door was shut tight. I peeked through the dirty windows but could not see much beyond the posts of the balcony. From a postcard I have at home, I knew that the pulpit was in the front of the church. This is where our father preached every Sunday. Here, my parents spent happy times together before the horrible war destroyed our lives, along with so many other people's. I realized that I could have had a more normal childhood in this home, with both of my parents present, my siblings, and a church community—only to be reminded of the bitterness of war and its violence that had come so early in my life. I had lived through it all and been carried through the fire and along the roads without being able to reflect on the experiences as they happened. I did not know how to express what I saw and felt. Words alone could not help anyway; I had no words yet. I saw it all but did not understand it on the inside. Stories retold by my family carried only a skeleton of the full emotional impact, hidden for a long time. I was too busy with life. I was too busy listening to other people's memories and problems. I could not look at my internal images alone. It was too much for anyone to listen to, I assumed. It would take too long to explain to someone.

"It was bad enough, why talk about it?" one of my brothers once said, speaking for himself and our mother. He meant that opening up the old wounds does not change anything; it will not bring back loved ones. He was right about not bringing loved ones back, but what about the living?

It had taken over fifty years to return to the place of my birth in Breslau, Poland. It had taken years for me to dig out from under the rubble, to take this trip and speak through writing: sentence after sentence, memory after memory, reflection after reflection, conclusion after conclusion, feeling after feeling. First, I would verbalize my memories in a cautious, tearful tone eventually to reach a louder pitch and find a stronger resonance.

There were a few intangible treasures in our family that no fire could burn, no soldiers could destroy, and death could not stop. One was a strong belief in a merciful God, a faith lived out with insistence, and practical expectations of blessings for our daily life. The second was a deep respect for education and learning, "which nobody can take away from you," as Mother used to say. This mandate was loaded with high expectations for achievement in order to maintain our family pride. The third treasure included the presence of music in our lives. Music provided a connecting phrase to the prewar years, a mirror of our culture, a home. It was a constant with us wherever we lived. Music became for me the sound with which to express feelings. The voice, the human instrument, is able to mirror life from the deepest loss to its highest celebration, from a hushed whisper to a passionate scream. With it and in it, unspoken emotions and beliefs, memories, images, and spiritual assurances can be expressed and communicated.

However, to express these emotions freely meant coming out from under the rubble, and therefore posed a conflict in retaining the silence. Spoken and sung words kept tightening my throat. Spontaneous writing, however, would allow the small child inside me, the one with a timid voice, to be heard, because writing starts in silence.

Mother hung on to her faith in God, which connected her to our father throughout their years together. From the start, it had been the spiritual basis for their relationship. I could not experience such trust and comfort, could not develop much of a belief in God without a father present to model it. I had to reconstruct who I am and where I come from by revisiting my childhood on location while daring the process of trauma recovery on the inside. I recognized that I could hear the voice of God in music whenever I was not distracted. Why had it been so difficult to talk?

For various reasons, the silencing started early on in my life. We were told not to say anything about our family life or whatever was discussed in the home out of fear of being spied on, first by the Gestapo, then later on by the Communists.

After the war, silence became a fitting way of self-imposed punishment for the atrocities committed by the German people during the Hitler regime. Our teachers did not talk to us about their past experiences. It seemed that they were not allowed to mention anything that had to do with the Hitler years. I know for sure that they did not want to say anything out of fear that they might still be brought to justice for their own atrocities committed during the war. All signs of a Nazi presence were destroyed—even swastikas on family pictures had to be scratched out. The swastika was the most hated symbol from then on; it stood for everything evil under the sun. The black, red, and gold flags were put away; too much flag waving had been connected with the massive parades during the Third Reich. We were taught not to be proud of our country, just silent and critical. The history lessons usually stopped either with Bismarck or with the end of World War I. When Germany lost the war, I concluded as a child that the defeat meant losing your right to speak, to have a voice. I had ended up on the wrong side of the war survivors, the side that is identified with being a child of the perpetrators, the Germans, citizens of a nation that had started the war under an evil leader and had created blind followers. Millions had gone along with the political propaganda; that included my parents and my grandfather.

After the end of the war, silence became an important response in the face of my mother's suffering; she was hurting so deeply. She struggled with such determination to feed us and to lead us to freedom. How could I heap any demands or needs on her in the face of such chaos of survival? I figured that my silence was a way of helping her, taking care of her the best I could. I was ashamed when I could not live up to these perceived expectations. From deep within, a larger shame emerged for having been part of a people that lived out such evil. I knew that I could not repeat such actions. Was I capable of such behavior, too, under the right circumstances? Was I responsible for their choices? I concluded that it was best to be a quiet person without ever giving anger a voice. That way, the evil forces would be stemmed at least during my lifetime.

Self-imposed shame merged with silence and with geographic distance, as if, this way, evil could be avoided even more effectively. In 1966, I left Germany for the United States, a soothing distance from the lingering trauma of history. I hoped to escape the possibility of any further wars, or at least to be on the side of a world power. In my new country silence engulfed the past even more. It became a tool for helping to hide the years that I did not want to remember. The first time Winfried and I walked on Fairfax Boulevard in Los Angeles in

1966 and I heard an old Jewish man and a woman speaking Yiddish at the street corner, I wanted to disappear from the surface of the earth. I did not want to be recognized by my accent. I thought that I would be verbally attacked and spat at. We went quietly into the famous Canter's Deli and had matzo ball soup and a pastrami sandwich on rye bread. Nobody threw us out.

Did I believe the silence would be a life-long atonement? The Jewish tragedy remained before us, the suffering and struggle retold and remembered with new discoveries of losses and family tragedies. Even after more than fifty years, business ventures in Germany are scrutinized, moneys are discovered somewhere hidden in the Swiss banks, and synagogues are still smeared and burned. Is there no end to this?

*I guess I had to come here, to start over, to seek a connection to my father, my mother, and our family. It was safe now to talk about their ordinary lives, their joy and their suffering. I could unburden myself from here on knowing better who they had been and what they had lived through. Pictures, letters, and collective memories had led the way for me to get to know myself better. I would have a chance to speak through writing it out in phrases and floating words. I had arrived at a place that was my first home.*

The sun was beginning to set, and it bathed the neglected house and my father's church building with a golden glow, a reminder of returning and constant warmth in the middle of rubble and trash.

We spent the night in Breslau in the birth house of Dietrich Bonhoeffer. It had been purchased by an elderly Polish couple and transformed into a bed-and-breakfast inn. A simple plaque on the outside wall marked the date of his birth, February 6, 1906. What a time to honor this famous theologian who had participated in the German resistance movement, and was executed for it a few days before the war was finally over in May of 1945. He had paid with his life for what he believed in.

The next day, we explored the *Hala Ludowa*, the People's Hall, used for sports events and exhibitions. The gardens led to a pond with a central water fountain, surrounded by a walkway along the arcades.

"We used to come here a lot when we lived here," Klaus said to me as he took out his camera to catch that special angle of the hall. "It was the most avant-garde building of its time."

I bent down to touch the water and see my reflection. The sun was warming my back in the early morning hour. The park was quiet, the tables and chairs of the café had not been set up yet.

*I have been here before. I recognize this place by the shallow water and my fear of falling in. It is not deep at all; I can almost touch the ground. I recognized the thought, what I had told myself when I was little. The park and the water are still here. I have been here before. I have visited this place with my family. I had forgotten all about it . . .*

We headed toward the inner city. Our walk led us past the market hall, crowded with food stands and filled with fresh vegetables and fruits, to Sand Island and the *Marienkirche*. We walked toward the Cathedral of St. John the Baptist, hoping to climb the tower and get the panoramic view of the city.

A woman pushing a stroller with a child passed us. She looked at us, and without a word, pointed to a sign she was carrying: *Money for milk, please.* I looked away, feeling interrupted in my nostalgic contemplations and bothered by a woman beggar. We ignored her and entered the cathedral to admire the baroque, carved choir loft and the stained-glass windows in the lifting heights of the Gothic structure above us.

The magnificent view from the tower led our eyes in all directions. On this bright summer day, the river Oder, below us, hosted ferryboats waiting to transport visitors. Red roof tiles still covered many old, historic buildings that stood right next to the postwar, cement apartment complexes. Their ugly shapes and gray presence disrupted the silhouette of a once-beautiful city.

"See that bridge over there?" Klaus pointed toward the river.

"Yes?"

"That's where I stood when Hitler came and paraded through town in a caravan. I saw him there driving by and waving. I had forgotten all about it." He shook his head.

"How old were you?"

"I must have been about seven or eight."

We looked at each other, took a deep breath, and sighed. Traces of the past were everywhere, good ones and traumatic ones, easy ones and uneasy ones. These memories were permanent, nonerasable.

"See down here, that large brick building. That used to be the city hospital when we lived here. Herbert and I had to stay there for about three months because we had diphtheria and needed to be quarantined. Our mother and father were not permitted to visit us, so we had to stand by the window and see them waving at us while they stood on the sidewalk. Well, *das war halt so.*" He smiled without saying more.

"How did you feel being away from the family?"

"All I remember is looking out the windows in the back of the building toward a large park, you can see it there."

Other memories had been washed away, or words could not be found for them right now.

"It probably was the hospital where you were born," he added.

I stood a long time at the railing, staring at the place where I was most likely born and welcomed by my family. The red brick building with its high windows harbored stories of beginnings and endings, maybe mine included.

*Oh God, I had forgotten about my mitzvah mandate—the woman with the child at the entrance of the cathedral who wanted money for milk! She was in need and I had ignored her. I had walked away from her. I don't like beggars, but here in this place, the place of my birth? I was once in great need, too, our mother could not feed us. How could I ignore her? I had more money than one dollar in my mitzvah fund. It had grown with what I had received yesterday.*

After we left the cathedral, I began to look for her. The streets around the church grounds were deserted. It was too early for the daily tourists to arrive. The woman with the stroller was nowhere in sight. I had lost a chance to fulfill my mitzvah in this city—I was too busy with my own story, trying to connect my feelings, taking in all the sights in one day. I walked toward the hospital building, which stands near the oldest church in Breslau, named after St. Gidius and built in the twelfth century, and next to a brick arcade called the *Knödeltor*. Klaus and Winfried busied themselves with their cameras, taking some more pictures of the cathedral.

Suddenly I saw the woman pushing the stroller around the corner. She was walking in the other direction, not paying any attention to us anymore. I ran after her until I caught up with her. She stopped and looked at me, bewildered, when I quietly offered her the money. No words were spoken; only our eyes met when she opened her hand. A smile was her answer. Then she left in a hurry. I began to enjoy the thought of how the dollar given to me back home by the woman in my office was stretching nicely all the way to Germany, Poland, and beyond.

We entered the Greek Orthodox Church of Saints. Cyrillus, Methodius, and Anna next to the cathedral. A man welcomed us, inviting us to enjoy the artwork, the icons, and the many liturgical items. We had lit some candles near the offering plate when he approached me and handed me a painted egg hanging from a red string. He just gave it to me, and shook his head when I offered to pay for it.

"It is for you," he said.

I clutched it in my hand as we left this holy place. His kindness had touched my heart. A gift for me. Did he know?

We spent the rest of the day in the middle of town, walking around the decorative city hall surrounded by rebuilt patrician houses with richly painted gable roofs. The open café served coffee and cake, and it gave us a chance to watch the locals and the gypsy children begging for money. One little boy played the accordion while he squeezed his eyes shut; his "blindness" was only a temporary state while his sister held out her open hand to anyone passing by. The children's parents sat at a nearby fountain, giving instructions and collecting the money. The waiter chased them away.

Klaus wanted to go back to the old neighborhood once more to look for the building that had housed his school. He did not say much when he returned. "It was hard to make out the building, I was not sure. Everything is so different."

I thought that he wanted to be by himself for a while, to let the impressions sink in. He never said much more after that. He did his mourning in silence, too.

Down by the street corner, a woman stood alone in an alcove and sang her heart out. She just stood there in her long, black dress and sang selections from *La Bohème* and other arias of dying divas. Her strong voice echoed in the marketplace. She sang without accompaniment, not even a tape recording. People passed her and smiled, or ignored her; she remained unperturbed. The marketplace was her stage. I recognized her music, her effort, and her need to practice in front of people. I was happy to reward her with a tip.

In the late afternoon, the beer gardens on the plaza began to open. The wooden benches and tables filled with people as they visited with each other on this warm summer evening. We joined in and sat down at a table, allowing the day to sink in. In the distance someone played the guitar.

We left the city the next day, this time turning west toward the German border. I wanted to stop in Bunzlau one more time to purchase a blue-and-white ceramic teapot, a reminder of our visit to the old *Heimat*. The gaudy-looking gnomes still grimaced at us as we passed the dusty corner lot.

We were hobbling along on the bumpy freeway about three kilometers past Bunzlau when Winfried said, "The needle is going into the red, something is wrong."

The engine was overheating; white steam was drifting from under the hood. We had to stop as soon as possible. We rolled into a dirt exit along a forest, most likely a place of relief behind the trees. The men carefully opened the hood. No village in sight to walk to, no gas station along the road, no AAA Club to call here in Poland. We would not be able to communicate with anyone in Polish.

Both men bent over the motor. Klaus had taken out his toolbox from the trunk and poked with his pliers at various hoses and containers. Both men were quite calm about the problem. I got a bit nervous.

"Most likely the water hose . . . see over here . . . a hole . . . watch out, it is hot!"

They agreed on the diagnosis. Winfried had been correct about problems under a car's hood many times in the past, I thought.

I began to look around to see what trash articles could be helpful in fixing the leak. Amidst bottle caps, old tissue paper, nails, and pieces of tire was quite a bit of thin copper wire that I picked up. Klaus brought out his first-aid kit and got some Band-Aids and an old rag to wrap around the broken hose. Luckily, we had carried water with us for refill.

"It should get us across the border, unless we have to stop a few more times to refill the water," Winfried said calmly.

"Let's hope this is the only problem," Klaus said, wiping his greasy fingers on an old rag.

We drove on, our eyes fixed on the temperature gauge, which held steady.

We rolled into Görlitz, the German border town advertising a modern Renault service station, and found a great brewery where we ate *Knödel, Rouladen,* and *Rotkraut* while the car was being repaired. The local beer washed away my fleeting fears; the food was a welcome comfort. We were back in familiar territory.

We rolled toward München, leaving the city of Leipzig on our left. *I need to go there and trace those years some more . . .*

# CHAPTER FIVE

# *The Day the Man Came (1947)*

They said he would come the next day. We had waited for some news about my father, whose last postcard, written in Yugoslavia, had arrived two years ago in 1945, and was addressed to Klaus. After that there was no more mail, no letters and no official announcement concerning his whereabouts. Finally, tomorrow, we would hear where my father had been for the last few years and when he would come home.

A flash of excitement appeared on my mother's face; her warm smile spoke of sudden hope, although her eyes were burdened by years of waiting and sadness.

Grandfather had been told about the news, too. He sat quietly at the end of the sofa in the living room, his eyes fixed toward the window, the street. His thoughts were dark, his heart was heavy. Karl, his other son, who had served in the SA troops, had been killed in the war in November of 1943, at the Russian front. The family had been told soon after his death; his young wife was left a brokenhearted widow. We were told that our Onkel Karl had bravely fought for the *Vaterland* and was honored in death with the medal of a hero. Grandfather was told that his son, who was a paramedic on the battlefields, had died on the island of Krim while helping a comrade who had been mortally wounded in the heart by a bullet. Onkel Karl's widow, my Tante Elfriede, had a picture of his grave in Karatschi. Grandfather had written these lines in his diary, reflecting, in light of his faith, on her loss: "All her joy in life is now in ruins, and her life seems so useless. Only our God, the Lord, can comfort, and he will do so! Amen."

Grandfather had envisioned a great future for his son. He was proud of him and believed that his service in the SA force was "the only way to get somewhere in the world." He had been serving his *Vaterland*. My grandfather's dreams had died with his son's death; the loss of a son in combat buried his tears. My father had been ordered into the military in 1939 like all the other eligible men. He went because he had to go. Onkel Karl, however, wanted to be a soldier and help other soldiers at the front. I did not know what all this meant; I just saw the sadness on Grandfather's face.

Sometimes my family would visit the *Völkerschlachtdenkmal*. This huge war memorial from Napoleon's time had been erected during the last century and was located not too far from where we lived with my grandfather in Leipzig. It was enormous in size but gray and grimy on the outside from years of pollution and neglect. A park surrounded the memorial honoring the dead who had fought in previous wars. Despite the heavy stone walls, there was open space all around and a full view toward the city once we reached the high platform. The flowerbeds in the gardens always looked dry and neglected in the summer; they were overgrown by weeds. Few flowers bloomed there.

I liked this place away from our small apartment even though it gave me a solemn feeling. It was not like visiting the cemetery. There, we were in the presence of the dead and ought not to laugh out loud or have too much fun running around the graves. Here at the memorial, however, I could run about and climb the stairs and see the sky. I could not think of any other dead heroes except my Onkel Karl.

Visiting the war memorial was helpful in many ways. We searched for edible weeds and greens such as sorrel, which we picked and stuffed tightly into the bags we had brought along. To carry them home felt good because it meant another meal on the table that night. Once home, Mother emptied the bags into the bathtub, where the greens were repeatedly soaked and rinsed before being placed into the largest pot in the kitchen. I was always amazed at how much stuff we had picked and how little food finally made it onto the dinner table. All the leaves had boiled down to a green, creamy mass and had to be shared around the table. There were my three older brothers, my mother, my grandfather, and my two aunts (my father's sisters), who had moved out of the apartment when we moved in two years ago. However, Tante Lottel and Tante Johanna came back to the flat daily and ate with us. The dining table was not big enough for all of us to gather around. Tante Lottel often watched us eat while sitting on the edge of the sofa or leaning against the door. I never saw her eat a lot. She was very tall and thin; her straight, dark hair was pulled back into a bun. Mother said she received some food at her workplace and ate there. She always invited her to sit down with us at the table and was irritated with her for watching us eat.

"Sit down, Lottel, there is enough room here next to me," Mother said with a harsh tone.

"I am on my way to work," she said and watched us some more.

"You are so thin, you are not eating enough!" A silence followed. Tante Lottel looked away.

My brothers had figured out that as the older siblings in the family they should be entitled to receive proportionally more food than their little sister. It seemed hard to share, especially when there was not enough to go around. So we watched over the portions each one of us received while being reminded by our mother that we had to share. On a special occasion such as a birthday, a cake was placed in the middle of the table to be carefully sliced and divided. I thought my mother was very fair and knew how to cut all the pieces the same size. She left the middle piece for the birthday child, and I know for sure that she sacrificed her own portion, saying that she was not hungry anymore.

Preparing food and cooking was an ordeal by itself. Electricity was still rationed. On some mornings, a pot of milk rice was prepared when the electricity was turned on. The hot pot was placed on a couple of bricks right in our beds and covered tightly with blankets to keep it warm for *Mittagessen*, lunch, or dinner the same day. I thought nothing of it and remembered to be careful when climbing into my bed for an afternoon nap. The warmth in the bed left behind by the pot of rice was both welcoming and comforting in the wintertime. My favorite foods were potato soup and *Kartoffelkuchen*, a yeast-based sheet cake made with potatoes, sugar, and butter, if available. *Reibekuchen*, potato latkes, with applesauce on the side was also a special treat. The whole apartment was engulfed in the smell of burned fat when the women pan-fried them in the kitchen. The balcony door was opened wide to let the fresh air in. I also liked fresh, dark bread with salted lard and bacon bits on top; we called it *Schmalzbrot*.

The adults were always concerned about where our next meal would come from—I saw it on my mother's face, the worry in her eyes, her thoughts somewhere else. She talked to the neighbors and my aunts about the rationing, the unpredictability of the stockpile in the stores, the quality of the vegetables, and the scarcity of everything, even such items as new shoelaces. They worried about where she could find a special grocer who had received a shipment of goods. I don't exactly know how we survived during those years. Maybe I tried not to notice because it was a scary thought, not having anything to eat tomorrow. Mother said it was our faith in God that got us through the *Hungersnot* (famine).

During the winter of 1945, Mother had been invited to join Herr Wedel, a church organist, and Frau Zieschang, a violinist, on several concert tours into the countryside. It was more like musical *hamstern*; the trio would make music in various villages and be given potatoes and carrots by the farmers for their performance. I was allowed to accompany my mother on two of those trips. Their concerts were held in bitterly cold village churches; no coal was available to heat them. I could see my own breath when I talked. Herr Wedel had to warm his fingers with his gloves in order to play the organ. I held his hand and led the way because he was blind. He needed help to find the steps into the church building, but he always knew how to open the organ and pull the stops next to the keyboard. He was at home at any organ. My favorite place was sitting down by the organ, where I could watch his feet move swiftly over the pedalboard while joining my mother in singing various arias such as Handel's "Largo" and Giordani's "Caro mio ben." I always wondered what the "ben" had to do with, not knowing that it meant "bliss"; I thought it was *Bein* (leg).

At the beginning of each concert, Mother said, "You cannot sing now, you have to be quiet." I understood what she meant and kept silent during the concert. The wailing sound of the violin echoed in the high ceilings and bounced off the stone walls of the cold churches. Because I sat close to the organ bench, I could not see the people sitting and listening. Every concert opened in deep silence and ended in deep silence. There was no applause in a sanctuary. I heard someone open the creaky doors, then a shuffle of steps and an occasional, suppressed cough. This was the house of God, to be entered in deep reverence. God was to speak to us in this place, even in the silence. I was not sure if God would be offended by my sitting on the floor by the organ pedal; it felt very safe.

We slept in people's homes where the beds were ice cold, the thick feather beds clammy, but I was with my mother and spared of being homesick for her back in Leipzig. We shivered as we climbed into the old, creaky beds. We returned to Leipzig by train with food and money given to my mother by the farmers. I felt that we were begging for food, depending on the charity of the villagers. They did not have that much either. I knew though for sure that there was less food in the city than in the countryside. I was embarrassed for my mother and I tried to be nice in return to everybody.

Near the train station in Leipzig, people traded food for goods; it was called the black market. We all knew of this risky business because the government officially prohibited the citizens from selling goods, and if they were caught, the police arrested everyone involved. Some people were being caught trading cigarettes and western currency. I hoped none of my family members would ever go there; the thought of it frightened me.

Sometimes our friends at the Methodist church helped us out when there was extra food to share, such as fruit or vegetables from their

*Schrebergärten.* Many people went *hamstern* too, which meant they took the train to the countryside to trade goods such as jewelry, china, or watches for potatoes, eggs, and sausage. Mother had food stamps in her wallet that dictated our rationing for bread, butter, milk, and occasionally some meat. We were entitled to three pounds of bread per week. Sometimes she would take me shopping to some of the local stores in the neighborhood, which rarely displayed any goods in their windows. The stores only opened when there was something to sell. One time, we stood in a long line outside a store that had received a shipment of cucumbers. When we finally got up to the front of the line, someone locked the door from the inside. They had run out of cucumbers, and we went away empty-handed.

Our bread was carefully rationed for each day. There was a time when we received two slices at suppertime with some spread on it. Occasionally, Mother gave us a piece of blood sausage or liverwurst which we pushed on top of the slice of bread up to the final, last bite. We called it *Schiebewurst.* One evening, as we sat around the supper table and the meal was finished, I said to my mother, "I am still hungry!"

My oldest brother answered quickly and sharply, "If I am not hungry, then you can't be hungry either!"

I was very quiet after that. I knew how little food there was for all of us and that I should not have asked for more. I should not have said what I felt because there was nothing anybody could do to change it. Keeping quiet meant not burdening my mother with questions and making her more worried. We all knew what the food rations were.

A sudden gift of food was always considered a small miracle in our home, and each night after our meal, we would give thanks to God for it and pray for the next day. We could talk to God about having no food and ask him for it, but I could not say how I felt about maybe having nothing to eat tomorrow. When I kept seeing my mother worry while she prayed out loud, I worried with her but kept silent to protect her from having to deal with me too. I was to believe that God would take care of us, whatever would come, today or tomorrow . . . *Give us this day our daily bread* . . . It was hard to believe when I saw so little food in the cupboard. Mother said that we would not be forsaken—she knew that for sure.

At our daily devotional times, usually after supper, we opened our Bible and each one of us read a few verses, one after the other. I could not read much then but was expected to participate anyway. I knew many Bible verses from Sunday school and would recite them when it was my turn. I also knew some handy biblical phrases that I could freely recite at any time if needed: "And Jesus said to his disciples . . ." or "Therefore I tell you . . ." And of course I could say "hallelujah" and "amen." I could fill in with these when it was my turn to read from the Bible and could feel that I was a part of the family.

Things got more complicated for me when we were reading from the Old Testament, where verses might have a sequence of difficult names, as in 2 Samuel 23:24–39: "Asahel the brother of Joab was one of the thirty; Elhanan the son of Dodo of Bethlehem, Shammah of Harod, Elika of Harod, Helez the Paltite, Ira the son of Ikkesh of Tekoa, Abiezer of Anathoth, Mebunnai the Hushathite, Zalmon the Ahohite, . . . Uriah the Hittite: thirty-seven in all."

Much later I found out that my brothers had quickly assessed the reading sequence around the table beforehand, strategizing so that I would end up with the hardest verses; then they would laugh sheepishly at my struggle.

A *Stille Zeit* followed our nightly readings from the Bible, a quiet time, a time of silence and reflection. I did not really know what to reflect on, it was such a long silence. We were to listen to God, Mother said. I thought of things I had done wrong that day and confessed them. Some days I could not find much to confess and God did not talk to me either. I tried very hard to listen but there was only more silence. I did not really understand how God would talk to me in my silence and what I was to listen for. I figured that my mother would know, and she would tell me what to do and how to be helpful and nice. Maybe it was because I had chewed my nails again, and my mother had sternly inspected my fingers that afternoon. I felt really bad about it and was ashamed. I tried to do better the next day. Maybe God would talk to me if I would be really good that day. It never occurred to me that my mother had sinned and needed to confess for anything. I looked at her standing in the kitchen every day, wearing her apron and worrying about the next day. In my eyes she had done nothing wrong, ever. Our next meal was on her mind, and so was money and our community, the church. She was seeking God in her prayers. Most of all, she was waiting for our father to come back from the war. Our nightly devotion was the only ritual connecting us to our father wherever he might be because we knew he would also pray for us. All of us prayed so hard for his safe return from the war. I squeezed my hands together and shut my eyes tightly. I tried to beg God with words.

When we had our own Sunday afternoon worship service, I had a more active part in it. My brothers would move the dining table chairs in a row and I would gather my dolls and bears to be the audience. It was usually Herbert who took over the designated pulpit duty. Klaus served as the organist at the piano, and Gerhard helped out as a second preacher for the day. I sat with my dolls, listening as well as joining in the congregational singing. We knew the routine well because we had already attended a service in the morning at the Methodist church. Herbert turned out to be an eloquent preacher, long-winded, full of powerful oratory and waving gestures to convey his message. The content of his sermon was based on a scripture reading freely interpreted. It was difficult for the second preacher to get a word in. When Gerhard finally got a chance one day, he began his proclamations: "And Jesus said to his disciples . . ." Then he bent forward to ask us congregants, "What did Jesus say to his disciples?"

All the preaching was over my head. I did not follow the sequence of the homemade homiletics but the service was solemn and respectful of the word of God. I believed that in this way, our father was present through ritual and gathering.

Our family life had remnants of our familiar routines from back home in Breslau. My brothers played the piano and Mother started to sing again. There was flute music dancing in the air, sometimes mingled with the scratchy whine of the violin. They practiced the same scales over and over again, made the same mistakes in the finger runs of the Clementi sonata. I covered my ears when the brothers practiced their instruments at the same time. I listened to these concerts while sitting on Grandfather's sofa in the living room.

Together we sang hymns in church and at home. We stood around the piano harmonizing. They let me sing the melody because it was the easiest part and I was the youngest. I liked the sound of Christmas best. The melodies became light and joyful, the words full of magic and shine. The sound of small bells hung in the air. This happy time was unfortunately over much too soon with January 6, Epiphany Day, and the commemoration of the arrival of the three wise men in Bethlehem. Even there, the cruelty of life was present in King Herod's rage.

Music mirrored and carried many of our unexpressed feelings. I heard it in my mother's voice. Her singing voice colored the words with longing and sadness, with tears and memories. Her dark timbre took on the warmth in the phrases as the long sustained notes carried the sound. What was she remembering? The singing with my father, the loving times in their home?

On many Sunday afternoons she would stand by the piano and sing with Klaus accompanying her. Both of my brothers would play trios with her. Sheet music returned into our home: collections of vocal, choral, and instrumental music, mostly classical music from the Baroque and Romantic eras. Our favorite composer was J. S. Bach, whose music we listened to on the radio. My brothers said that he was really a much better composer than G. F. Handel, more sophisticated in style and more spiritual in content; I believed them. Bach's Passions according to St. Matthew and St. John were revered in my home as the most perfect and divine music ever written. Performances on the radio were not only listened to, but were reviewed and eagerly critiqued by all of us as to the style of the singers, the interpretation of the text, the tempi of the various pieces, and the quality of the instrumentalists. Mother knew the names of many oratorio singers and conductors at the time. We became music critics. By the time I was six years old, I could read and follow the scores of Bach's choral works and arias. I was familiar with his works and waited for my favorite chorale. Sometimes I lost my place on the page. The many parallel lines of the orchestra scores were filled with too many fast-moving notes!

Every year during Holy Week, the week before Easter, J. S. Bach's *Passion according to St. Matthew* was performed on the radio. The week of Jesus' passion and death was faithfully observed in our home—no coloring of Easter eggs before Saturday afternoon at three o'clock! We gathered around the radio in Grandfather's living room, score in hand, and followed the painful events of Jesus' death, scene by scene, from the first recitatives to the last aria, singing along all the chorales and the mighty choruses. The drama unfolded . . . three hours long. We sat in silence. No one spoke during the performance. It was a three-hour worship service. I was always so relieved when Jesus finally died after being so mistreated; death arrived as a release from his suffering. A moment of silence followed. Afterwards the heavens opened with an earthquake and the curtain tore apart in the temple. Jesus was gently laid to rest with the most wailing and comforting melodies. My soul understood grief but I had no words for my feelings. Sadness echoed in these wonderful musical sighs that carried words of comfort!

It was so hard to hear Jesus die like that with people hating and killing . . . the Jews killing Jesus . . . to be reminded of it every year! Our Sunday school teacher had taught us the stories of the last supper, the betrayal, and the trial. Jesus had been condemned by his own people, she had said. They had screamed, "Crucify him, crucify him!"

Jesus' death was the reason for the ongoing persecution of the Jews in the world, a two-thousand-year-old curse. That was the conclusion

I formed in my mind from what I heard. I was ashamed of the harshness and hate toward a people, but, nevertheless, in the face of the death of God's persecuted son, revenge seemed sent from God. Justice would prevail. I did not ask questions; I did not ask my mother, either. I did not question the Bible but rather accepted these Christian teachings by listening and watching. The silence among us covered reason and feeling. My childhood was full of traumatic and dissonant melodies, and suffering was an acceptable virtue.

*Here I found my own base of anti-Semitism, the foundations of hate laid out by the teachings of my church within a country that had carried out revenge toward the Jewish community in an evil manner. The Jews had killed Jesus two thousand years ago, each year to be commemorated? Why did I silently accept such thoughts of revenge in the name of God? I never questioned my own conclusions, or the biased teachings of the church I attended, or my own capacity to accept the foundations of anti-Semitism. I felt hated too in the middle of fire and homelessness. Power, revenge, and hate had become unchangeable facts of our life that I had no control over. As a result, I hid in silence under the rubble of the emotions and the painful implications of my history. I was silent and timid. That way, I would not be noticed.*

*I am humbled and ashamed, mindful of the slippery road of prejudice and ignorance. To become aware is a step toward recognition and change.*

The glorious music at the end of Jesus' suffering pointed toward eternal life full of hope and resurrection, comfort and peace . . . I waited for that every year. The music became rich in harmony and depth, a reminder of perfection within us, of wholeness in a time of brokenness. Our silent grieving was expressed through the music of tears. *In tears of grief, dear Lord, we leave Thee* (J. S. Bach, *Passion according to St. Matthew*).

Tomorrow we would know for sure if he would come home and when. It was easier to wait for the man's arrival when I was playing outside the apartment with my friends in the neighborhood. The sidewalk along the street had curbs to sit on. I sat there and watched horses pulling carts, people passing by, and military vehicles patrolling the neighborhood. Sometimes the neighbors ran after the horses with their buckets to catch the droppings, so-called *Pferdeäpfel,* to be used as fertilizer for the tomato plants in their *Schrebergärten,* the small gardens outside the inner city.

We used white chalk to mark our favorite hopscotch games on the sidewalk. There was a number game from one to nine, but I enjoyed the more difficult ones which spelled out the days of the week, or the one with all the months of the year. On one leg, I jumped into the marked squares following my throw of the rock. I was good at it.

The games my brothers played outside in the backyard were less solemn, in fact were rough but nevertheless exciting. On a few occasions, I was invited to participate. The boys in the neighborhood played war, an action game between Russian and German soldiers; it had a fast-moving pace and strict rules. The basement of an apartment house was designated as a prison and whoever was caught during the game had to be jailed there. An old sheet hung on the wall to mark the location. I ended up there once because I could not run fast enough.

The building at the corner of our block was still in ruins, and the boys had cleared away some of the rubble to establish a fort. They had smoked some dry grape leaves there, too, and I was not to tattle about it at home. I even tried once myself but it tasted horrible, and I felt sick to my stomach. The games involved lots of screaming, running, hiding, and chasing up and down the staircases through the various apartment buildings on the block. Sometimes we played *Klingelputzen,* which consisted of pushing all the doorbell buttons at once near the entrance of a building and then running away as fast as we could before someone looked out the window. At a certain time of the year, on *Tauchscher,* these games involved standoffs of one neighborhood block against the next. I was scared for the safety of my brothers. They, in turn, would send me home early to play with my dolls so I would not get hurt or caught by the gangs. Things got out of hand each year, fights erupted, threats were made, kids got hurt; I was afraid. I think my mother was afraid, too.

Being afraid of what went on outside in the neighborhood was nothing new. I overheard my mother and my aunts whisper about the Russian soldiers with their guns who had attacked women and done something terrible to them. They thought I did not hear them talk about it but I understood. They said out loud, "Make sure you are home when it gets dark outside. You could get lost."

I knew it was more than getting lost in the dark; you could get killed or snatched away. I had heard that the Russians would take prisoners to Siberia, far away, where the ice never melts and the winter never leaves. I decided I would rather get killed than be hurt and taken away by the soldiers.

I felt that my brothers would protect me from other kids in the neighborhood if I were ever to be bullied around. I was proud of their assurance and did not mind when they teased me on occasion as the little sister.

One day, Klaus left me with a puzzling challenge. When I was standing in front of the big grandfather clock in the living room, he said to me "Watch out, if you make a silly face at the time the clock strikes the hour, your face will forever look like that!"

I thought about his comment for a long time, and one afternoon I dared to stand in front of the clock at the time the chimes went off, exactly at four o'clock. I grimaced and twisted my cheeks, stuck out my tongue, crossed my eyes, held my breath. The chimes rang four times—I stood up straight counting to four. I had dared the spell!

Once in a while the Buchholz family invited us to their house in the suburbs of Leipzig. After a trip on the streetcar we arrived at their beautiful freestanding house, surrounded by lush trees and quiet streets. The roses were carefully groomed and the trees gave shade in a beautiful garden. They shared food with us. In the hallway stood the most beautiful dollhouse I had ever seen. Not only did the wooden staircase lead up several floors to a cozy attic, but lacy curtains covered every window. Chandeliers and houselights were in working condition. Antique furniture filled every room; dainty armoires were filled with china cups and tiny silverware. A rocking chair sat next to the *Kachelofen*. The roomy kitchen had a large stove, complete with pans and baking sheets. The kitchen clock never changed time. For that moment time stood still for me, too. I touched and played and forgot fears and war. I never forgot that house in the sunshine.

The day had finally come. My brother Gerhard and I had waited in front of the house all afternoon when he finally arrived. His name was Karl Kirchner. He wore a gray suit, not the uniform I had expected. I got a good look at him as he walked toward the house to ring the doorbell and ask for my mother. He shook her hand and looked straight ahead. Then he headed for the chair in the living room. My grandfather and my mother sat down too, waiting to hear his report. He started slowly. "I came to tell you what I have heard about your husband, Herr Schnädelbach."

He took a deep breath and looked at my mother. "We were stationed together in Croatia in April of 1945, when we were attacked by a unit of Tito's partisans on our retreat back to Germany. The fighting was fierce. On April 15, our division was encircled; some of our comrades were captured. The next morning, Herr Schnädelbach and I found ourselves in the area of Esseg in an unknown village near Nasice, in Croatia. We captured the village in order to pursue our flight plan. Fierce fighting erupted in a canyon. I tried to climb up a hillside with him, but could not get myself up there because my legs were swollen from an accident the day before when a transport vehicle had driven over them. Therefore, I went on to another, less steep hill and lost sight of him. Soon after that I was captured by the Russians. When we were put into a prisoner-of-war camp, I started to look for him and asked some of our comrades if they had seen him. One man, Robert Guenther, had seen him fall on that hillside following a gun battle with the partisans . . . shot by several bullets. Herr Guenther said,

'He moved only a few times and was most likely dead right away.' " He looked down. "It all happened on the sixteenth of April, a few weeks before the war was finally over. Nobody knew what happened to him after that. There is little hope that he ended up as a prisoner of war since the partisans killed all the soldiers left on the battlefield who were unable to walk. I am very sorry."

Then he got up and left quickly. My mother had listened attentively to the man, her face motionless; she covered her mouth with her hands. Nothing was said at first. Gerhard and I stood in the doorway and watched her.

She started to weep into the silence, bending over in her chair. I had never seen her cry like this before. Grandfather wept too as he stared at the window. I suddenly realized that our father was not coming back to us, ever. Tears trickled down my face but I did not know what to feel. My brothers wept quietly. Heavy silence descended on all of us in the room, the beginning of a frozen state of emotions and images. I stood quietly by the door and looked at my mother but could not join into the deep sadness on her face. She covered her face with both hands. Her bent back was shaking. I heard her weeping and gasping for air but I did not know what to say or do. No one could help her in this dark moment. I did not want to be a burden to everyone by standing there crying, too. Therefore, my brother Gerhard and I went quietly downstairs to play some more on the sidewalk. We tried to laugh and jump on the hopscotch squares, but it did not feel right to have fun while my father was dead and my mother was sad. Gerhard thought that our father was not really dead but that his buddies had just seen him fall down. We did not know that *gefallen* meant having been killed in action.

"The Lord never gives you more to bear than you can handle," Grandfather declared that same day. "He will take care of the widows and orphans as is promised in the scripture." My mother was now a widow, and we were war orphans.

Grandfather had lost another son—this time, though, without a medal or a picture of his grave somewhere far away. We all fell silent.

*. . . never gives you more than you can handle . . . This phrase hangs heavy and dark. It never made sense to me but Grandfather believed it. It is the voice of helpless faith and utter resignation. In the face of death, the silence rings in familiar words and images, to claim a power greater than grief. But why?*

Later on that day we ran out of food; no more bread in the house, nothing to share anymore. I heard high-pitched chatter and sensed restlessness around me. The adults fussed in the kitchen. "No rationing stamps left for this week. It is only Wednesday. The store has no goods to sell. No money. We have run out of it, nothing is left. Who ate the bread?"

Mother paced the floor, her face frozen, her eyes swollen from crying. She did not know anymore what to do and where to get help. She paced through the apartment, then suddenly grabbed her coat and ran down the stairs, out of the house and down the street. In the past, she had always told us when she was leaving, but not now. I looked out the window and saw her walking away. I was terrified and started crying. She walked away from us and did not even look back. I called her but she could not hear me because the window was shut tight. So I called my brothers and told them what I had seen from the window and begged them to follow her because I could not run fast enough to catch up with her. Klaus and Herbert ran after her. I saw them reach her and start walking along beside her.

They kept going toward town, along the roads and streetcar tracks, in the direction of our church. My mother just kept on walking; it must have been panic and desperation that led her way. At one of the intersections, they ran into Herr Buchholz, the choir director of our church. He listened to her despair and said, "Go on to the church, I heard some CARE packages just arrived from America and there will be food for you."

They hurried to the church, going faster and faster until they were running. Her coat fluttered in the cool afternoon breeze as if she had been given wings of hope. The heaviness and despair began to lift when she finally stepped into the church building. Herr Buchholz had been correct. The packages from America had arrived, all of them stacked up in a neat pile in the corner of the sanctuary.

That day she brought home the first of many CARE packages sent by a Reverend Zurbuchen in America and containing what we needed most: milk and egg powder, rice, brown sugar, raisins, oatmeal, cans of meat called Spam, Lipton's noodle soup, coffee, and cigarettes. There were also red-and-white-striped hard candies in a can, colorful crayons, an oddly shaped football, and a paper dress-up doll with many cutout clothes. The packages were sent from a Methodist church Sunday school class in Temple City, California.

From that day on, the packages kept arriving, often containing personal greetings and photographs from the senders, whom we never met. They smiled at us.

"The food saved us from starvation," my mother said to all of us. "They saved our lives."

We promised never to forget this day. Despite the announcement of our father's death, God had not forsaken us and had sent us food. Mother was right; another miracle had happened, and we were grateful that night in our prayers: "*Give us this day our daily bread and forgive us . . .*"

We all grieved over our father's death quietly and by ourselves. I was not quite sure what to be sad about. I only recognized him from the big family portrait taken during his last visit with us in March of 1944. He had been sent home from the military service for a short time due to a severe case of bronchitis and associated numbness in his face. The *Abschied* from his family after that had been so difficult and now seemed so final to my mother.

Soon after the fateful day that our father's death report reached us, Mother's friends in the congregation conducted a memorial service in our church. The main part of the sanctuary was still in ruins but was used as a playground while services were conducted in a temporary barracks, a wooden structure with a pulpit and chairs in it.

Pastor Witzel and other church members conducted the memorial service and spoke for a long time, saying many wonderful things about my father: "a faithful servant, a spiritual counselor to his congregations . . . a father . . . in heaven . . . with God."

Our family sat in the second row up front. My father's picture was standing on a table with some flowers placed next to it. I sat next to my mother, leaning on her soft coat. I had a hard time sitting still; my legs just dangled back and forth. Mother's hand touched my shoulders to stop me from wiggling. I could not follow all the words the adults spoke. The service took so long. Mother clutched her handkerchief; it was twisted into a round ball.

We sang our favorite hymn, "Jesus, my joy, my heart's delight," an old chorale with a steady and powerful melody. It spoke of assurance and protection despite "a world of ruins, even when sin and hell are threatening."

We sang loudly, especially during the third verse: "even when facing the dragon of death with its huge jaw. All our fears will be overcome by God's power. Despite all suffering I stand here and sing with inner peace." Those were the words of the hymn.

The words held true. We stood up and sang. Mother's voice was shaking as she sang the words of comfort to us. Her warm, deep tone had changed to a husky and ashen whisper. She wiped her eyes and with a sudden quiver lifted her head and looked straight ahead at the picture of my father. It was as if her voice had found the familiar melody once more; her faith supported her breath from that moment on, even alone.

The superintendent of the regional church office had sent a special condolence letter to my mother. Herr Georgi wrote, "Herr Schnädelbach was fully ready for the eternity!"

My brothers were angry at his remark. They interpreted his comments as his spiritual approval of our father's death. We all needed him to be here—not in eternity. I did not know what it all meant but I saw the anger on their faces.

My father was from now on in heaven with all the angels he knew. Yet deep inside, I remembered that the Red Cross had sent us a letter that he was missing in action very soon after Herr Kirchner had visited us. I hoped against all odds for his eventual return with other prisoners of war, so my mother would be comforted. This flickering hope stayed with me for many years.

Grandfather made sure we received the allotted pension since Mother was now a war widow. He also handed her a savings account with money in it that he had put aside over the years, designated for his son. His heart ached even more so since his wife had passed away in 1941. He was homesick for her. The last few years of the war had been horrifying for him. The city of Leipzig had been bombed six different times between 1943 and 1944, the worst attack happening during a night in December of 1943. Five hundred English and American fighter planes dropped bombs and thousands of lives were lost. The inner city was totally destroyed; people had been buried under the rubble. Churches, hospitals, and cultural buildings were in ruins. His church was also destroyed, the organ burned to charcoal. Pictures of total destruction stayed in his mind. He felt that this was not a war but rather "a foreign demonic action" against his *Vaterland*. The attackers would surely be punished in time, he believed. He had prayed to God.

But in May of 1945, the war was finally over. The bitter end was different from what Grandfather and many other German people had hoped for. Hitler and his henchmen killed themselves, although they hoped for an *Endsieg*, a final victory, during the last few weeks. The Nazi leaders had to be forced to stop the bloodshed and capitulated in death and defiant silence. All German troops alive were declared prisoners of war. Grandfather was devastated. He said that God had not heard our prayers for victory, and therefore the German people had to face deep sorrow and distress. He conceded in his diary: "We have heaped great sin on us and deserve punishment. We certainly received what we deserve."

I knew what he meant about punishment. In August of 1945, I had sat outside the house door overlooking the street. The grownups upstairs were talking about a horrible event that had happened in Japan and been reported in the newspaper. The American soldiers had dropped the atomic bomb on Hiroshima and Nagasaki a few days earlier. The adults said the bombings of our cities were nothing compared to what had happened in Japan. Everything had been melted down and forever destroyed. Nobody even had a chance of survival. A huge cloud had descended on the whole city. This action was meant to force the Japanese to surrender, too. Although the war was already over for us, I expected that we would be the next targets for the atomic bomb by the American soldiers. It would be the ultimate punishment for us who had lost the war.

Listening to my grandfather's comments about the lost war and watching my mother's despair following the announcement of my father's death, I came to this conclusion in order to find some order in a world of chaos: my father had died as part of God's punishment for having started a war and for the horrible things the Nazis had done to others during the war years.

After the war, I had heard the adults whisper about starving people in camps, the killing of Jews and other prisoners, huge graves filled up with corpses. They said they did not know the extent of all this horror and could hardly believe it. Mother said that the Russians had been even worse, crueler and more sadistic than the Nazis. Stalin was the worst of all, Mother said, because the Communists did not even believe in a God. But in the end, the German *Reich* had been defeated. We deserved what we received: famine, homelessness, and most of all living with shame for what we had done as a nation. Our father had been killed because he participated in fighting a war for Hitler. His death was ultimately God's will according to the teachings of my faith: . . . *thy will be done on earth as it is in heaven.* That was my conclusion, although I never talked to anyone about it over the years. It was my way of making it all go away because it was hard to see my father as a bad person. Maybe he deserved to die? Nobody talked about it and I did not ask. Deep inside, over the years of growing up, I felt ashamed of his conduct as a soldier and became angry with God for punishing us. My silence became layered with guilt and resentment, a blanket of numbness for a life meant as a celebration. There were no simple joys but rather more layers of sadness as time went by.

Because of the order by the Allied forces to denazify the German nation through reeducation and democratic instructions, nobody wanted to talk about their experiences. Nobody wanted to be labeled a Nazi by his neighbors or by the leaders of the occupying forces. The new leaders in the eastern part of Germany began to introduce Communism as the ideal society.

*Over the years, I carried my shame quietly, strove to be good and pleasant so nobody would ever suspect me of being part of a nation of perpetrators, the daughter of a soldier for Hitler. Since I am not seen as a victim in the eyes of the world, I could be a part of the justifiable process of punishment through suffering in silence. That way, evil would never rise again— at the cost of a healing resolution. That way, anger and aggression would be eliminated—at the cost of a healthy integration.*

From the time of his memorial service, our father lived in our memories only, of which I have none firsthand. In turn, I listened to the stories and memories of my mother, my brothers, and my grandfather. But they were not my stories. I knew that Mother had a bundle of letters that my father had written to her and to friends during the war. She never read them to us. They were the private remnants of their relationship. I thought she held onto them as a tangible proof of their precious moments of intimacy. In addition, the letters contained many spiritual thoughts and insights, which I would not have understood; he had been a preacher and a theologian. I did not intrude into the last remnants of their marriage.

So I listened attentively as my family remembered and talked about him as a person, not as a soldier. I joined in the laughter at the funny stories the brothers recalled and heard my mother's sadness in her voice. I could not say good-bye to a person I did not know. I never grieved for the void in my life. His death had been tangled up in the last few weeks of the most horrendous years of our century, one person killed on a hill in Yugoslavia, my father. For me, he was gone forever and thus had not been alive.

Grandfather had written a diary, starting in 1931 and going through 1951, which included comments about his life, reflections on the political events of his time, and significant events in our family. In addition, there were letters saved by my mother and other relatives, which helped me to paste together a picture of my father, creating concrete images and adult conclusions. Over the years, the stories and remembrances of others had become static in my vision, and we children idealized him as our heavenly father. However, he was fully present through his absence. Mother cherished every dream she had in which he appeared; her mood was lifted visibly, her broken heart gently comforted for a short while in the morning. She wrote them down in a special diary. These dream visits helped her feel his closeness and soothed her feelings of deep abandonment. One entry from 1969 reads: "Every time I dream of Vati, a huge weight falls off my shoulders."

In 1970, she wrote down a pivotal dream that she had had in 1945. She claimed that she had the dream at the time he was killed in Yugoslavia, in April of that year: "I stood in a washhouse and was washing clothes, could look toward a street leading up toward the washhouse. Suddenly, I saw Vati coming toward me on the road. I quickly dried my hands. Vati came through the door, in uniform, took me into his arms and kissed me affectionately. Leaving . . . and waking up followed immediately. I looked for such a house (washhouse), so the dream could come true. Sorry . . ."

I began to look, too, for traces of him in pictures and old letters, accepting that there can be no good-bye and no healing before the silence is broken through speaking and acknowledging hidden feelings. It could become a healing burial for a person I know, a belated eulogy to my father, who is a part of my life even in his death. The final goodbye took the form of a letter never to be sent or received, of course, but written as an acknowledgment of his death; the time of waiting for his return had come to an end.

# CHAPTER SIX

# Blessed Is the Man

San Diego, California

Dearest Vati,

I hardly know you . . . You hardly knew me . . .

I am sitting in the middle of thousands of white gravestones at the Rosecrans Military Cemetery in San Diego, California. The Pacific Ocean surrounds this peninsula with the bluest of water. The graves have been decorated for this special day with flowers and a sea of American flags. It is Memorial Day, the day of commemoration of veterans throughout the years, celebrated in remembrance of the fallen men and women who fought in various wars. Looking down the walkway, I see people preparing for a patriotic celebration with bands and colorful parades of veterans, officials giving speeches, and children's choirs singing. Next to the sidewalk, someone displays paramedic equipment used by the medics during the invasion of Normandy in 1944.

I chose this place and the early morning hours to remember you and read this letter aloud among the graves of other soldiers. I know we are far away from where you died, even on the wrong side of the firing line, but in the end, every stone here indicates one life, one father, one brother or son, one mother or sister, one person missing in someone's life. In the end, all have died and lie buried in the earth, a homecoming of sorts. So, it may be yours today.

You died as a soldier in Yugoslavia, but for me you have a place here, too. This country is my home now—so you are with me. My throat is really dry; it is hard to read out loud. I am scared to start crying . . . so I clutch on to my tissue. But then, I could not cry at your memorial service, I did not know how and why. Mother was not crying much either; she had to be strong for us. I had to go back and get to know you through letters and papers and find you in pictures, places, conversations, and reports. I am sure I only caught glimpses of your life, but I hope they will glow for me and my children forever.

I know you were born on August 12, 1901, in Leipzig, the oldest son of Paul and Helene Schnädelbach. You had five younger siblings. Grandfather did not allow any of you to obtain a higher education (past the age of fourteen), since he planned a family business and expected all of you to become a part of his enterprise. In accordance with this plan, you were sent to an apprenticeship at a local business. As World War I was ravaging Europe and coming to a devastating end, you were diagnosed with tuberculosis, from which you miraculously recovered. In 1919, Bishop Nuelsen, a Swiss Methodist, was looking for an assistant and you received this assignment, which you held for the next seven or eight years. While in Lausanne, Switzerland, you completed your secondary education by attending night classes, and finished with the official *Abitur*, an academic prerequisite for any university. What effort and determination you showed! Mother was always proud of you for your efforts to study in such a disciplined way. You entered the University of Zurich and studied theology for four semesters under the mentorship of Professor Emil Brunner, a theologian who was famous at the time. The leaders of the Swiss churches offered you a pastoral appointment in Thurbenthal, which you did not accept, mostly out of obligation to your church and your family back in Germany. Mother confessed to me later that she may have talked you out of this job offer, and following your death suffered severe guilt feelings about it. She thought that she could have prevented your death had we all lived in the neutral and safe Switzerland during the war. She talked about it again and again, even at the time of her death. She blamed herself bitterly. I tried to console her on several occasions, to no avail. Can you comfort her now?

. . . *who trusts in the Lord* . . .

You met her in Leipzig through friends. Your special talent of playing piano must have opened her heart to you.

"He was a wonderful accompanist, you could always feel secure singing with his playing," she said repeatedly, and her warm smile would express her feelings of admiration.

The music of Chopin was especially close to your heart, with its unique, flowing and romantic phrases. Your fingers moved so smoothly over the keyboard. Mother would sing, standing beside you, the lieder of your favorite composers: Schubert, Schumann, Brahms, and Wolf. Where did you learn to play the piano like that?

"Nothing was ever too difficult for him to play," Mother said.

Music became the language of your hearts and souls. A deep faith in God connected you even over long geographic distances.

. . . *whose trust is the Lord.*

You were ordained a deacon in the Methodist Church in 1933, in Germany. Then you married our mother on August 31, the same year. The bishop assigned you both to a Methodist church in Altenburg, about thirty kilometers outside Leipzig where my two older brothers were born. You lived on Oswaldstrasse 58, today Heinrich-Heine-Strasse 58; that's what my brothers told me. The church was a living hell, so I heard. People were fighting just like in churches I have been to all my life. There were hostile arguments over the complete truths in the Bible and whose opinion was the correct one in the eyes of God. Members of the congregation debated the timing of the last judgment and who was ultimately accepted by God's grace. Long and bitter fights erupted over such issues as repentance of sins, forgiveness, sinning, and holiness. They were fighting to find religious truth and the way to be a disciple. While they were fighting, they lost each other here on earth. Why? To enter the portals of heaven justified and righteous?

Amidst this debacle, there was no money in the collection plate for your family to live on. Mother remembered that on any given Sunday, a few marks that were left in the plate were for your salary that week. For months, no other money was assigned to you by the church organization. At Christmastime, the parishioners came to church with their shopping bags and expected gifts in return for their attendance and contributions during the year. You were told by the church officials to "trust in the Lord, and pray for guidance. The Lord will not forsake you". What kind of test was this?

"When Klaus was born, I had only a few marks in my wallet," Mother said later, bitterly. "But somehow we made it through".

What happened to your faith? I heard there was a woman in the congregation who demanded your pastoral attention for weeks with her religiously crazy and manipulative, at times threatening, behavior. Today, we would say she was obsessed with you, and used you for her not so Christian intentions. Mother was still mad at her later on because she demanded so much of your personal time. I guess she was jealous. Your time with Mother and us was so precious and fragile.

One year, the church conflicts became so intense and ugly that you despaired and wanted to kill yourself—Mother took the rope out of your hand! She told me so during her later years of life. It was sort of a secret in the family that you became full of despair despite your faith and your faithful intentions. I can fully understand such depth of depression and hopelessness. Mother used to say that you were *sensibel*, which meant you were a very sensitive and compassionate person. Her description of you also carried an undertone of irritation. Maybe she meant you were too sensitive in her eyes, not always so stoic. I am glad to know this because I can see these qualities in myself, often directing sensitivity by helping others and not necessarily applying such compassion toward myself. Maybe you were just plain mad and could not show and express disgust and disappointment. Mother saved your life for the time you had left.

How difficult this time must have been for you and Mother. Why did you stay in such a thankless job? Was your call so strong that you were willing to sacrifice your life and your family's happiness?

*His delight is in the law of the Lord.*

Finally, in 1937, a new appointment by the bishop sent you to Breslau, in Silesia. I understand that the annual conference of the Methodist Church each year was the time when pastoral appointments were announced. It was not unusual for the bishop to read a change of appointment on Sunday afternoon just before the close of the yearly meeting. Everyone was curious and anxious in anticipation of his or her assignment, and all the changes were discussed afterwards at length. Moving was part of your job in the tradition of the circuit system of the Methodist Church with its limited itinerary. Mother was used to it from her own family. I am too, having married a Methodist minister. Congregational moves have been difficult. It is hard to uproot and start over again and again.

The city of Breslau was a welcome change for our family. You were pleased with the congregation you found there, and the enriching, cultural atmosphere of the city. Friendships grew, people understood your preaching and accepted your leadership. Our family lived in a flat in the third floor with no garden. The apartment house stood right in front of the church building, on Paradiesstrasse. You and Mother built a sandbox in the backyard just for us, which caused many raised eyebrows among the parishioners. They said it was too close to the entrance of the church. I finally have visited the city of Breslau and have seen the house with my own eyes. Not much has changed there. The years left grime and brokenness everywhere.

Your third son, Gerhard, was born in 1939, just a few weeks before the beginning of World War II. Until then, you and your family had lived a fairly normal life with work and family time, vacation, visitors, and anticipation of holidays and celebrations. You were known for your sense of humor and the funny sayings you repeated at opportune times, a kind of stamp of approval to the more mundane things in life. You'd say to the boys when they were asked to take a letter to the mailbox, "Now go to the mailbox and don't fall in".

Do you know that your second son, Herbert, still repeats this? He not only remembers your favorite sayings but also has his own collection by now. He recites them word by word, and then laughs loud and heartily. You'd be proud of his quick mind. Did you laugh, too?

Evening and bedtime in Breslau included a nightly potty routine for the three boys, so I hear. All of them stood on the bed next to each other while you held the chamber pot in front of them for their use. You'd say, "Now hold on to your *Böpse* (fannies), so they won't fall down!" The boys stood up straight with one hand holding up their *Böpse*, the other hand directing the stream.

You knew how to make the simple things in life fun. Although the space was so limited in the flat you lived in with your family, there was room for an electric train to run under and around the boys' beds. Your piano stood in the living room, so you could keep playing and accompanying Mother. Songs and prayers were said each night at bedtime. Mother told us that the two of you had a close, spiritual relationship that included intimate moments and the search for closeness through your faith in God and angels. Klaus told us that he saw an angel sitting on his bed one night, just being there for him to see. From then on, he believed in miracles and messengers from the other side. You must have taught the boys about guardian angels and heavenly friends keeping watch over us all. Even later, there were always pictures of angels in our home, not just at Christmastime—angels dressed in flowing robes with feathery, colorful wings, holding harps or flutes, and praising God. In my home now, you can find pictures of them on the walls, a colorful collection of angel postcards from various museums, and a carved cherub sitting on a table. The heavenly hosts come out at Christmastime, to announce the birth of Christ in full force.

*He is like a tree planted by water* . . .

In September of 1939, life changed forever. You were ordered to enter the military service and you had to join an active construction battalion in Poland. After the invasion of Poland was completed you were sent home to Breslau.

Again, you took care of your congregation and conducted regular church services; several times, you were interrogated by the Gestapo, who, in search of people of Jewish descent, asked for names of your parishioners. I understand that you did not hand over any lists of members as demanded. I am proud of you for your resistance and the risk you took by remaining silent. The Gestapo also came and attended worship services to be sure you showed the politically correct respect for the Führer.

During that time, a couple wanted to join your congregation; the man came from a line of Jewish ancestors. Since he wanted to be baptized into the Christian faith, the elders of your congregation held a meeting. They debated this delicate and potentially dangerous situation, weighing their Christian faith and political views, and finally voted not to allow him to be baptized in the church. In protest, you held a private ceremony in our home with the man's family present, and you baptized him with water, in the name of the Father, the Son, and the Holy Spirit.

Like most Germans, you held high hopes for the future of the German *Vaterland*, starting in 1934, with the strong economic recovery under Hitler's economic war machine, his clear plan for a heightened identification with the Germanic tradition, a necessary cultural cleansing of the German values with the establishment of a perfect, Aryan race, and the elimination of all Jews. He had written it all down in *Mein Kampf*. I know for sure that you never joined Hitler's party. I wonder how much you understood of his real intentions. The Führer was seen by many and most likely by you as having been blessed by God in a special way, and each charismatic message was faithfully listened to on the radio. I remember such an event. Many people said after the war, "His voice was so beguiling and magnetic".

I know now, that he promised you all a perfect world, a happy place where everyone would have what was needed to live a good, clean life. I know that Hitler told you that the family was at the core of the new nation. He wanted God on his side; he wanted your Christian support and your total obedience to the ideals of the new nation. Mother remembered his speeches. One unified nation, undisturbed by uncontrollable elements, cleansed of unwanted people, including the weak and sick ones—a strong nation to rule the world. These goals justified his methods of evil pursuit, of which you may or may not have been aware. How clearly did you see good and evil? And did you know of the scapegoats in the neighborhoods? I cannot tell what you knew because you could not write freely, as I can these days. You had to worry about the censoring of your letters by your superiors. For Hitler, war and violence became acceptable and justified tools for the good of the nation. Did you know about it? Did you hear the underground whispers of the resistance movement?

The grown-ups huddled around the radio in order not to miss a single word of Hitler's speeches. At times, the crackling and static on the airwaves would interrupt his screaming oratory. I can remember it vaguely while we stayed in Damsdorf. There was excitement in the house: "Hitler is giving a speech today!"

I tried to join in but tired quickly of his screaming.

The strong censoring of all radio stations and the press did not allow for any objective information at the time. The rumors of concentration camps, deportations, vandalism, and markings of Jews and other unwanted individuals most likely began to seep into your awareness around 1943. That's what our mother later told us. You must have found yourself a helper of the Führer, supporting his evil actions through being forced to be a soldier and, at the same time, wanting to protect your family and your homeland. With heavy heart you had to follow the orders of your government. How did you appease the voice of your conscience? How did you live with it every day? I, too, have a hard time living with it all. I lived with it by not thinking about it, leaving it behind in the old country when we moved to America in 1966. But it kept following me wherever I lived because of my German descent and accent. I had to start facing it straight on: looking at pictures, meeting the eyes of the victims, and reading about silent trauma and the guilt of survival.

Following your return to Breslau after the invasion of Poland by the German army in 1939, your military commander assigned you to a prisoner-of-war camp for English soldiers. You worked there as an interpreter; you must have spoken English fluently. I know that you traveled to America once, maybe in 1923, on a trip to the East Coast, when you worked for the Swiss bishop. It amazes me that you were comfortable in another language, the language I speak now.

In September of 1941, I was born in Breslau. The brothers told me that you were very happy when you came home from the hospital to announce my birth to them. You stood there at the door with your hat in your left hand, a big smile on your face, and said to them, "You have a little sister!"

Klaus's seventh birthday happened to fall two days later. Due to the excitement around my birth and Mother's stay in the hospital, he did not get his traditional birthday cake. He never forgot about it and told me so later many times, laughingly, of course.

Shortly after my birth, three officials from the local Nazi Party came to the house. They were dressed in full uniform and announced their arrival with the "*Heil Hitler!*" greeting as mandated. They asked for our mother to come to the door and started their ceremonial introduction: "In the name of the Führer, we are most pleased to present you with the *Mutterkreuz* in honor of your gift of four children for our Führer!"

Then they opened a case they were holding. With utmost care, they took out a special cross with a swastika hanging from a blue-and-white ribbon, which they placed around my mother's neck. She stood quietly in the door, looking down on her stained apron. She accepted the medal and blushed. Another salute to the Führer followed, and then they went quickly down the stairs.

After the war, she smiled about the incident but I never asked her what she really felt. Was she proud of it? Did she like to receive an honor for giving birth to four children? Why did she stick the medal into her brown leather bag to be carried into freedom, much later, when we crossed the border to the West? Your grandson, Peter, found it in Mother's desk after her death and asked if he could have it as a personal token to take back to America. I was so scared that the customs agent would find it on our trip back to Los Angeles that I almost did not allow him to hide it in his suitcase. I was afraid of being labeled a neo-Nazi. I wanted to have nothing to do with this part of my past. But it is our past together and to acknowledge it has connected me to my history, to myself.

I knew about the slogan of the Nazis—*Ein Kind für den Führer!* (A child for the Führer!). I also knew that I was not meant to be a gift for the Führer, to be used as *Kanonenfutter* for the war machine, or to become a future *Deutsche Mutter*, a German mother. I know that you both were happy to have a little girl after the three boys in the family. I often wondered what you really thought about having a child born in the middle of a horrible war. Was I not an additional burden and an extra mouth to feed?

*. . . that sends out its roots by the stream . . .*

In 1943, the rumors about the war turned dark and sour. Again you were ordered to enter the military service, this time into combat in the Balkan to fight Tito's partisans there. You were forty-two years old. Many letters were written back and forth between you and Mother, only to vanish later in the fires of Breslau and Dresden. So many of your ideas and insights burned. You must have felt the end when the emptiness and the darkness of the soul began to set in. You left Mother and my brothers with clear and strong memories of loving times together as a family. You took these memories with you.

I found this letter telling of our last Christmas together. You sent it to your sister, Gretel, and her family in Budapest, Hungary.

Breslau, January 3, 1944

My dear Ones in Budapest!

In the meantime Christmas has passed. In midst of our four children, we cannot be sad. Let me tell you, they celebrated the holidays! They are still celebrating as long as the Christmas tree is standing in the living room and the gift table is up. And our Gerhard, who loves to sing, keeps singing Christmas songs all the way into the spring. Last year on Easter, he still wanted to sing *Kling-Glöckchen, Klingelingeling* . . .

The highlight for Püt (Herbert) was his ¾ violin he received as a present. Klaus plays the piano quite nicely; Herbert should learn the violin along with it. Gerhard was so excited about the rocking horse he received; he has been riding it ever since. And our little Maria was most interested in the little grocery store she quietly used and emptied as consumer, seller, and buyer all at the same time throughout Christmas Eve. In between, she also sampled from all reachable goodies such as apples and ginger cookies. Since she had already helped her Mother with the Christmas baking days before and had not left her side, eating cookies day and night—the end had to come in form of a "Christmas illness". Her little stomach tipped over and needed to be emptied out. But after a few days, the damage was resolved. Our little Gücke, this is what her brothers call her, is a lively rascal, always busy, a real sunshine!

The big event this Christmas was the puppet show theater Leni constructed out of lumber material. She was able to find several puppets, and the older kids are eager to play *Kasper und Seppel* (Punch and Judy) stories. The little ones sat in the audience and frequently interrupted the stories by getting up and shaking Kasper's hand.

A lot was going on here during the last few months, not only the festive church services but as usual, we have many visitors. We must have been putting up about 200 people during the last year. Last January, our living room became the delivery room for a young wife of an officer who happened to visit him while he was recovering in town from an injury. The baby arrived 6 weeks too early!

For us parents, the best Christmas present was that we could be together. It was always so, and has never changed—

Your brother,

Herbert

*. . . and does not fear when heat comes . . .*

In early 1945 the nights and days of terror, flight, and fire came for all of us. Your last letter to Mother was written in March of 1945 and sent to Dresden but did not reach us until months later.

March 16, 1945

Leni Dearest,

Today marks the day, one year ago, we said goodbye to each other in Vienna. It was so difficult! At that time, we fortunately did not foresee *how* long we would be separated from each other and what all was going to happen.

There is still no mail from you. However, a letter arrived from my friend, Brother Georgi, to let me know that your house in Dresden is no longer standing, and that there is no trace of you all. My soul turned pitch dark, especially since I could not feel any spiritual connection with you as has been in the past.

Finally, two nights ago, I received a special gift. For over one hour, you were with me in a vision (not in a dream), and you kept saying to me: "Dearest, my dearest Vati, we are not dead, we are alive! Do not worry about us, we are well taken care of." Only where you were, you did not say. Since then, I am glad and feel comforted. The last few weeks have been excruciatingly painful. I hope there will be some mail from you, soon!

In never ending love and kisses,

Your Herbert

Give the children a kiss from their Vati

*. . . for its leaves remain green, . . .*

Three days later, you wrote this postcard to Klaus, who had written you from Raschau. We had fled there after the Dresden bombing in February of 1945, and he informed you of our survival.

March 19, 1945

My dear, dear Klaus,

Your little letter, written on the 5th of March has reached me two days ago. You cannot imagine what a great joy this message brought me. This is the first sign of life in many weeks, telling me where you are and that you are still alive. My dear Klaus, I will never, ever forget what you have done for me. Such a burden fell off my shoulders, now I know where you are!

Surely, our dear Muttilein has written to me also. However, it is terrible with the postal service here in this region. Hardly anything reaches us, probably because of the many bombing raids. I would like so much to come home on furlough. As soon as I receive news from Muttilein, I will try to arrange my application. It would help to have a notarized telegram, signed by the Party, or the police, as a document.

I hope you have peace in Raschau, and you are comfortable there. Until now, the good angels have led us; they will continue to do so. Along with your letter on March 5th, I also received a note from my friend, Herr Georgi, written on February 21, to tell me that you escaped Dresden. But what happened to Oma? I am waiting for more mail from you. I wonder how you are doing? How is our dear Muttilein? And Herbert? And our Gerhard? And our dear, little Maria. I want so much to be home again with you all!

Give Mutti a kiss from Vati and to the others, also. In deep gratitude with greetings to all,

Your Vati

*. . . and is not anxious in the year of drought, . . .*

One month later, you lost sight of us forever—and I lost sight of you. From then on, your enlarged portrait, taken from our last family picture in 1943, hung on the wall. It hung above Mother's bed, the frame decorated with dried flowers, or with a little wreath hanging on a velvet ribbon. On the back of the picture frame, Mother had taped a piece of paper cut out from a death announcement with a quotation on it that reads: "We shall not mourn that we have lost them, but rather be grateful that we had them. Yes, we still have them, since he who returns to the Lord, stays in the community of God's family and has only gone ahead" (Hieronymus 331–420).

*From that picture you smiled down at me, wearing that soldier's uniform with the swastika on its lapel, but I could not smile back. I looked at Mother and saw her deep sadness, her grief and her tears. A big part of her had died with you. Her heart was broken from then on. I heard it in her crying at night in bed when she thought I was asleep. We shared the same bed until I was ten years old, and the same bedroom until I was eighteen. And later on, she collapsed two times from exhaustion, hard work, and caring for us four children alone, and had to spent time in the hospital. On certain days during the year, such as your birthday, your wedding anniversary, the days of terror in the fires of Dresden, and the anniversary of your death, our home was flooded with deep silence and tension. I did not know what to say to her because she was trying to hold back her tears. To bring up the subject of your death would have made it worse. I felt guilty for being so numb inside and for being unable to comfort her during those days. Therefore, I tried to stay out of her sight, because I felt her sadness, not my own. Her voice seemed cold; her words were short as if she was angry with us for not joining in her grief, and for not helping her. Klaus knew best how to say something to her which helped a bit. I was always glad when these commemorations were over, and our life went back to normal.*

In 1981, two years before Mother's death, she entered these comments into her journal of dreams and reflections:

> Had a talk with Maria about Vati's last letters and gave them to her to read. Letters that continue to stir me and bring up the old guilt.
>
> Maria sees these letters as a balance sheet of life that our Vati wrote down, emptying his heart during a night watch. A tremendous account of life, not without hope, but with a willingness to accept whatever may come. His worries focused on his family. The mail rarely reached Yugoslavia by then. He knew nothing about us after the bombing raid on Dresden, the 13th and 14th of February, 1945. Klaus did finally relieve his worries with his postcard from

Raschau, letting him know that we were still alive. That was the last news he received from us. On April 16th, 1945, he was killed.

Mother's last entry in her journal is dated April 16, 1983, the thirty-eighth anniversary of your death. She wrote: "Vati's death anniversary. Just read 'Dying is so different'. Much I don't understand . . . "

The anguish never left her; recurring questions were never answered. She comforted herself with the thought that you died knowing we were alive and safe for the moment. You were killed—we survived the whole ugly disaster. You paid the price—we received the gift of time and life.

I was with Mother when she died in September of 1983. She waited for me to visit her that summer, and suffered a heart attack two days before my departure back to the United States. She became disoriented the day before her death and pulled out all the tubes. She muttered, "Herbert is coming tomorrow!"

Was she thinking of her son or of you? I sat next to her bed the night the hospital called me, held her hand, and stroked her face as she passed away. All I could say was, "You may be comforted now." She nodded and said quietly, "I know."

After that, the numbers on her blood pressure monitor went down. I sat quietly holding her hand, stroking her arm. When she had slipped away, I took off the wedding band you had put on her finger. Your name, *Herbert*, is inscribed in the ring along with the date of your engagement: 23. 2. 31. I took the ring with me as a reminder of your love for her.

I hope you received her at the threshold to the other side, her suffering over and her longing fulfilled. Her sweet and smiling face is in my memory, forever.

We had a small but dignified service for her in the cemetery chapel in Bad Bergzabern. The low, warm bell of the Protestant church tower rang in her honor. All of your children and most of your grandchildren were present. Your grandson Peter was with me and stood by my side. Of course, we sang our family chorale: "Jesu, my joy, my heart's delight . . . Despite of all suffering, I stand here and sing with inner peace . . ."

And we gave thanks for her life.

I did lose sight of you from then on. My image of you had died with her. I was alone now. She had kept you alive for us the best she could; I had no image without hers. I took your picture along with me to America but for a time forgot where it was stored in the garage. Then for a while your picture hung on the wall in your granddaughter Lisa's bedroom. She calls you Opa. You smiled down on her when she slept. During our next move, the picture disappeared again into a box in the garage.

I have so many questions for you and so few answers. I could not ask you why this entire trauma happened to the German people and us. I could not ask you why you did not try to do something about the whole bloody mess in our country, to stop the bloodshed, the gassings, the beatings of innocent people, the killing of children, the hate, the insanity—as if you could have fixed it all. I resented you for not standing up more like those brave men and women of the resistance movement in Germany, in and outside the church. They were willing to risk their lives, and died for their efforts to stop the evil of Hitler and his followers. There was Dietrich Bonhoeffer, a Lutheran minister, who was imprisoned in a concentration camp and killed a few days before the end of the war. He is now remembered as a saint. Last year I visited the concentration camp of Flossenbürg, where he had been hanged according to Hitler's order. There is a memorial plaque near his last cell. A mountain of ashes speaks of all the burnings. Did you know about him during the war years? He died for a courageous cause, and is honored as a hero. But you died alone, a drafted soldier, somewhere on a hillside in Croatia while trying to get home to us. I wanted to be proud of you for being just and heroic. At least, I would have liked for you to rest in a cemetery for veterans, under a white tombstone with your name and a cross on it, not a swastika. Just like the cemetery I am visiting this Memorial Day morning. We had no grave to remember you by. I don't even know where they threw your body—I could not say good-bye to you. Sometimes I did not believe you were really dead. Maybe you were alive in Russia, I thought, somewhere in a prisoner-of-war camp. I even imagined that you had deserted us for another family, but no . . .

I could not ask you about the decisions you made in your life, your faith, your family, your ideas and values, your music, your memories of me—I could not ask you any more. I could not ask you why you baptized the Jewish man in our home in Breslau, why you did not stay in Switzerland following your studies in Lucerne, and what you saw and heard in the English prisoner-of-war camp outside Breslau. I could not ask you about the last days of the war, your despair when you wanted to die in Altenburg, and your thoughts about carrying a rifle. Did you shoot and kill someone? I cannot ask you anymore. I am so sorry . . .

*. . . for it does not cease to bear fruit.*

I wanted to be proud of you and you to be proud of me. Not for you to miss my first day in school or the day I learned to tie a bow on my apron. When I was hurt so bad and whimpered in the refugee camp, I needed you with me. I wanted you there when I crossed the river to freedom with Mother, and I could not swim. Or later on, when I learned to swim and rode my bicycle, alone. Or when I could not do my math in school and nobody had time and patience. We needed you to take the load off Mother who worked so hard to get us through school. Not for you to miss my singing, the music you knew so well. Or much later, when I studied at the university in Heidelberg and graduated with a degree in psychology. There was no celebration when I finished my studies. I wanted you to conduct my wedding, to be present at the birth of my children, your grandchildren and great-grandchildren in another country. For you to hear their laughter, watch their ball games, join all of us around the Christmas dinner table, enjoy their graduations and their weddings. You would be so proud of them. They are wonderful children, and I am proud of them for you, too. Can you imagine? I have four little grandsons and one more baby on the way, all under the age of four. What happy sounds! I wanted you there to hold my hand, and share these special moments in my life.

I did not give your absence a lot of thought before. It was a fact of life with no replacement possible, ever. How your absence affected me would take a long time to understand. It is difficult to think how our lives would have been different with your presence. What I missed the most was a sense of protection and safety, to run into your open arms . . .

You hardly knew me . . . I hardly knew you . . . I am sure you wanted it, too. You were on your way home to us!

Some years ago, we sang John Rutter's *Requiem* on a Memorial Day weekend church service. The last movement is called *Lux aeterna*, eternal light, and has the most floating of melodies and gentleness of sound. I always think of you when I hear or sing this special music. I am sure you would have liked it as an invitation and assurance of your rest.

I heard a voice from heaven saying unto me, Blessed,
Blessed, Blessed are the dead who die in the Lord,
for they rest from their labours . . .

I chose the text from Jeremiah 17: 7, 8 and Psalms 1 and 2 to interweave in my letter to you because you wouldn't have wanted it any other way but to say good-bye with the ancient words reflecting our long history of blessings and perseverance in times of terror. You did not lose your faith; I am beginning to recover mine.

It is much easier now to smile back at your picture on my desk, and at all the other pictures of you with Mother during your courtship, on your wedding day, and with us children. My favorite picture is the one where you stand with me in Breslau at the open window in our flat, a few months after my birth, holding me in your arms with the sun in the background. You hold me in your arms, close to your heart. You wore a suit that day, not a military uniform. Thank you for that special moment caught in a picture. A man of the cross—not of the swastika.

*Blessed is the man* . . .

In 1983, when Mother died, I had your name and the years of your birth and death placed on the same tombstone on her grave. Between your birth and death years stands the iron cross (*Eiserne Kreuz*), a sign of your death in combat and of faith, struggle, and hope.

. . . *for they rest from their labours.*

Your portrait has been taken out of the box in the garage, cleaned and dusted off, and you will receive a new wreath on a velvet ribbon this upcoming Father's Day. I found you in my heart. May you rest in peace now, assured of my forgiveness and love.

Your loving daughter,

Maria


We said good-bye to Klaus in Dachau at the end of our traveling days. I felt like we had been gone for a very long time and had come back from the past, back from intense memories, even inner images of war and loss. In his quiet way, Klaus had revisited a part of his personal history, but more as a curious observer on the surface than as a mournful seeker. I had found the traces of my childhood, had confirmed places and old feelings of fears.

"It's amazing what we saw after all these years," he said during breakfast the last morning we were there. The Bunzlauer bowl he had bought for his wife was sitting on the table. She had unwrapped the package the night before with a smile and had said, "*Ja*, we can use a new salad bowl."

"So little has changed . . . Well, that's how it was," Klaus said while shaking his head. "I don't think I need to travel there again." With that he passed the basket stacked with fresh rolls and brown, crunchy pretzels.

My feelings were bundled up in excitement and a sense of family connection. We had shared a revisit to our past as adults. I would never forget this trip to the East.

He headed for the piano in the living room and started playing some Chopin and Joplin as if to return to the music he had left behind for a few days. "Let's be sure to sing some lieder before you go," he said as he pulled out his favorites from a stack on the floor. I got up and we played and sang old familiar melodies and lines. His fingers moved swiftly along the keyboard, his lips pressed together in concentration. My voice soared a little more easily.

*"He was such a good accompanist . . ."*

"You should learn Dvořák's biblical songs," he said.

Later that day, he showed me Grandfather Schnädelbach's diary in its original handwriting, all of it written in the old German font called *Sütterlin*. His wife, Elisabeth, had deciphered it and had begun to type it on the computer, so we all could eventually have a complete copy.

"It is quite a job to read and type it," he said. "She has spent many hours."

I was grateful for her contributions. I held back my tears as we hugged and said our good-byes. *Abschieds* are always so hard; it never gets easier. It is always a loss of the familiar, the present moment that has been.

"I'll send you some pictures," he said before Winfried and I drove off, heading west toward the Rhine Valley. The silence in the car was a welcome break.

"I am glad you went with us although this was not your history nor your mother's and father's," I finally said to Winfried while he was enjoying the speedy ride on the autobahn.

There was a long pause.

"I want to visit several people in my hometown, Sinsheim, who would remember my parents. You know, Helene Schmutz and Werner Rudisile." He paused. "Life changed forever after my mother died in 1948 and our father did not come home. We moved to our grandparents' and nothing was ever the same." He stopped himself from remembering his growing-up years, filled with loneliness and unexpressed needs.

"You have at least your parents' letters," I said quietly.

"I know, I should read them when I get home."

"How many are there?"

"There must be at least six hundred between them. They numbered their letters so they could tell if one was missing. He sent hers back, including some with my early scribbles and drawings. Haven't you seen them?"

I nodded. I thought of the drawings of military trucks, airplanes, and soldiers that he had sent to his father.

"When did they start their correspondence?"

"Around 1939 . . . the last letter came in January of 1945 . . ."

"These letters are really a gift for you. You can find yourself in them. You can find your parents in them too, if you want to revisit those years. With them will come memories of hardship, the suffering of your mother . . ."

He interrupted, "You know, Hoffenheim and Sinsheim had quite a Jewish population. Each had a synagogue that was destroyed in the *Kristallnacht*. Some of my aunts still remember this fateful night. Long after the war we would still buy *Berches* at the local bakery every Saturday."

"You mean that braided, white bread with poppy seeds on top?"

"Hmm. Now I am sure it was their challah bread, a reminder of the Jews that once lived there. I think my aunts will remember how the Jews lived in town and when they disappeared. All I need to do is ask them."

He did not say much more. I had heard about the time when, as a six-year-old, he took a short train ride to visit relatives, and the train was attacked by American fighter planes. Some people were killed, others wounded; he was badly shaken.

I reached for his hand. I was sure the time would come for him to uncover the past and to heal old wounds.

We crossed the Rhine near Speyer and arrived at the massive Romanesque cathedral. The burial crypt of the house of Habsburg, the emperors of the Middle Ages, is located under the sanctuary. Stone steps lead into a past of sarcophaguses and statues with inscriptions edged on marble plates. The musty coldness offers a relief from the summer. It is almost as if you can breathe the centuries of life and death.

The sanctuary received us with full rays of sunlight breaking through the high windows. Streams of light fell at our feet. The plain yet majestic design leads the eye to the enormous, golden crown suspended over the altar area. It has always been a sanctuary of homecoming for me because of its powerful yet simple beauty and the city's proximity to the area where my mother lived for the last years of her life and where she is buried.

Winfried and I were heading toward Bad Bergzabern, to visit the little town and to pay our respects at her grave. Over the years the local springs had attracted many visitors with multiple ailments, and therefore the town was declared an official spa.

My plan also included picking up my father's letters at Gerhard's house in Böhl. I wanted to study them, take them back home with me, and maybe even translate them for my children.

*Nothing has changed much here. The vineyards are in full foliage at this time of the summer. The narrow roads are the same, the old trough is still at the street corner in Pleisweiler. It used to be a dirty village in years past, but now the windows are decorated with flower boxes in full bloom.*

*Driving toward the small town of Bad Bergzabern, nestled in the woody foothills, takes me back to the first time we all arrived here in 1949 . . .*

# CHAPTER SEVEN

# A Piece of Home (1949)

The train finally came to a screeching halt at the station. Through the white steam drifting by the window I tried to get a first glimpse of our new hometown. Mother had said that the train would stop at the end of the tracks, in a small town. Once we were there, she would take the job of the director of a children's home, and we would have our own house to move into. With my nose glued to the thick and dusty window, I could make out the red brick train station. A huge sign spelled in large white letters the name of the town, Bergzabern. The stationmaster stood in full attention next to the open iron gate, his red stop sign lifted up high, and yelled for all to hear, *"Endstation Bergzabern!"*

"Someone is supposed to pick us up," my mother said to my two brothers and me as we gathered our few bags. I carried my new, shiny leather suitcase, the one I had just received for my eighth birthday a few days ago in Frankfurt. We stepped off the train onto the platform, where people gathered outside the gate to the street. The train doors slammed shut behind us and the puffing of the steam engine came to a gradual stop. I noticed how closely the town was located to hills covered with thick green forests and that houses were nestled in between vineyards and orchards. Two church steeples were barely visible in the distance. All seemed so quiet here, no roaring airplanes in the sky and no sirens to disturb our arrival. The late afternoon sun threw large shadows on the gravel along the train tracks.

"That must be her, over there." Mother walked toward a woman standing by the fence, a wagon in tow.

"I am Fräulein Kitzmann," she smiled. "You can call me Tante Gerda. I am here to pick you up and take you to my house. You will be staying with me, isn't that right, Frau Schnädelbach?"

She looked at us. My mother nodded as she introduced us one by one. I shook her hand and curtsied politely. Then we put our bags into her country cart and started to walk toward town. Fräulein Kitzmann was a heavyset woman with red, round cheeks; her dark shiny hair was pulled back into a bun. Everything about her was round. She seemed to be waddling more than she was walking and swayed steadily from one side to the other. Her short-sleeved dress tightly covered all the curves. With each step, her wide skirt fluttered in the early fall breeze. I had noticed that she spoke a different dialect. Her words sounded gruff and harsh, very different from the soft, drawn-out accent of my family and friends in Leipzig. I was beginning to wonder if all the people in this new town talked like Fräulein Kitzmann.

We walked along the main road, which led up to a large building flanked by two round towers and an arch-shaped staircase going up to a front door. By this time in late summer the flowerbeds around the steps were all dried up and overgrown with weeds.

"This is where you will be going to school." She looked at me, pointing toward the building with the two round, fat towers. "A very long time ago it used to be a castle."

I was excited about going to school in a castle with two towers and the forests nearby. She must have seen my smile, because she said, "There are many castles in these woods over there. Some of them are very, very old and only their ruins remain. But they are fun to visit."

I only knew castles from fairy tales, places where knights and princesses lived and robbers and wolves roamed nearby in the dark of the woods. I did know about ruins.

I noticed the thick cobblestones and the distinct sidewalks leading into the quaint town. On our walk through the streets, I had seen several small shops such as a bakery, a butcher store, and a dairy. Their windows displayed sausages, cold cuts, and liverwurst, apples, grapes, cucumbers, and fresh bread. Nobody seemed to be waiting in line outside the store to get food; I was amazed. As we turned the corner, we had to pass by the Protestant church, the *Marktkirche*, and the *Rathaus* across the street. Coming up the steep hill, we headed toward the Catholic church, *St. Martinskirche*, and turned left, going toward the edge of town. The road was leading uphill toward the vineyards. I began to wonder how far we were going to walk. I had liked the cozy town with its narrow streets and welcoming shops.

Finally, on Gartenstrasse, Fräulein Kitzmann turned right. As we entered the street, the wagon wheels started to rattle and rumble on the dirt road even more. She stopped in front of a large, two-story stone house surrounded by a high fence with a gate.

"Here we are. This is where I live!" she said proudly.

With that she opened the enclosed entrance double doors and showed us around. The main house door opened into a dark hallway leading up to her parlor on the left, the *Gute Stube* we called it later on. The curtains were drawn, and several fine chairs and a canopy had been covered with delicate crocheted lace. The bay window, which I had noticed from outside, was dark, the frame outlined by a few rays of sun. It all looked very elegant and mysterious to me. Nobody seemed to live in this room. I could not understand that, since all of us in Leipzig had lived crammed into one flat.

"You are not to play in this room," she said, as we walked by the open door. Apparently, she did not want us kids dirtying her private living room.

Her kitchen was located in the basement of the house with a door leading to her garden. "This will be your kitchen, too," she said to my mother, following her downstairs.

We were not the only refugees Fräulein Kitzmann had taken into her home. Frau Maurer, her three daughters, Helge, Almut, and Heidrun, and their grandmother also lived in this house upstairs under the roof. With our arrival, sleeping arrangements had to be discussed. Oma Maurer had already been living in one of the bedrooms on the first floor. From now on, we had to walk through her room to get to our bedroom where my mother, my brothers, and I were to sleep. The five of us were to share one double bed. That was nothing new, I thought. I was used to sleeping quietly, not moving too much during the night, and sharing the blanket. But then we were only to be here for the next three months until the children's home would be finished and fully operational. That's what my mother had been told.

The garden next to the house was laid out in flower and vegetable beds with steppingstones placed between them. A cement encasement around the various beds made the garden look orderly and clean, except for the messy wooden shed in the corner and the gazebo near the hedge by the street. The gazebo looked gray and chipped; maybe it needed a new coat of white paint. A round table and three benches had been placed in the middle; all were piled high with boxes filled with garden cuttings and thin branches for firewood. Nobody seemed to have used the gazebo, anyway. I hoped to be allowed to play there, but Fräulein Kitzmann said, "Do not jump around in the flower beds or step on the vegetable plants, and remember to stay on the cement walkways out here. You kids can play on the street, outside the gate."

Her cat, Kater Büh, however, was allowed to stroll through the whole garden, climb trees, and come in and out of the house as he pleased. We had never owned a pet before nor had we lived with an animal in the same house. Kater Büh had gray and white stripes in his very soft fur, and sang with the loudest voice for a special morsel of food. At dinnertime, Fräulein Kitzmann, or Tante Gerda, as we called her by now, sat at the table, her plate loaded with food, while Kater Büh jumped on top of the table and sat right next to her plate to wait for his prechewed piece of meat placed on the rim of her dish. We had to laugh out loud when we told each other what we had seen; we knew that our mother would never allow us to do this. I can still hear Tante Gerda call for Kater Büh by the garden door, "Beeeeeeeevel, Beeeeeeeevele!"

A few days after our arrival in Bergzabern on the sixth of October 1949, my second brother, Herbert, finally joined us. This time, it was our turn to welcome the new arrival at the train station and to show him our new hometown. I was relieved to have all my brothers together again after a time of separation and our different escapes from Leipzig. Herbert also seemed glad to tell us about his adventures since we had last seen him leaving from Leipzig on the train to Frankfurt/Main. It so happened that someone in church had given my mother a one-way train ticket to Frankfurt on a Sunday morning in August, at the end of the Technical *Messe* (the annual trade show in Leipzig). The next day, Herbert was on his way, alone, carrying his violin case, his coat, a decal from the Technical *Messe*, and a small suitcase, leaving for the West with twenty *Pfennige* in his pocket.

Herbert said, "I sat in the train compartment that day with my violin, when, in Bebra, a Russian soldier came in to check my papers, my ticket, and my permission to cross the border to the West for a 'vacation' with my relatives. He saw my violin case and told me to open it up. He asked me if I play the instrument, and when I nodded, he asked me if I could play something for him. I shook my head, afraid of what he might do next. Then he said something like, 'Should I alone understand this?' and left me alone. I did not understand what he meant; maybe his German was not that good. Then he just went on . . ."

"The next morning, we arrived in Frankfurt where I was told to take the streetcar, number 1, marked 'Ginnheimer Landstrasse,' to the end. I used the twenty *Pfennige* for the fare. I found the Wunderlich house [the home of my mother's brother, Friedrich Wunderlich, and his family]. I met my cousins. They have a motorcycle, which they run without a gasoline tank. It stopped after a brief run in their yard in need of some more gas. After three days, they shipped me off to the *Hardmühle*, in Kandel, a farm with a mill where I knew no one. They told me that the family were good Methodists and would be able to provide for me until you all would arrive here. I had to work in the fields, help with the wheat harvest. I played the Harmonium for them during the church services and they liked it. Herr Günter, the owner, was a nice man, but teased me about my accent. He said, 'You old Saxon!' and laughed. The worst was that I could not understand them really well. They speak a strange dialect, '*pfälzisch*,' and then they laughed when I could not get their jokes. There was plenty of food to eat. I could eat as much as I wanted . . ."

Herbert knew how to tell stories but suddenly he looked angry as he went on, "I don't understand why the relatives shipped me off to this farm; I did not even know them. Onkel Friedrich, though, gave me twenty marks before I left in Frankfurt."

He complained bitterly. He would never forgive our relatives for that. Deep inside, all I cared about was to have him back with us.

Then he wanted to know how we all had gotten across the border to the West. My oldest brother, Klaus, told him how he and my third brother, Gerhard, had also taken the train to the West, leaving Leipzig shortly after his departure in August with a special permit for a "summer vacation." The plan was to remain with Mother's other brother, Paulus, and his family in Neheim until she and I could join them. Klaus, who was fifteen, and Gerhard, who was ten, passed the border without problems but missed their train connection in Bad Hersfeld, and spent the night in the waiting room of the train station. The next morning, they were able to travel on to the relatives' home without further delay. "The waiting that night was strange, we were tired and all by ourselves," Klaus said.

I looked at him. He sounded so serious and I imagined how scared he and Gerhard must have been. He did not say much more after that but then, he has always been brave; he is the oldest brother.

My mother finally told them of our flight through the night, how we saw the Russian soldiers while we were sitting in the fields, and the mysterious event when the guard dog did not bark. She talked about God's guidance and protection for us that night. They laughed at her comments about my excitement on the way to Kassel in the brightly lit train. I was so glad; we were all back together again.

It was my brother Gerhard who explored the new neighborhood. I watched him from behind the sheer curtains of the window facing the street as he met and talked with some children standing in the middle of the road. One of the boys had a bicycle, and a girl rode a scooter with one foot. Gerhard convinced me shortly thereafter to join them outside for jump rope and ball games.

The Wirt family lived just across the street. Herr Wirt was the music teacher in the local *Gymnasium*. I could hear him playing the piano while I stood on the street. I became friends with his three daughters, Gerlinde, Reinhild, and Irmtraut. Gerlinde had the most beautiful blond hair, and her manner was poised and sweet; Reinhilde was the most talkative and lively one of them, while Irmtraut was generally filthy and on the wild side. Her clothes never seemed to fit and my mother had noticed that green snot ran down her nose most of the time. "Their mother does not seem to care," she muttered.

The Wirts owned the most overgrown garden I had ever seen. Nobody had trimmed down any bushes or hedges for years; everything was growing wild and free. Thick branches covered up old flower beds and grass. The walkways were barely noticeable to the eye. The garden seemed endless, leading up to a nearby creek. To me it was like an enchanted garden with unconquered territory, a place where hidden animal eyes were staring at me, or small gnomes peeking through the tree trunks. I had seen such places only in picture books.

There were no streetlights in our new neighborhood. The garden became an ideal place to play hide-and-seek when darkness fell. I never went too deep into the Wirts' garden. I preferred to get caught early in our games rather than face the darkness and the unknown in the thickest part of the garden. Our favorite game started by someone yelling, "Lumbo out, come out of your house . . ."

Then the search would begin. As I sat behind the bushes, the rustling, the running, the moving shadows in the dark, the screams, the laughter, and finally the catching touch would make my heart beat in my throat, even though I knew it was just a game.

The Maurer family upstairs in the house where we lived kept quietly to themselves. Their father had not returned from the war either. Heidrun was about my age and I became friends with her. She showed me the quiet corners in Fräulein Kitzmann's garden, especially the woodshed, where we could crawl into hiding and talk. The spicy scent of freshly cut vine branches was all around us. She knew where babies came from and told me about it. We discussed anatomical differences between boys and girls. One day, we checked our own . . .

Her older sister, Almut, stayed close to her mother most of the time and hardly joined our play. One afternoon, I saw her fall down in the garden, her arms and legs flailing uncontrollably, foam around her mouth, her body thrashing against the ground. I was very scared and could not watch her. I ran into the house to get help. They said that she was retarded because of her epilepsy, and she was having one of her seizures. On many occasions, I saw her mother sitting with her at the table in the pergola, teaching her to read and studying with her.

Another family, Frau Hei and her two daughters, lived in the house next to us. She was a very short and heavy woman who never yelled at us for bouncing the ball into her yard. Her husband, too, had not returned from the war. She had been told that he had been killed and was buried in a grave far away. In her living room, she proudly showed me his picture and his military cap displayed on a small table. I liked to talk to her about the picture and her husband but she always became very quiet and I did not want to bother her with my questions. I realized that we had no grave for our father to remember him by, no uniform or cap to look at . . .

"Next June, you can come and help me pick the cherries on my tree," she said to us shortly after our arrival in the neighborhood. She allowed us into her garden anytime we wanted to come, and kept her promise about the ripe cherries the following year.

Our street ended in a walkway that led to the lushest meadow I had ever seen. I could see the soccer field on the right, and behind it the local dump framed by the soft, green forest at a distance. Straight ahead in the foothills stood a large mansion surrounded by several small houses. The French soldiers were stationed there. The occupying forces were to keep peace in the region, I was told.

"They are not dangerous. They are rather stupid and noisy," the people in town said. I was still leery of any soldiers and did not like to be close to them. Sometimes, I went to the sidewalk on the other side of the road in order to avoid them.

The building site for the children's home and our future home was located at the end of that meadow to the left. I was very excited to think of living so close to the forest and the vineyards, and imagined how we could play there.

Shortly after our arrival, we all walked up there to inspect the children's home but discovered that there were no buildings at all—only dirt piles, pipes, a standing tractor, tipped-over wheelbarrows, and wooden boards left everywhere. As we came closer, my mother's face dropped; she became very quiet. No one was working there to build our home. The construction site looked deserted and messy, garbage and beer bottles scattered all over the ground. The concrete basement walls had been poured, including stairs and frames for doors—but no walls, no windows, no roof. Wooden boards led down into the basement. I could not imagine how these foundations could grow into a children's home in three months. My mother's face had turned serious; she looked straight ahead, her lips tightened. She walked around the property and started describing to us where our home would be. Then she pointed toward an area for her garden and a dog run. A cherry tree stood in the middle of all the building material. The vineyards started next to the property line. I was stunned. I saw my mother's face and did not want to ask any questions. I had hoped for a home to move into with my own bed to sleep in, a house with windows and curtains, a kitchen, and a place to play . . .

"The view toward town will be spectacular from the terrace, the sound of the church bells will reach us loud and clear," she said softly. "It will be a short walk to the town and to your schools through the park."

But then, we could wait for three more months until the children's home and our home were to be finished; that's what Mother had been told. It did not seem that long.

The new school year had already started in late summer. In order to be enrolled in the appropriate grade, my two older brothers had to take an entrance exam at the local *Gymnasium*. Their academic performances were so good that they did not need to be held back a grade level, as first suggested by the principal.

My third brother and I started in the elementary school, located in the old castle with the two round towers. My second grade teacher was Fräulein Schläfer, a nice and soft-spoken woman who smiled at me approvingly. As a new student in class, I had to catch up on my reading and spelling. The class had learned different ways of reading and writing, and I was lost. We were to start cursive writing on white paper with soft gray lines; my lowercase letters and words did not want to fit between these lines. My fingers could not hold the pencil tightly enough to avoid erratic smudges. I was frustrated with my writing and had to correct it with an eraser, only to leave lumpy, black marks on the paper. The ink on my fingers would leave prints on the white paper. My writing never looked as neat as Gisela's and Waltraud's, my new friends in class.

I noticed that people in town called us *Flüchtlinge*, refugees. They openly referred to my mother as the "widow woman with her four children," or, in the local dialect, "*die Flichtlingsfrä mit denne vier Kinnerlin.*"

In school I was aware of being a newcomer, too, and had to find my way around the courtyard. Fortunately, my new friend, Reinhild, also went to my school, and we would start off together in the morning. Her classroom was located on the first floor in the Catholic part of the elementary school, while I went to my classroom on the second floor, the Protestant section. A high, wooden fence divided the large playground. During recess, the Catholic children played separately from the Protestant children. I did not understand why we could not all be together since we played in the same neighborhood, on the same street. The teachers said it was because we were required to have separate religious instruction provided by either the local priest for the Catholic children or by the pastor for the Protestant children. Twice a week, the local clergy would hold religious classes for us. Our pastor taught us Bible verses and hymns, discussed church history, and talked about the division of the church, starting with Martin Luther some centuries earlier. I wondered many times which religion practiced the real faith or manifested the truth best; I never found the answer.

I stood outside by the wooden fence one day, squinting through the panels, and could not see any obvious differences between the children playing over there and us on our side. I felt my family was very different from both groups because we were Methodists; I did not know why. However, I was assigned to stay with the Protestant section of the school and attended religious education twice a week. On Tuesdays and Thursdays, Dekan Rettig would arrive with his violin case and accompany our singing of staunch Lutheran chorales with his violin. His bow produced the screechiest whine I had ever heard, but his eyes filled with tears as he proclaimed his faith to us in word and song. I wondered why he was moved to tears. Some of my classmates snickered behind his back or wrote jokes to each other during class.

To my great surprise, real food was served during break time in the schoolyard. We were told it was part of the school food programs sponsored by the American government to help us after the war. We had to bring our own bowl and spoon, then queued up daily for this *Schülerspeisung*. It consisted of *Kakao* (hot chocolate), a *Weck* (a roll), and many other wonderful treats. My very favorite meal was served each Wednesday: thick chicken noodle soup, steaming hot and ladled into my bowl. Gerhard not only ate his own portion each day but also finished up the leftovers of his friends. My other brothers laughed about him. Mother cautioned him not to do so; she said it was not hygienic. I knew that for the first time I could eat until I was full.

I had already learned in school that the whole town was very conscious of its religious affiliations and divisions. On occasion, I was allowed to go shopping but my mother would say, "Make sure you go to the Protestant bakery!"

And so it went with the butcher and the dairy store. As a Protestant you were obligated to support the merchants in your congregation. After Mother's instruction, I felt uncomfortable when I walked into the Catholic butcher shop because I did not want to offend the owner with my presence. Since people knew each other by name, I could not cross the religious lines without being noticed. We all ate the same food, after all. The Catholic sausages looked just like the Protestant sausages in the display windows, and so it was with the bread at the bakery and the milk at the dairy. I looked forward to being sent to the butcher because he never forgot to slice off a piece of bologna from a big sausage with his shiny knife; then he would lean over the counter and place it in my hand. He smiled at me, too. I said, "Thank you!," hoping for a big piece. I heard from Reinhild that the Catholic butcher did the same for all the Catholic children.

Although I made some new friends in school, there was one boy who began to pester me. His name was Gerd. Day after day, he threatened to beat me up after school. I could not understand why he did this. I tried to be friendly and could not remember ever offending him. I had noticed that Gerd was always in trouble with the teacher. He was sent outside the classroom, at times punished with the paddle. He looked ragged in his dirty clothes; foul words fell out of his mouth like hardened dirt. His blond wild hair rarely got a trim. Each day, as the afternoon school bell rang, he looked around for me. I hoped that he would get distracted by what other kids were doing. In order to avoid his threats and unpredictable chases after school, I hid behind a fence or waited outside the school gate. Sometimes, I quickly ran into an open courtyard next to the school building. His anger and fury scared me. I worried about it even before I went to school in the morning. Fortunately, I could run fast, and on several occasions he could not catch up with me. Sometimes, though, he did.

Finally, I told my mother about it and she went to discuss the problem with my teacher, Fräulein Schläfer. After that he stopped chasing me. I kept wondering why he hated me so much. Maybe because I was a refugee, maybe I looked scared, maybe I was not wanted in town. I knew I spoke with a different accent and looked different. I felt like free game. I saw him treat the gypsy children that way, too, the ones who came to town with the circus for a couple of weeks each year. They moved on as suddenly as they had appeared in town. Maybe Gerd thought I would do the same.

Once a week we girls in class had a special hour of sewing instruction, called *Handarbeit*. Frau Meyer was an older woman who taught us to knit, crochet, and embroider. She sat at her desk in front of the classroom, and guided us with her loud and gruff voice through various ways of twisting the yarn, holding needles, and counting loops. One day, we had to bring a piece of white linen to school in order to learn a special stitch, which required a fine needle and thin white thread. It was called *Hohlsaumstich*. "It is a useful skill to embroider handkerchiefs with, table linen and towels," she said.

I sat at my desk, trying very hard to count the stitches and sew a straight line along the border of the cloth. Frau Meyer walked up and down the aisles and suddenly stopped at my desk. She bent down to inspect my work.

"Your cloth is dirty, your stitches are uneven," she said.

She told me to come up front to her desk where she gave me a hard whack on my hand with the ruler. I was glad it was not my left hand. I was very ashamed as I went back to my seat. The cloth had turned dark from the sweat in my hands while I was trying so hard to stitch perfectly.

One special day, our teacher carried a heavy movie projector into the classroom for an important lesson in history class. A white screen was placed at the front of the classroom and the curtains were drawn. The teacher said to us, "Today we will see a special event in our recent history on film. It is a required lesson for everyone."

I had not ever been to the movies and was quite excited about seeing one. The teacher made no further comment, and the movie started. The screen flickered with white and gray lines until the first pictures came into focus. Many people stood behind barbed-wired fences, crowded next to each other, staring into the camera, grinning with ghostly smiles. Their clothes were ragged; their arms were reaching through the openings of the fence. They had long thin arms and fingers that could barely wave; some people looked like they were reaching out. More men stood inside a large courtyard, huddled together, wearing filthy, striped outfits and no shoes; they just stood there and waited. The next section showed more people jammed into barracks, lying in bunk beds, one body next to the other, their faces looking like skeletons, emaciated, with smiling, hollow eyes; they seemed barely alive, too weak to walk, naked. Dirt piles and open trenches were filled with dead bodies, small bodies piled up on top of them, lifeless. There were rooms with ovens and open doors, ashes and bones in their openings, chimneys and shower rooms for gassing . . . and children, women, and old men. It was a place of death. The camera showed the torn-down buildings.

". . . stench of death," the reporter said. American soldiers were standing in the middle of this ghostly mass of people. According to the reporter, this was a documentary of the liberation of the Dachau concentration camp on April 29, 1945, by the Allied forces at the end of the war. Millions had previously been killed; these people on the screen barely survived the ordeal. What had happened? More faces grimacing . . . more bodies, mass graves, and piles of body parts. And on it went.

The reporter said that the camera had caught the results of the cleansing of the German nation under the Nazi regime. Hell and death stared at us from behind the barbed-wired fences. The crimes committed by the German people were documented here for us children to see and never to forget, ever. The Germans—my people—had carried out these atrocities.

There was dead silence in the classroom. You could have heard a needle drop as we witnessed this moment frozen in history. The documentary was shown to us in order "[t]o honor the dead, [as] a mandate for the living" (*Den Toten zur Ehr, den Lebenden zur Mahnung* is the inscription on a memorial monument in the Dachau concentration camp).

I was horrified and sat quietly watching the moving pictures of anguish and death.

No one said a word after the film ended. No one asked a question. I was afraid to think about what I had seen, too afraid to ask my teacher, too afraid to ask my mother. No further explanation was given by anyone—just the pictures of horror and then silence. The class was dismissed for a break after the movie. The images would become forever imprinted in my memory. Later on I learned that this history lesson was a prescribed part of the denazification program, mandated in the American- and French-occupied section of Germany. It was meant to teach the German children the facts of the atrocities of the Nazi regime and introduce the general principle of democracy. Some kids said afterwards that their parents told them the movie had exaggerated the facts, and that these camps were just reeducation camps for foreigners and criminals; of course at the end of the war, they ran out of food. I was so shaken by it all that I had nightmares. Deep inside I felt ashamed of being German, a child in this country. I comforted myself by thinking that we had escaped the Communist part of Germany with my mother and could be free from now on in this part of the country.

My mother and I still secretly waited for my father to return from the war despite all the information we had of his likely death in Croatia in 1945. Prisoners of war were still being released in Russia, and I had heard of men having recently returned to their families from Siberia. Seeing the suffering and jubilant people standing in front of the soldiers in the Dachau documentary, I hoped to recognize the face of my father somewhere in the crowd. Maybe he had been imprisoned there without our knowledge and miraculously survived somehow. Maybe he had died there, too. I could not see his face anywhere . . .

The impact on my family of the events during the last few years seemed insignificant after I had seen the horrors on the screen; my own dread began to fade. No words could describe the expressions on these prisoners' faces. I had recovered from my burns with only scars. We had survived the bombings and the famine. Mother and I had made it safely across the border, and so did my brothers. I had no reason to complain.

"It was not that bad," my brothers said.

We still had our mother and maybe a new home soon. The past was turning gray and our eyes were focused on the future. The war was over. I was to seek comfort in our faith, it was expected from all of us, as expressed in the words of the hymn: *God is faithful, his heart is like that of a father who will never forget his own* . . .

We took pride in our religion. There was order, control, and meaning in the world of faith if you had grown up a Methodist. Tragic events in life could be explained with the words "it was God's will." Our pastor Mann said in his sermon that the war with its terror was a part of the *Endzeit*, the final years before Christ's coming in glory to judge the quick and the dead. Of course, I wanted to be included with the "quick"; I guessed it meant the living. I began to wonder what other plagues and wars would be ahead of us before the end would finally come to all of us survivors. Many unanswered questions about the war and its aftermath lingered on, and shredded images of doubts remained. I remembered how Gerhard and I, back in Leipzig, had waited for the coming of Christ and for the atom bomb to fall on us. Neither of these predictions had come true; that knowledge gave me some comfort and curiosity. We had survived, but for what? I also sensed that we Germans would be forever indebted to the Jewish survivors and their children. I figured we would eventually be punished for it all; in the meantime I would live being ashamed of who I was.

Mother was busy with getting the children's home completed. I saw her standing on the grounds of the partially completed basement, talking to the architect and builders, looking at blueprints, and occasionally pointing toward the adjacent basement walls of our future home. The days had grown shorter and the damp fall weather arrived with lots of rain, fog, and chills. Nearby, in the vineyards, the farmers came to harvest the grapes in huge buckets; the smell of sweet fruit filled the air.

On rainy days, the workers at the children's home wouldn't show up at the building site because the water had formed puddles everywhere. After each downpour, the workers had to wait another day before they returned to the site and were able to continue their project, always making sure that there were full beer bottles stacked in crates and wheelbarrows. I noticed a particular worker who stood in one spot most of the day, hands on his shovel, one leg crossed behind the other while he followed the activities of his coworkers with a grin. He looked like a statue of a construction worker. Nobody seemed in a hurry except my mother. The foreman gave instructions by yelling, but the responses came in slow motion, one shovel of dirt, one piece of material, and one dirt pile at a time.

Mother had said that we had only to wait for three more months until our house would be finished.

The month of December blew in with cold winds and long, dark evenings. The first candle of Advent brought a glimmer of warmth into Fräulein Kitzmann's home, where we continued to live. There was little room for all of us but there was enough to eat. We still were not allowed to play in her living room upstairs since it was reserved for special occasions. Maybe on Christmas Day we would be invited to come in.

My brother Gerhard and I began to think about our wishes for Christmas. He began dreaming about an electrical train set with fancy locomotives, cars equipped with interior lighting, train stations and turntables, and tracks and switches controlled from a central panel. Back in Leipzig, my mother and I had talked about St. Nikolaus and his importance at Christmastime. I knew that many of my friends thought that he was a real person who would bring presents and goodies on St. Nikolaus Day, the sixth of December. He would know all about us children, the good ones and the bad ones, and either reward us with treats or give us a swatting with his switch. The worst thing he might give us would be a pile of stones. A black pile of stones meant that you had really messed up all year long.

Nobody in my family believed in this story. Only small children believed in St. Nikolaus. My brothers said that St. Nikolaus was just a figure representing a famous bishop who had lived a long time ago and who was gentle and kind to all. In fact, he was still kind to all the children each year. St. Nikolaus was usually accompanied by his servant, *Knecht Ruprecht*, a rough-looking guy. He usually wore a dark, heavy coat with a hood covering his head; he rattled chains and carried all the goodies in a large burlap sack. This was the figure I was most cautious about. He could just show up on St. Nikolaus Day in the evening somewhere in town, scare us with his gruff voice, remember our name, and know our sins, too.

Despite my contemplations on this matter and my scrutiny of all the facts, each year we polished our shoes with special care on the evening of the sixth of December, and placed them outside the door in hopes that St. Nikolaus would come by late at night and leave us sweet treats. In previous years, we had found our polished shoes filled with goodies. All this lore was familiar to me from my favorite Christmas story, "St. Nicholas in Need" ("*St. Nikolaus in Not*"), by Felix Timmermans.

I loved it when my mother read this story to us on a dark December night and all the characters came to life in my mind—Cäcilie, the night guard in the tower playing sacred songs, and Trinchen, falling into the apple bin at the sight of St. Nikolaus and *Knecht Ruprecht*. And there was the gaunt poet with his long hair and his declamations of philosophical theses, reciting his insights hours on end.

I knew many of the lines in the text by heart, and waited for their turn. My brother Herbert always laughed out loud when it came to the poet's dramatic recitation of his prose and his references to Dante, Milton, and others he expected to see in heaven. I was so relieved when the story ended on a peaceful note and Cäcilie received her favorite gift.

According to our German tradition, the Christmas presents we received on Christmas Eve were delivered quietly and secretly by the Christ child as a sign of love and sharing, not dropped off by St. Nikolaus through the chimney; we did not have open chimneys anyway. Therefore it was the *Christkindl* who needed to know about our wishes, and it was to him that we wrote our wish list. That year, I wrote the following letter, illustrated by colorful drawings:

Dear Christkindl,
I would like a watercolor set.
And a plate of goodies.
And a doll carriage.
And a sewing machine for the doll clothes.
*Maria*

We handed this list over to my mother, who knew exactly how to deliver the information to the right source. And then we waited for magical signs of arrival, dreaming of fulfillment. We watched for packages showing up in the house and hoped for encouraging questions such as, "Now, where did you see this baby carriage?" I also saw my mother hiding her knitting under the pillow. At night, before sleep came, colorful toys and baked sweets danced in my mind, floating gently along the inner screen.

"My mother invites you to come over to our house tonight," my friend Reinhild told me on December sixth in the afternoon, while we were walking home from school.

I was very excited about a visit to the Wirt family across the street. I expected to learn some new crafts from Gerlinde, Reinhild's older sister, in preparation for Christmas.

On this pitch-black night no moon and stars sparkled above us; only thick clouds of fog drifted in the air. The Wirts' home, however, was warm and cozy. The grand piano in their living room, stacked high with sheet music, was Professor Wirt's workplace. He was a wiry man with thin, stringy hair. In fact, he could never sit still for very long, and talked in short phrases, already thinking ahead and seemingly distracted by something. My mother had explained to me that he was nervous this way because he had seen many terrible things during the war years as a soldier that he could not forget. He had been at the Russian front. That night, he rushed around even more than usual, walking in and out of the house and slamming doors on the way as if he was in a terrible hurry.

Reinhild led me and a few other friends from the neighborhood into their dining room, where the large wooden table was set up for our crafts. The lamp over the table provided dim yet sufficient light, marking soft shadows in the room. After Frau Wirt brought each one of us a cup of hot chocolate, we started to cut paper strips for colorful chains, and flattened straws to be transformed into stars; we could hang these ornaments in our windows or on the Christmas tree.

Suddenly, there was a loud knock at the door. I heard a rattle, clanging chains, and the sound of a muted bell. Heavy footsteps came nearer.

"*Sankt Nikolaus* is here!" someone shouted.

The door flew open. Out of the dark emerged a hooded figure carrying a heavy sack, holding a switch in one hand and a golden book in the other. I dropped my paper strips and stepped back toward the wall. Reinhild and her sister Irmtraut started to giggle. The figure stepped into the dimly lit room. I could make out the huge hood covering most of his face; I noticed a trimmed, white beard. When he turned toward us, his blue eyes looked piercingly at each of us; for an instant, I thought I had seen these blue eyes before. But then, this could not be, I said to myself.

"I have come to see if you have been good children this year," he said in a low, loud voice.

All of us nodded eagerly and someone said, "Yes, we have been good." More giggles from Irmtraut followed. No one else spoke for a while.

In the silence that followed, St. Nikolaus dropped his sack on the wooden floor with a thud. I was totally startled by now. He said, "Let me check in my golden book. Everything is written up in here, all your good and all your bad behavior. I have heard it all. I know every one of you." He looked around, nodding at each of us.

I began to feel scared. What if he knew about the bad words I had said, or the time I did not return all of the change to my mother after an errand? Or the time I was late to school in the morning?

In the meantime, he had opened his thick, gold-covered book and stepped closer to the light coming from the hanging lamp over the table.

"Is Reinhild here?" he asked.

"Yes." She raised her hand.

"My book says that you have not always practiced the piano as told; you also have not studied as diligently in school as you should. You must improve this next year. Do you remember what you have been told?"

"Yes, St. Nikolaus," she said quietly. Then she started to giggle again and whispered something into her sister's ear, covering her mouth with her hand. "I bet it is him," I heard her say softly.

"Where is Heidrun?" he went on.

"I am over here," she answered.

"Heidrun has been a busy and good girl. She does not complain and follows her mother's direction. You all should be like her. She has been a perfect little girl."

On he went, naming each of us children written up in his large, heavy book. One of the boys was told he would get the switch next year if he did not shape up in school. I started to worry that St. Nikolaus would call on me, too. I wondered if by any chance he had not caught up with me yet, because I was a newcomer in town. Maybe he did not know me at all because I did not really believe in him.

"Where is Maria?" he said, looking around.

"Here."

Now my heart was beating fast. I anticipated a scolding and a switch. He checked his book, then looked up again to make sure I was there. "You need to keep up your studies, your homework, and practice the recorder each day. Do you understand?"

"Yes, I do," I responded quietly, very relieved that he did not mention anything else. Then he went on and asked where Irmtraut was.

He checked his book once more and I got another look at him. His loose hood covered his whole head—all of his hair and most of his forehead. The heavy brown coat was tied at the waist with a thick rope. By now, his blue eyes sparkled with the gleam of light.

With a faint smile, he finally closed his book with a loud clap. "You all have been fairly good children this year. Now help yourself to the goodies!" He grabbed the burlap sack and threw it on the table, then swiftly turned it upside down and emptied it. Apples and nuts flew in all directions, along with candy and chocolate; everything was rolling toward us as we stood at the table. I held up my hands to catch as many apples and nuts as I could. We all started to scream; Reinhild and Irmtraut had already crawled under the table to pick up any candy that had rolled down.

By the time I had gathered my goodies into the pockets of my dress, the visitor was gone. No good-bye. I had not even noticed when he left. I had missed a chance to get a glimpse of him.

"I know who it was," Reinhild said out loud. "I was not scared of him at all."

"Yes, it was Herr Jung!" someone blurted out.

Herr Jung was the principal of the local school, the *Gymnasium*, which my brothers attended. I had met him on several occasions, but at this moment I had not been sure who the visitor was. The face under the hood had looked faintly familiar. But what was most important was that I had seen St. Nikolaus, the saint who, with the help of his book, knew all about us. He had rewarded us with red apples and goodies . . . and it was St. Nikolaus Day today!

Frau Wirt brought out some more hot chocolate from the kitchen and turned up the light a bit. Gerlinde showed us how to make small St. Niks using a round red apple for the body and a walnut for the head, all stuck together with a match. Then we glued some white cotton to the walnut for the hair and beard, and topped it off with a red paper cone hat. We laughed and ate and debated some more who this visitor could have been.

"Don't tell Irmtraut, she still believes in St. Nikolaus," Reinhild said later to me as I left the house to go home. I nodded quietly, wondering myself . . .

That night, my brother Gerhard and I placed our polished shoes outside the door, only to find them the next morning filled with goodies, chocolates and fruit, decorated with a small branch of evergreen. No switch or coal had been left for us next to our shoes. That year, I had met St. Nikolaus and knew for sure that Christmas was coming.

Christmas arrived with familiar carols and more wishful preparations. Mother had picked up a tree-cutting permit in city hall, and so we went into the woods to cut a Christmas tree. The area had been marked for us by the forest ranger, the *Förster*.

Fräulein Kitzmann finally opened her special living room the day before Christmas so Mother could make preparations to set up the tree. I got a good first glimpse of the preparations inside the *Gute Stube* by peeking through the large keyhole; it quickly got covered from the inside by a cloth. From then on, I relied only on what I could hear from outside the closed door—the rustling of papers, some humming of Christmas carols, the music coming from a radio.

Christmas Eve finally came with the smell of baked *Stollen* filling the house. Mother had actually been able to find all the necessary ingredients to bake the "best *Stollen* ever": enough sweet butter, raisins, almonds, cardamom, flour, sugar, and more butter. The whiff of tangy tangerines and the fresh fragrance of the noble fir drifted through keyholes and walls. On Christmas Eve around six o'clock, we were finally allowed to enter the special living room. The tree had been decorated with white, lit candles, shiny silver balls, and tinsel. We sang "Ihr Kinderlein kommet" as we walked into the parlor, *die Weihnachsstube*, the Christmas room, Gerhard would say. Once a year

Fräulein Kitzmann would even take the covers off her furniture to display the flowered fabrics on her sofa and her armchairs. I missed my grandfather back in Leipzig, picturing how he would be sitting on the couch, smiling at us and puffing on a well-cultured cigar.

To my relief, despite our recent arrival in Bergzabern and the many preceding moves, the *Christkindl* had found us after all. Special gifts had been wrapped and labeled with our names on them. I had been introduced to chocolate as a treat and had slowly gotten used to its rich, sweet taste. From this year on, our traditional plate of goodies contained one bar of chocolate, wrapped in colorful paper with fairy tale scenes printed on it. My chocolate bar had a picture of *Hänsel und Gretel* standing by the gingerbread house with the witch watching from between the trees.

I received the watercolor set I had asked for, a doll carriage, and some dolls with new outfits my mother had knitted for them. I had seen her crocheting and knitting in the weeks before Christmas, and now I knew why. I had asked her what she was knitting and she had said, "A pair of knickers for the rooster."

"The rooster wears knickers?" She just smiled and looked away.

It was a happy time. I was allowed to stay up until midnight on New Year's Eve to hear the fireworks go off in town, and to listen to the festive bells from both churches ringing in the new year. Catholics and Protestants celebrated the same holiday yet in separate churches.

By the middle of January, the first snow had arrived. The whole town was covered with a thick layer of white powder. Some of the trees' heavy load drifted down in a gentle, white shower. A hardened, black crust of ice covered most roads. Car tires had carved grooves and ditches. The snow formed magical designs in the Wirts' garden: intertwined, white branches climbed up walls and trees, leading into nowhere. Tile roofs and church steeples were softly silhouetted against the gray winter sky. I could hear my shoes crunch on the frozen ground.

During those winter days, life in town was very quiet except for the special prayer week that was held each January. It was called the *Allianz Gebetswoche*, and involved nightly meetings to pray for the

unity of the church and ask for harmony among the Christian denominations. I thought we prayed to get along with each other, the
Catholics with the Protestants, and the rest of them with us. We prayed
to share our faith with others and not to insist on being the keepers of
the truth. The services were attended by about thirty people in town,
mainly old women and a few men, and led by different clergy in the
community. Even the Mennonite farmers from the estate near town
arrived for this special yearly event. It felt like the gathering of a select
group of believers in town. All of us huddled together on a cold winter
night to pray for our *Seelenheil*, our personal salvation, and to be saved
from a sinful life. I understood that it all had started with Adam and
Eve, as described in the first chapter of the Bible, when they listened to
the temptation of the snake, ate from the forbidden fruit, and, conse-
quently, were driven out of paradise. No one ever spoke of our political
trauma during the last few years or our personal histories or prayed for
the survivors. Politics was not mentioned. All these events were a part
of God's will.

The gathering room was usually overheated, the stove gurgled,
and the lectures were lengthy . . . my eyelids would become heavy.
Pastor Mann's prayers went on and on, his voice getting louder and
louder with each new supplication. To us, his prayers sounded like
growling barks in the night. He really got excited in his prayerful com-
mentary about the just-completed sermon and his own repeat of the
preacher's main points of the text. He must have mentioned *the blood of
Christ* about ten times in his barking. Gerhard and I could not look at
each other; one of us would have burst out laughing. I squeezed my lips
and tightly shut my eyes, hoping for the mighty *Amen* to come soon.

The heavy snow cover transformed the children's home into a mysterious mountain. All the tools and building supplies left by the workers
disappeared under the clean snow cover, including all the trash. Not
much construction had gone on during the last few months. Day after
day, the workers stayed away because of the harsh winter weather.
Mother waited patiently for sunshine and warmer temperatures. Month

after month passed. But then, we were only to wait for three more months until our home would be finished; that's what my mother had been told. It did not seem that long . . .

The month of February came. I heard Irmtraut singing on the street while she played in the snow:

*Wenn Eis und Schnee im Febr'ar kracht,*
*Im Febr'ar kracht, im Febr'ar kraaacht,*
*dann freut sich all's auf Fasenacht,*
*auf Fasenacht, auf Fasenacht,*
*dann freut sich all's.*

(When ice and snow crackle in February, everyone is looking forward to Mardi Gras . . .)

"What are you singing?" I asked her later on that day.

"We celebrate *Fastnacht* [which means Mardi Gras, Shrove Tuesday, or Fat Tuesday]—no school that day. We all get dressed up and go around town to get candy. Are you going with us?"

I checked this invitation with my mother who explained to me that *Fastnacht* was a Catholic custom, a time to celebrate one more time before the season of Lent. After Ash Wednesday there was supposed to be no more partying and celebrating until the Saturday afternoon before Easter, some forty days later.

Now I understood that the Catholics in town were making preparations for the Mardi Gras celebrations; they had already started last November. In the small town hall, a festive ball was planned for Fat Tuesday. A few weeks earlier, the Fastnacht Club in town had chosen a king and a queen. This year, the owners of the clothing store on Main Street, Herr and Frau Bossert, were to be the honored royalty. Reinhild said that even the local priest would be in attendance for the crowning. Every guest would wear elaborate costumes, fancy makeup, and even masks to hide their identity.

Days before *Rosenmontag* and *Fastnacht*, all my friends had been thinking about what costumes to wear. A feeling of excitement was in the air. Mother said that it was one more excuse to get drunk, to dance, and to do foolish things. I did not quite understand what she meant by that; to me the whole thing sounded exciting.

"We Methodists don't do this," she said with a serious tone in her voice.

"Can I get dressed up anyway?"

She did not answer me for a long time but finally agreed that I could get dressed up in a costume if it was not too wild or offensive. I could do nothing too outlandish such as dress up like a gypsy woman or a grotesque witch with wild hair and makeup on my face.

"Be sure not to pass by Pastor Mann's house in town," she said. Then she muttered, "Your grandfather Wunderlich would have been appalled by such nonsense. He would have said, 'The devil is at work here.'"

"I promise," I said quickly and ran out the door.

I wondered how the devil could possibly be at work on *Fastnacht*, although I did hear that kids were planning to get dressed up as devils; they would be wearing red outfits and horns and dragging long tails. Was my grandfather correct after all?

The long-awaited Shrove Tuesday finally came. It was a holiday in town; the schools were closed, just as Irmtraut had said. Reinhild, dressed up as a French harlequin, wore tights and a colorful shirt and held a white fan. Irmtraut was a chimney sweep for the day, complete with a black top hat and attached clover leaves for good luck. Heidrun was a witch, carrying a basket and a switch. Werner Dietz, my friend from school, came dressed up like a girl, with an apron, a scarf, and a handbag; he resembled a babushka and looked really funny. He reminded me of a figure right out of the Punch and Judy stories.

My mother had glued some golden stars and moons on a blue sweatshirt I wore, along with a shiny paper hat. Since I was not disguised as someone else, my mother allowed me to join the festivities in town. Despite her approval, I was a bit uncomfortable about the whole affair, knowing that we Methodists were not supposed to participate in such folly. I made sure that I stayed away from our minister's house in town, and hoped that nobody would recognize me and tell on me.

We paraded up and down the main streets and stopped at various shops where we received candy. The goodies we received that day were plentiful. Our neighbor Frau Hei had the best *Fastnachtsküchle*, a round fritter filled with jam, fried in oil, and rolled in white, crunchy sugar.

The next morning, Ash Wednesday, the whole spectacle was over. A solemn silence fell over the entire town. The Catholics were confessing their sins at the six o'clock mass. Some sinners even went to church in their costumes. Reinhild and Irmtraut also attended mass that morning and later returned with black, ashen crosses on their foreheads, a sign of penitence. As the day went on, Irmtraut's cross slowly dissolved into large, black spots dripping all over her face. She did not seem to mind. For all of us school started at about ten o'clock in the morning; the big cleanup in the town hall had already begun hours earlier.

In early spring, to my surprise, Mother allowed us to adopt a black kitten. She had bought a dog, a German shepherd named Ria, to guard the children's home property during construction. The kitten, however, was allowed to live with us at Fräulein Kitzmann's house, and I was very happy about that. It was named Mohrle. One sunny Sunday afternoon we held a baptism for her. My brother Gerhard dressed in the vestments of a minister, complete with a black robe, a white *Bäffchen*, a collar, and a hat, and carried a liturgy book. I brought a basket with the kitten in it to the garden; Heidrun and Almut were the godparents present. During a short outdoor ceremony, the kitten was carefully baptized with water, named, and blessed.

Another three months had passed and the children's home was still not ready. By now the wooden scaffolds were in full view, barely outlining windows. The buildings took on a skeletal, transparent presence, hollow and promising. Each day, my mother went to the construction site, talking to foremen and architects, masons and roofers. Progress was painstakingly slow.

"It will be done this summer," the foreman said to her as the workers moved their equipment—shovels, nails, bricks, dirt, and large wooden beams. The cement mixer ran all day without a break, a deafening noise filling the dusty air. Some of the workers still continued to admire their own work by standing around the lot or watching each other. They drank beer by the crates.

Spring and summer came. With the help of my friends I learned to ride a bicycle on the dirt road in front of Fräulein Kitzmann's house. I had a hard time balancing the whole bike while pedaling with my feet and holding on to the handlebars at the same time. A few times I fell and crashed into the hedges along the road, but in the end my perseverance paid off. I rode the bike up and down the dirt road.

"There will be a big procession in town this Thursday," Reinhild told me one afternoon.

"Can I come, too?" I asked.

"I am not sure about it," she shouted as she tried to avoid getting tangled up in the jump rope which was being swung under her feet. Finally, she stepped closer to my friend Heidrun and me and said, "Maybe I should not tell you this, but this Thursday is *Fronleichnam*, Corpus Christi Feast Day, a very holy day in my church. There will be no school that day. Every year a festive procession moves through town, stopping at several altars decorated with many flowers. We all get dressed up, carry flowers, lay them down at the altars, and sing as we follow the priest and his monstrance with the Host. Irmtraut gets to wear her first communion dress one more time, and she is allowed to carry her white candle in the procession." She took a deep breath and started skipping around on one leg.

"This sounds like fun. Can we come and watch you?"

"That's exactly the problem. They told us at our last lesson at church that *Fronleichnam* is a very old church holiday with magical powers over you Protestants."

"What could happen if we watch the procession?" I insisted.

"They said that when the priest carries the Host past any of you Protestants, and you look at the Host in the monstrance, you will fall on your knees and become Catholics, instantly. Maybe you better not go."

I was startled by her comments, and tried to question her some more about this fateful procession in town. But by then, she had hopped into the flying jump rope again, and was not one bit interested in church, magic, and conversion. I did not ask my family about it either, but decided to go and watch the procession on Thursday morning with my friend Heidrun in order to test the power of Reinhild's church.

*Fronleichnam*, the Thursday after Trinity Sunday, arrived with the brightest sunshine in June. No clouds drifted in the sky. A quiet hush, anticipation of this special day, hung over the entire town. Heidrun and I had gotten up early and walked together toward the middle of town. I could see the storks flying in and out of their big, round nest on top of the Protestant church roof. Their base was a wagon wheel, now filled with branches and soft pluckings for a nest. There must be young ones in there, I thought. I loved their smooth flight, their enormous wings, and their orange-red, thin legs with knobby knees.

"Don't get there before nine o'clock because we will first be having Holy Mass in the church," Reinhild had said to us. "After that, we will be walking in the procession and you can see us."

Heidrun and I did not get very far into town. The streets were blocked off and all the stores closed, including the Protestant shops, the bakeries, and the dairy. No traffic was allowed through town any more.

We positioned ourselves just across from the butcher shop, which had totally disappeared behind a high wooden scaffold. Steps led up to an altar; a red carpet was laid out past the sidewalk into the street. A white-laced tablecloth was draped over the altar table, and a wooden cross had been suspended. I had never seen so many flowers arranged in one place. All the Catholic gardens in town must have been picked bare that morning. The altar panel was totally covered with flower petals from roses, peonies, and hydrangeas. Their pungent scent was mixed with the fresh fragrance of the birch branches placed on each side of the altar. More flowers, such as delphiniums, snapdragons, and carnations, had been placed in vases and lined the walkway to the altar table. The most beautiful roses had been arranged in fancy vases and placed on the altar.

"People said there are two more altars in town," Heidrun told me as we were waiting, taking in the sights and scents.

More people had joined us standing on the pavement; other children sat down on the edge of the sidewalk in order to have the best view. I remembered Reinhild's predictions of the mighty power of the Host and decided to stand a little farther to the back. This morning, the town had been transformed into a holy place filled with anticipation of a mighty demonstration.

The church bells began to ring, signaling the conclusion of the mass at St. Martin's church and the beginning of the procession. In the far distance, the music of the brass ensemble announced the arrival of the pilgrims. The hymn they were playing was familiar to me; it was one that we Protestants also sang.

The procession was now in full view and moving toward us. The pilgrims followed the musicians. A group of children led the way. All the girls wore white dresses and matching shoes and carried white, burning candles. Small, lacy veils had been fastened to their hair. The boys wore black suits and black, polished shoes, their very best attire. Everyone was singing and holding a hymnal. Some of the older boys carried long birch tree branches. Others wore acolyte vestments, beautiful red garments layered with white-laced chasubles, while they swung shiny incense holders back and forth on a chain. I saw Reinhild walking in the middle of the children's group. I hardly recognized Irmtraut in her first communion dress, her hair combed and her face cleaned up; no snot was running from her nose.

Then came Herr Herzog, the mayor of Bad Bergzabern, to lead the procession of adult pilgrims. He looked very serious in his black suit and top hat, holding his hymnal and singing. People around him either sang along or held their hands in a prayerful position. All the men walked together, followed by all the women. Everyone was dressed in black. They all moved solemnly to the tune of the brass band. I noticed that the beginning of the procession was about half a stance ahead of the tail end. It did not seem to matter to any of them.

The procession stopped in front of the flower altar; the crowd spilled over into the sidewalk area where we were standing. Finally, several men announced the arrival of the priest by carrying and waving enormous flags made of white satin, framed by golden fringes. I could see the picture of a lamb with a cross on one of the flags. Then four men held up the poles of the baldachin that provided a canopy for the arriving priest. He carried the monstrance containing the Host. The priest was dressed in the shiniest and most flowing vestment I had ever seen, a miter on his head. The chasuble, all made of white, red, and golden tapestry, reached his knees. He looked straight ahead while leading the prayers of the people. I recognized the paternoster they all muttered but did not quite get the prayer about the Holy Mother Mary. As he came closer to the altar, the pilgrims began to kneel down, bowing their heads while the monstrance with the Host passed by them. The priest stepped up to the altar and began to recite long prayers in Latin, words that I could not understand. On several occasions, he turned around and lifted up the golden monstrance for all to see. It looked like a golden shrine with shiny rays around it. The Host was shown to all the people present. Every time he turned toward the pilgrims and the rest of us, the ringing of handbells filled the heavy, incense-laced air.

That's when I remembered the fateful prediction that I would fall on my knees at the sight of the Holiest of Holy. I looked at Heidrun, who was watching the procession next to me. She was still standing, other people were standing, and so was I. My knees were not giving in, the viewing of this holy ceremony had not made me become a Catholic instantly, nor was it breaking me down in paralysis and repentance. I stood up straight and watched the holy ceremony—music, incense, prayers, gold, and all. I was relieved to still be a Methodist, although

I loved all the fancy outfits, the flowers, and the show of godly power in front of me. There was nothing so lavish in our small church—maybe one bouquet of flowers in a vase was placed on the altar, and even that seemed unnecessary.

In the meantime, communion had been served to all the pilgrims present kneeling on the hard pavement. Even the *Bürgermeister*, Herr Herzog, knelt down in homage. His granddaughter, my friend Waltraud, knelt right next to him.

Later that afternoon we all played outside again, swinging our jump rope and riding our bikes up and down the street. Irmtraut still wore her white dress, although by now it had turned slightly gray, showing dust, dirt, and the leftovers from food she had eaten following the procession. She had been running through the garden, and her shoes had turned black. Her blond hair was back to its old tricks, with tangled curls and loosened strands hanging all over her face. She smiled.

"I wonder why her mother never wipes the snot off her nose," Mother said.

Summer had come and Frau Hei's cherry tree was loaded with plump and juicy fruit.

"You can come into the garden, climb up the tree and eat all you want!" she said. We all did follow her invitation: Reinhild, Irmtraut, Heidrun, and the rest of the neighbor kids. I found a special branch in the tree to sit on, surrounded by dark, ripe cherries and fluttering leaves. I ate until I was full. We spit the pits as far as we could.

The children's home was still not ready. In fact, only now were the wooden beams for the roofs ready to be hoisted up so that the project could be finished before the fall and winter arrived. In addition to the masons and their daily helpers, the journeymen carpenters had appeared on the scene. Their clothes were different from those of the other workers; they wore bell-bottom pants with tools hanging from their belts and had handkerchiefs stuck in their back pockets. Their wide-brimmed hats provided protection from the sun or the rain.

Mother had scheduled their arrival, and was excited to finally see them climbing up and down the ladders, moving beams and nails. The hammering went on all day long, echoing a pounding rhythm. Several weeks had passed when my mother finally announced, "This Friday, we'll have a ceremony in celebration of the raising of the roof!"

When I returned from school that day, the rafters were in place, the crest decorated with a small pine tree. Colorful paper streamers fluttered in the summer breeze while the workers' party was in full swing. Thick, white smoke came from the barbecue station where the men grilled knackwurst and bratwurst. A large laundry basket had been filled with rolls but by now was almost empty. Crates of beer bottles had been emptied, too, and the mood was generally happy and boisterous. The roofers' foreman had given a speech; so had my mother. A representative of the Methodist Church was talking about the future of the home and the important mission of caring for children. Everyone nodded and drank some more.

Mother did not like all the drinking and carrying on that day. She did not want me to be part of it either. She explained, "I don't like to buy all this alcohol and see the workers drunk. But this is what they do around here and I better not get them mad at me. They might do something crazy or steal stuff from the property. My father would have been very upset to see this drinking party at a future church-related home. He was absolutely against any alcohol, he was a teetotaler, you know." She shook her head and sighed.

That summer, I learned to swim but not right away in the public pool. One afternoon, Reinhild brought a stool outside which she placed in the middle of the street, then showed me how to move my arms and legs in order to stay above the water once I got into it. Lying belly down on the stool, I could dangle my arms and legs freely to practice the movements of the breaststroke. I was well prepared when I finally got into the shallow end of the pool to try my swimming strokes. One day it just happened. The water carried me easily.

After the raising of the roof ceremony, the construction site of the children's home became very quiet. The brick walls promised an outline of the rooms (the kitchen and bedrooms) and the layout of our home. I loved to walk through the open rooms and imagine how we would live there. I would share a bedroom with my mother, while my brothers would have one together. The view toward the vineyards was going to be special, the cool air of the forest refreshing on a hot day. Even our dog, Ria, would have a kennel from which she could watch over us and the property.

But we still lived with Fräulein Kitzmann in her house. Mother was very quiet about the children's home building project. She looked serious and her enthusiasm was gone. She stopped going up to the construction site every day. None of the workers had shown up for days, anyway. No cement mixer was running, no yelling by the foreman could be heard; there were not even empty beer bottles lying on the ground.

"We are waiting for more money to complete the home on the inside. We ran out of funds a few weeks ago. The expenses were already too high. Everything costs more than we thought." She sighed. "We'll have to wait for another American rebuilding grant. This means we have to wait a few more months until the money arrives," she said to us children one night. I did not want to ask her any more questions because she seemed so worried and sad about the postponements and the money problems.

So we kept on living with Fräulein Kitzmann in her house, crowded into her space, her kitchen and bedrooms (as I have said, the Christmas room, the *Gute Stube*, stood empty all year long).

I came home from school one day when both my mother and Fräulein Kitzmann were very upset. They did not speak to each other as I entered the kitchen; their faces looked tight and serious. "I am very sorry that I broke your favorite cup," I heard my mother say. "I will replace it, I am so sorry."

Fräulein Kitzmann sat at the kitchen table, her face carved in stone while she stared at her favorite coffee cup, a white porcelain cup decorated with blue flowers. A piece was missing but the handle was still attached. The saucer, usually reserved for Kater Büh's milk, was not broken, either. She did not answer my mother and just looked away.

The next day my mother went into town, to Frau Turner's china shop, to find a replacement for the broken coffee cup. She could not find the exact one with blue flowers on it but tried to match it as best as she could. Fräulein Kitzmann put the new cup into the cupboard and continued to use the cracked one, which she could still fill about half full. There she sat at the kitchen table staring at it, silently sulking about the loss of her favorite coffee cup. Her patience had been shattered; her resentment was overflowing. She was mad and nothing could make it better. In silence, she resented all of us and the loss of privacy in her own home to us strangers. She had shared everything she possessed with us refugees for over a year. Three months had stretched to more than one year, with no end in sight. Now she just sat there, bitterly holding the broken cup and insisting on drinking from it. I sensed her anger. I was afraid she would punish us by sending us away. Where could we go this time?

My mother disappeared into our bedroom. She closed the door, sat down on our bed, and began to cry uncontrollably, tears running down her face. "I can't go on anymore . . . can't go on anymore," she cried out loud. "I can't take it anymore."

With that she slumped down on her knees.

The tears just kept on flowing down her face into her hands, onto the bed and down to the floor. It was like a dam had broken and opened up a flood; stored tears began to flow after her many years of suffering in silence and hardened feelings of sadness and fear. It had all been covered up by her strong will of survival for us children, by her pure determination and blind faith. She began to break down while memories and unspoken images flooded her heart. She could not stop weeping and frequently gasped for air. Her cup of tears had been totally shattered, and there was no comfort to be found. Nothing could replace the loss of her loved ones and her homes. Nothing would have been good enough to make it whole again, just as Fräulein Kitzmann's new cup did not replace her loss. So she sat there, unable to stop the tears until her body shook in pain.

We four children stood next to her and could not help. I did not know what to do. She did not ask for help, either. Maybe I was in the way, a burden? I was afraid of what might happen next. Fräulein Kitzmann sat downstairs in her kitchen; my mother was up here slumped on her bed—a broken world all around, a broken heart inside.

My brother Gerhard finally announced, "I'll go to the pastor and get help."

He ran out of the house, jumped on his bike, and pedaled as fast as he could until he arrived at our minister's home. When he reached the house, he rang the doorbell and blurted out, "My mother is really in bad shape, please come right away!"

The pastor arrived shortly thereafter and sat down next to my mother to talk to her. He closed the door so that I could not hear what was said. He stayed with her for quite a while and left only after she had calmed down and fallen asleep. I did not know what to say after that or where to be. So I waited outside on the street.

From then on, the tension in the house was almost unbearable. Icy silence and unspoken resentments gave way to feelings of hurt and intrusion. We stopped eating meals together with Fräulein Kitzmann. The lack of privacy and ownership had gnawed away any patience and Christian tolerance and left raw despair, anger, and hopelessness. Nothing much was said to us children. Mother just went on as best as she could.

It was our pastor who contacted the church officials in Frankfurt/ Main to inform them of our plight and the financial problems hampering the building project. My mother's brother Friedrich, who directed the church seminary at the time, was also informed of the financial delays and the ongoing lack of funds. Finally, definite plans were made to complete the home, but by this time winter had come, and the snow cover made it impossible for the workers to continue their jobs.

The icy weather had not only left slippery streets and icicles decorating trees and roofs, but also caused the *Stauweiher,* the pond by the forest, to freeze over. Only one corner, at the right side, was accessible to the swans and ducks that had chosen not to migrate that year. The people in town said that the pond had a warm well deep down in the ground that kept the water heated in the winter. That corner had become the birds' favorite hangout, while we children skated on the thick ice cover on the other side of the pond.

"Don't get too close to the edge. Some years ago, a boy fell through the cracked ice and drowned there," my friends said as we walked up to the snowy shore.

I did not want to hear it. Too awful to imagine, drowning in the icy lake, screaming . . .

I had never skated on ice before and I watched how my friends fastened their skates to their shoes with a special key. That winter, I learned to skate on this pond, the blades gliding along the shiny surface. Deep down beneath the ice was a shimmer of green. I made sure I stayed away from the water hole and the warm well.

The nearby forest offered a steep sled run we used during heavy snowfalls. Sometimes we tied several sleds together with a rope, and a leader would steer the lineup downhill, usually losing a few passengers in the snow. The hot chocolate we had afterwards tasted better than any I would ever have again.

I found these notes in Mother's diary: "1949–1951: instead of a fourth of a year with Fräulein Kitzmann, it took one and three fourths years—lived very crowded, but enough to eat. School attendance for the children is successful, music lessons possible. Bought dog."

We finally, finally moved into our house the next year, on July 13, 1951, the evening before Bastille Day, the French celebration of their revolution in 1789. At night, the French soldiers celebrated in their barracks, too, with fireworks, loud singing, and partying. Colorful rockets went off high in the air. We could see their firecrackers and sparkling spinning wheels. They carried on until late at night.

I was still uncomfortable having soldiers so close by. The locals called them *Göcklingers* (from the word *Gockel*, or *Göckele*, meaning rooster) because of the rooster crest on the sleeves of their uniforms. People laughed at these young soldiers because they were there for occupation purposes only, and did not really have anything to do anymore. They did not speak German and were labeled "stupid." Most of the time, they kept to themselves and patrolled the French border about eight kilometers away. People were bitter about having their land occupied and patrolled by soldiers from another country. But we had lost the war and this was part of the aftermath.

"They are celebrating with us," my mother chuckled as she looked out the window and started the fire in the cooking stove. "I can hardly wait to put tulips and daffodil bulbs into the flower bed this fall. Over there is a perfect place for a lilac bush. We can even plant a strawberry patch right here behind the house." She smiled. "My old family genes of running a farm are coming through. My grandmother managed the whole estate in Rüssdorf, you know?" She chuckled. "Grandfather was gone from home a lot, preaching and saving souls. There is nothing better than working in the garden! She knew that."

Mother envisioned a garden, flowers, a chicken coop to the left, and a sour cherry tree climbing right along the wall. Most of all, she dreamt of a lilac bush and roses over by the concrete slab. Eventually, there would be a table and chairs for guests, china on the table, fresh flowers, and a peach torte . . .

At a distance the peaceful yet noisy celebration of the soldiers went on and on. Inside the house, we sat down at the table for our first meal. We were together. Mother bowed her head and prayed, *Komm' Herr Jesu . . . Amen.* We held hands. *Guten Appetit!* We all chimed in. She looked at us and smiled. "We are home again."

Another entry from Mother's diary reads: "1951: House and Home built. On July 13th, we moved into the small house, great joy! No furniture but alone after seven years. Received 500 Marks from Papa

Zurbuchen, in America, I was not allowed to buy furniture. The money had to be spent on a piano! What luck!"

Fräulein Kitzmann had her home back but with her favorite coffee cup cracked forever. Drops of bitterness would gather in the cup for a long time. We hardly ever saw her at the children's home from then on. Kater Büh continued to sit in the middle of the kitchen table slurping his milk from the saucer.

The "little house," as we called it, had a living room, a kitchen, our own bathroom, and two bedrooms upstairs under the roof. The day we moved in, neither the electricity or the running water had been connected. We used candlelight in the late evening, and Mother went to the little well down by the cellar steps for our drinking water. We did not mind, the summer evenings were long anyway. Mother and I shared one bedroom and the three brothers the other one. For the first time in my life I slept in my own bed. As a matter of fact, we all had our own beds to sleep in. A basement provided ample room for coal, wood, bikes, shoe racks, and workbenches. The brothers planned to set up a darkroom. There would be enough room for Gerhard's model train set. Downstairs, a large, gray toad that had moved into the cellar during the long months of construction croaked a raspy welcome.

Our bedroom, which faced the vineyards and the dense, dark-green forest, overlooked the cherry tree in the garden and Ria's kennel. At night, I opened the window wide and saw the full moon hanging over the mountain ridge. The stars had decorated the sky into an unending tapestry. Ria was watching over us and occasionally howled to the moon. The cool fresh evening breeze found us. We had, at last, found a piece of home.

# CHAPTER EIGHT

# *Over the Ashes*

Not much ever changes in small towns. Not even new buildings can replace internal pictures and memories. I noticed that the old train station in Bad Bergzabern had been newly renovated. The old, reddish brick building had been restored and cleaned up. The diesel engine train was running again. People could travel again to the next train station in Winden, to catch a connection to a larger city. I had done so myself for a number of years when I lived here.

"Do you want to stop at the cemetery first?" Winfried asked as we drove past the old gas station at the corner.

"Let's first stop somewhere to get some flowers for Mother's grave."

It all seemed like a dream. I lived here many years ago. I took with me many memories and feelings. So much of my past is still here, alive and partly hidden from my eyes. My numbness tells me so. I haven't sorted it all out yet. Will I ever?

I saw that the old castle with its round towers had been washed and newly painted; the roses were watered and blooming. My eyes wandered to the upper floor, which had housed my third-grade classroom. I could hear Herr Judt, my teacher, screaming at the boys. I had been so afraid of him and of his sudden outbursts.

At the next street corner, the old Dietz's hardware store was still there but had changed ownership; it was now a stationery store. I used to pass by there every day on the way to and from school, wondering what it might be like to live so close to the school. My schoolmate, Werner Dietz, had graduated with me from the *Gymnasium* in Landau but then had died a few years later of cancer. He was the smartest of all of us students and took home a perfect report card at the end of each year. He was a whiz in physics, mathematics, and chemistry, subjects that remained mysteries to me. Once in a while I asked him for help and he never said no.

Down the street, Bossert's clothing store still displayed stylish dresses and expensive men's sweaters in its windows. Following the sidewalk, Winfried and I arrived at the little castle chapel where we were married in 1965. The old stone steps were worn from years of being walked on.

"We had such a simple wedding compared with the productions I see back home," Winfried said.

"I know, you went to Pfeifer's nursery that morning and picked up a bouquet of red roses and freesias, right?" He nodded.

"My aunt gave me some money that day so I could bail you out of the pub when your brothers had kidnapped you later that day." We both chuckled and held hands as we tried to open the heavy wooden door. It was locked. We took turns looking through the large keyhole and could see the altar area. We had sat next to each other on two chairs during the ceremony.

"Do you remember what the wedding sermon was all about?" I asked.

"Not really. I remember the music. Your brother Herbert played the organ and Klaus the flute."

I was remembering the beautiful dress I had worn and the matching white shoes. Winfried bent over and kissed me.

How fortunate we had been to spend thirty-some years together, raising a family and living without the horrors of a war separating us. My parents were married for twelve years only.

Back on the main road, the Protestant bakery and the Catholic butcher shop were gone for good, the space used for another type of business. However, both the Protestant and the Catholic churches were standing intact like beacons over time. Sidewalks were clean; flower boxes full of blooms decorated windowsills. I could see it all in my mind: still pictures of school, friends, and warm summer days.

We passed by the familiar children's home and the little house next to it. The property had long ago been renovated and now served as a retreat center for various church groups and family gatherings. The old sour cherry tree was still giving plenty of shade to the overgrown gardens. No one lived there anymore. It was almost as if I could hear the chatter of the children on the playground, the commotion in the kitchen with our cooks, Erna and Gertrud, fixing dinner, and Spatzehenner digging ditches near the meadow. I saw my mother sitting in the office near the front door and welcoming visitors and workmen. I thought of the dog, Ria, and the many other pets that joined us over the years. Unfortunately, the surrounding vineyards had been developed, and houses and apartments built there. The once-beautiful view of the hills was mostly obstructed by fences and bushes.

My mother, in her later years, had finally built her very own home a short distance from the children's home. As a war widow she was entitled to some building loan money, and she finally had the peace of home after all the years of fleeing, moving, and starting again. After her death her home had been sold, and I hesitated to walk by. I knew I would not find her there any more. The house was just a shell, and I wanted to remember it the way it once was. Those memories did not need validation, as did the many images and memories of my earlier childhood years in Dresden and Leipzig. I wanted to remember her home with our mother waiting for us.

The rose bushes showed off some red and pink blossoms, but the gardens were neglected, the grass overgrown with weeds, and the old lilac bushes covered most of the view. The once sparkly white paint on the outside of her house had weathered to a gray color, showing signs of aging and neglect. Someone living there had opened the window to her living room and the white curtains fluttered in the late afternoon breeze; but she was not there anymore to greet us with her warm smile. I could not go home anymore.

I could, however, return to this special place called Bad Bergzabern, somewhere in the gentle hills of Germany, six thousand miles away from my new home. I can come back here and connect with my family history and the years of growing up. The years we lived here as a family helped us recover from the worst but also formed scars to cover up painful experiences and deep losses. The wounds had stopped hurting but they never really healed. The trauma had not been felt through, talked about, sorted out so that it could be integrated and understood. We just went on living, surviving without recovering. I had started to do my part. It was going to be easier now that I had seen the countryside in Poland, and had visited Dresden, Breslau, and Leipzig. Validation of feelings and refreshed memories would lead to a more realistic acceptance of the past, a moving on in a less burdened way. Each one of us could choose to do so. My brothers had found their own way to live with the past; Winfried would do so in time. I had found my way to a richer and more meaningful present by reconnecting with a painful past.

I thought about how my children needed to hear the stories of their parents and grandparents, and, beyond the listening, how they needed to see us struggling with a world of evil that looms forever in our history and not denying the effect our childhood experiences have on our current lives. They should know of the lingering, underlying sense of shame, the forced and self-imposed silence, and the feeling of responsibility for the acts of a dead generation. Most of all, we needed to talk to them of the deep, often unspoken grief that was never expressed openly but was shielded by an avoidance of memories and images. That way old wounds were kept from breaking open but also could not heal. I learned that none of these efforts of hiding and suffering could atone for the past. As if crying over the ashes would lead to a cleansing of the powers that set the fire. As if screaming would wake the dead. As if silence would be a shield from harm's way. Instead the silent burden became the painful load. Life's burdens can never be forgotten—just carried, acknowledged, and shared. As if the past destroyed a future. As if there were no way out . . .

I began to see that there was not ever going to be an end to the pain of this history, just a courageous walking on for the sake of a defiant humanity in the looming presence of evil. *[N]ation shall not lift up sword against nation, neither shall they learn war anymore* (Isaiah 2: 2–4), the ancient prophet had proclaimed in the midst of war and dread. No one can ever take that hope.

I had more work to do in the next few years. I needed to reflect upon and sort out my feelings about my religious upbringing and learned acceptance of suffering as atonement for sin combined with the rigid instruction to blindly trust in a rather ominous God. What was I going to do with my childhood faith of a dependent yet imperfect child? The religious instruction I had received was not so far removed from a faith that involved blindly following a leader. I shuddered at the thought.

*Mother held on to her* Gottvertrauen *(trust in God), her conviction that God had saved us and that it was his will . . . Thy will be done on earth . . . I had also prayed.*

I needed to create another, more human God. I needed to know more about our Christian arrogance throughout the centuries, about the anti-Semitic prejudice that was justified by the death of the man Jesus two thousand years ago. How easy and handy it was to justify revenge in the name of God, to have a chosen group of scapegoats. It would take time for me to ponder and think. Maybe the absence of the old God would lead me to a richer understanding of a compassionate humanity, one that spoke in many languages and had expressions in many different images.

*I keep holding on to these familiar words: give us this day our daily bread and forgive us our trespasses as we forgive those who trespass against us . . .*

This trip back to my past had helped me to accept who I am and where I came from, to accept my parents' lives as they were lived and to mourn their deaths. In an awesome silence, I mourned the death of a nation as it was and could have been, the death of a people caught in evil and powerlessness. From now on, a model of mindfulness and social conscience in the face of fanaticism and religious slumber would be my guide. I would try to act on what I had learned by examining the past: the challenge to use power responsibly, practice tolerance, and accept the privilege to feel and reflect. It would be a task for a lifetime but it was never too late to start.

I held Winfried's hand as we walked past the heavy iron gate at the cemetery. Down the hill, Johannes Spatz—we called him Spatzehenner—was buried in his family plot. He had died in 1984, at the age of eighty-three. I smiled when I thought about his scrambled mind, about the time when he chopped our tree into pieces two days before Christmas Eve because he thought that "it was already over". I had to tell my children about him.

We passed the cemetery chapel on the right where we had gathered for Mother's funeral service after she died in 1983. *Herbert had played the organ one last time for her. We all stood to honor her. We sang her favorite hymns . . .*

The walk up to her graveside is an easy one. The pebbles on the walkways crunched with each step. We arrived at her final resting place. Colorful pansies and forget-me-nots bloomed in the bronze cast bowl at the bottom of her gravestone. I took the two small wreaths out of my bag and started to tie the blue ribbons to the bowl. One was for my mother and one was for my father—together in death. The wreaths, decorated with cornflowers and red poppies, reminded me of long summer walks through the fields nearby. Today, leaves blown by wind and rain decorated the grave. Tidying up the grave is one last thing I could do to take care of them. The heavy granite plate was the final cover to protect her fragile remains. Mother had wanted something that would be easy to keep clean and cared for as the seasons came and went. Were they resting in peace under the stone plate? I needed to let them rest in peace. It was going to be my job to see to it.

Their lives, which had contained laughter, love, and music, hope and disillusionment, tragedy and silence, were completed. I needed to let it be. May they rest in peace . . .

Winfried started to pick up the debris around the grave plot and went to get some water for the plants. It is one of the few places in my life where the tears just come, slowly, uninvited, freely. No effort to hold them back will do. It feels right to cry here—tears of relief for my parents that their incomplete lives are completed in death, tears of gratefulness that despite our harsh journey the beauty of life did not escape us, tears of bitterness that at a time of powerlessness the suffering seemed without end, tears of hope that our children and grandchildren are privileged to live in a new day of peace.

*I don't know how to thank you, except by never forgetting you and telling your story. I will be back . . .*

"We better get going, Maria! Friedel is waiting with supper for us. She promised us *Dampfnudeln*, dumplings, and *Weinsosse!*"

# EPILOGUE

## *The Mitzvah*

When we returned home at the end of the summer, our suitcases spilled over with letters and pictures and our minds with memories and vivid images of places and people. It would take months, maybe years, to sort them all out and write about them. I thought about the Madonnas in Dresden, the terrors, the fires, and the friendly face of Frau Freitag in Damsdorf. The remnants of our history remained shredded and gray, harsh and edgy, but clear enough so that they could be woven into a new tapestry for our children, who could come to know and find themselves in our history.

"I won't be back until next month," the Jewish woman said in my office as she got up from her chair. "I am on my way to Israel. I am leaving on Sunday for Tel Aviv and an exciting trip to Jerusalem. I have a chance to meet this important woman and interview for a two-year fellowship there. Then we'll travel to the Greek islands." By now she was beaming.

"Could you please take a look at this before you leave?" I said.

"Of course."

I handed her the first pages of my manuscript and asked her for corrections since I had quoted her.

She read silently, nodding a few times. She started to spell the word "mitzvah" in Hebrew and added to the meaning of it. Then she looked at me. "What are you writing about?" she asked.

"Oh, it is just a family project about my history and childhood in Germany," I replied, trying not to put too much attention on my work.

"You know, it really is not a problem for me to be here with you." She must have noticed my hesitation. "The Holocaust happened in a different generation." She paused. "Only one time, when I was traveling in Germany, I took the train and felt almost sick to my stomach, thinking about the many Jews that had been transported by train to the camps. But I just see you as a person. It sounds as though it is still a problem for you." She looked at me. "But the healing happens between two persons at a time."

With that she gave me the papers back.

*The ashes must be shared. It's hard to swallow them alone; the voice of peace is heard. The voice of peace is heard.*

"I would like to read it when it is all done." She looked at the stack of loose papers on my desk. I nodded but did not say anything else.

Then I pulled a dollar bill out of my wallet and handed it to her.

"In the meantime, here is your mitzvah!" I said. "Be a *schlichah mitzvah* and have a safe trip."

We hugged. We laughed. We had stepped over the abyss together.

"Thanks," she said. "No one has given me a mitzvah for my trip yet!"